THE CLAY SANSKRIT LIBRARY

FOUNDED BY JOHN & JENNIFER CLAY

GENERAL EDITOR

Sheldon Pollock

EDITED BY

Isabelle Onians

www.claysanskritlibrary.com

www.nyupress.org

Artwork by Robert Beer.
Typeset in Adobe Garamond at 10.25 : 12.3+pt.
XML-development by Stuart Brown.
Editorial input from Dániel Balogh, Ridi Faruque,
Chris Gibbons, Tomoyuki Kono & Eszter Somogyi.
Printed and bound in Great Britain by
T.J. International, Cornwall, on acid-free paper.

"BOUQUET OF RASA" & "RIVER OF RASA"

by BHĀNUDATTA

TRANSLATED BY

Sheldon Pollock

NEW YORK UNIVERSITY PRESS

JJC FOUNDATION

2009

First Edition 2009

The Clay Sanskrit Library is co-published by
New York University Press
and the JJC Foundation.

Further information about this volume
and the rest of the Clay Sanskrit Library
is available at the end of this book
and on the following websites:
www.claysanskritlibrary.com
www.nyupress.org

ISBN-13: 978-0-8147-6755-9 (cloth : alk. paper)
ISBN-10: 0-8147-6755-9 (cloth : alk. paper)

Library of Congress Cataloging-in-Publication Data
Bhānudatta Miśra.
[Rasamañjarī. English & Sanskrit]
"Bouquet of rasa" ; & "River of rasa" / by Bhanudatta ;
translated by Sheldon Pollock.
p. cm.
Poems.
In English and Sanskrit (romanized) on facing pages.
Includes bibliographical references and index.
ISBN-13: 978-0-8147-6755-9 (cloth : alk. paper)
ISBN-10: 0-8147-6755-9 (cloth : alk. paper)
1. Bhanudatta Misra.--Translations into English.
2. Sanskrit poetry--Translations into English. 3. Rasas--Poetry.
4. Poetics--Poetry. I. Pollock, Sheldon I.
II. Bhanudatta Misra. Rasatarangini. English & Sanskrit.
III. Title. IV. Title: River of rasa.
PK3791.B198R3813 2009
891'.21--dc22
2008042974

CONTENTS

CSL Conventions vii

Acknowledgments xvii

Introduction xix

BOUQUET OF RASA

Description of the *Náyika* 3

Description of the *Náyaka* and Related Matters 91

RIVER OF RASA

First Wave	Description of the Stable Emotions	129
Second Wave	Description of the Factors	151
Third Wave	Description of the Physical Reactions	169
Fourth Wave	Description of the Involuntary Physical Reactions	187
Fifth Wave	Description of the Transitory Feelings	201
Sixth Wave	Description of Rasas	249
Seventh Wave	Description of Rasas Continued	283
Eighth Wave	Miscellany	313

Notes 343

CSL CONVENTIONS

Sanskrit Alphabetical Order

Vowels:	*a ā i ī u ū ṛ ṝ ḷ ḹ e ai o au ṃ ḥ*
Gutturals:	*k kh g gh ṅ*
Palatals:	*c ch j jh ñ*
Retroflex:	*ṭ ṭh ḍ ḍh ṇ*
Dentals:	*t th d dh n*
Labials:	*p ph b bh m*
Semivowels:	*y r l v*
Spirants:	*ś ṣ s h*

Guide to Sanskrit Pronunciation

a	b*u*t
ā, â	f*a*ther
i	s*i*t
ī, î	f*ee*
u	p*u*t
ū, û	b*oo*
ṛ	vocalic *r*, American p*ur*dy or English p*re*tty
ṝ	lengthened *ṛ*
ḷ	vocalic *l*, ab*le*
e, ê, ē	m*a*de, esp. in Welsh pronunciation
ai	b*i*te
o, ô, ō	r*o*pe, esp. Welsh pronunciation; Italian s*o*lo
au	s*ou*nd
ṃ	*anusvāra* nasalizes the preceding vowel
ḥ	*visarga*, a voiceless aspiration (resembling the English *h*), or like Scottish lo*ch*, or an aspiration with a faint echoing of the last element of the preceding vowel so that *taiḥ* is pronounced *taih*[i]
k	lu*ck*
kh	blo*ckh*ead
g	*g*o
gh	bi*gh*ead
ṅ	a*n*ger
c	*ch*ill
ch	mat*chh*ead
j	*j*og
jh	aspirated *j*, he*dgeh*og
ñ	ca*ny*on
ṭ	retroflex *t*, *t*ry (with the tip of tongue turned up to touch the hard palate)
ṭh	same as the preceding but aspirated
ḍ	retroflex *d* (with the tip

	of tongue turned up to touch the hard palate)
ḍh	same as the preceding but aspirated
ṇ	retroflex *n* (with the tip of tongue turned up to touch the hard palate)
t	French *t*out
th	ten*t h*ook
d	*d*inner
dh	guil*dh*all
n	*n*ow
p	*p*ill
ph	u*ph*eaval
b	*b*efore
bh	a*bh*orrent
m	*m*ind
y	*y*es
r	trilled, resembling the Italian pronunciation of *r*
l	*l*inger
v	*w*ord
ś	*sh*ore
ṣ	retroflex *sh* (with the tip of the tongue turned up to touch the hard palate)
s	hi*ss*
h	*h*ood

CSL Punctuation of English

The acute accent on Sanskrit words when they occur outside of the Sanskrit text itself, marks stress, e.g., Ramáyana. It is not part of traditional Sanskrit orthography, transliteration, or transcription, but we supply it here to guide readers in the pronunciation of these unfamiliar words. Since no Sanskrit word is accented on the last syllable it is not necessary to accent disyllables, e.g., Rama.

The second CSL innovation designed to assist the reader in the pronunciation of lengthy unfamiliar words is to insert an unobtrusive middle dot between semantic word breaks in compound names (provided the word break does not fall on a vowel resulting from the fusion of two vowels), e.g., Maha·bhárata, but Ramáyana (not Rama·áyana). Our dot echoes the punctuating middle dot (·) found in the oldest surviving samples of written Indic, the Ashokan inscriptions of the third century BCE.

The deep layering of Sanskrit narrative has also dictated that we use quotation marks only to announce the beginning and end of every direct speech, and not at the beginning of every paragraph.

CSL Punctuation of Sanskrit

The Sanskrit text is also punctuated, in accordance with the punctuation of the English translation. In mid-verse, the punctuation will not alter the sandhi or the scansion. Proper names are capitalized. Most Sanskrit meters have four "feet" (*pāda*); where possible we print the common *śloka* meter on two lines. In the Sanskrit text, we use French *Guillemets* (e.g., *«kva saṃcicīrṣuḥ?»*) instead of English quotation marks (e.g., "Where are you off to?") to avoid confusion with the apostrophes used for vowel elision in sandhi.

SANDHI

Sanskrit presents the learner with a challenge: *sandhi* (euphonic combination). Sandhi means that when two words are joined in connected speech or writing (which in Sanskrit reflects speech), the last letter (or even letters) of the first word often changes; compare the way we pronounce "the" in "the beginning" and "the end."

In Sanskrit the first letter of the second word may also change; and if both the last letter of the first word and the first letter of the second are vowels, they may fuse. This has a parallel in English: a nasal consonant is inserted between two vowels that would otherwise coalesce: "a pear" and "an apple." Sanskrit vowel fusion may produce ambiguity.

The charts on the following pages give the full sandhi system.

Fortunately it is not necessary to know these changes in order to start reading Sanskrit. All that is important to know is the form of the second word without sandhi (pre-sandhi), so that it can be recognized or looked up in a dictionary. Therefore we are printing Sanskrit with a system of punctuation that will indicate, unambiguously, the original form of the second word, i.e., the form without sandhi. Such sandhi mostly concerns the fusion of two vowels.

In Sanskrit, vowels may be short or long and are written differently accordingly. We follow the general convention that a vowel with no mark above it is short. Other books mark a long vowel either with a bar called a macron (*ā*) or with a circumflex (*â*). Our system uses the

VOWEL SANDHI

Final vowels: a	ā	i	ī	u	ū	ṛ	e	ai	o	au	*Initial vowels:*
' â	" â	y a	y a	v a	v a	r a	e '	ā a	o '	āv a	a
' ā	" ā	y ā	y ā	v ā	v ā	r ā	a ā	ā ā	a ā	āv ā	ā
' ê	" ê	' î	" î	v i	v i	r i	a i	ā i	a i	āv i	i
' ē	" ē	' ī	" ī	v ī	v ī	r ī	a ī	ā ī	a ī	āv ī	ī
' ô	" ô	y u	y u	' û	" û	r u	a u	ā u	a u	āv u	u
' ō	" ō	y ū	y ū	' ū	" ū	r ū	a ū	ā ū	a ū	āv ū	ū
a' r	a" r	y ṛ	y ṛ	v ṛ	v ṛ	' ṝ	a ṛ	ā ṛ	a ṛ	āv ṛ	ṛ
' âi	" âi	y e	y e	v e	v e	r e	a e	ā e	a e	āv e	e
' āi	" āi	y ai	y ai	v ai	v ai	r ai	a ai	ā ai	a ai	āv ai	ai
' âu	" âu	y o	y o	v o	v o	r o	a o	ā o	a o	āv o	o
' āu	" āu	y au	y au	v au	v au	r au	a au	ā au	a au	āv au	au

CONSONANT SANDHI

Permitted finals:							(Except āḥ/aḥ)			
k	ṭ	t	p	ṅ	n	m	ḥ/r	āḥ	aḥ	Initial letters:
k	ṭ	t	p	ṅ	n	ṃ	ḥ	āḥ	aḥ	k/kh
g	ḍ	d	b	ṅ	n	ṃ	r	ā	o	g/gh
k	ṭ	c	p	ṅ	ṃś	ṃ	ś	āś	aś	c/ch
g	ḍ	j	b	ṅ	ñ	ṃ	r	ā	o	j/jh
k	ṭ	ṭ	p	ṅ	ṃṣ	ṃ	ṣ	āṣ	aṣ	ṭ/ṭh
g	ḍ	ḍ	b	ṅ	ṇ	ṃ	r	ā	o	ḍ/ḍh
k	ṭ	t	p	ṅ	ṃs	ṃ	s	ās	as	t/th
g	ḍ	d	b	ṅ	n	ṃ	r	ā	o	d/dh
k	ṭ	t	p	ṅ	n	ṃ	ḥ	āḥ	aḥ	p/ph
g	ḍ	d	b	ṅ	n	ṃ	r	ā	o	b/bh
ṅ	ṇ	n	m	ṅ	n	ṃ	r	ā	o	*nasals* (n/m)
g	ḍ	d	b	ṅ	n	ṃ	r	ā	o	y/v
g	ḍ	d	b	ṅ	n	ṃ	*zero*[1]	ā	o	r
g	ḍ	l	b	ṅ	l̃[2]	ṃ	r	ā	o	l
k	ṭ	c ch	p	ṅ	ñ ś/ch	ṃ	ḥ	āḥ	aḥ	ś
k	ṭ	t	p	ṅ	n	ṃ	ḥ	āḥ	aḥ	ṣ/s
gg h	ḍḍ h	dd h	bb h	ṅ	n	ṃ	r	ā	o	h
g	ḍ	d	b	ṅ/nṅ[3]	n/nn[3]	m	r	ā	a[4]	*vowels*
k	ṭ	t	p	ṅ	n	m	ḥ	āḥ	aḥ	*zero*

[1]ḥ or r disappears, and if a/i/u precedes, this lengthens to ā/ī/ū. [2]e.g. tān+lokān=tā̃l lokān.
[3]The doubling occurs if the preceding vowel is short. [4]Except: aḥ+a=o '.

macron, except that for initial vowels in sandhi we use a circumflex to indicate that originally the vowel was short, or the shorter of two possibilities (*e* rather than *ai*, *o* rather than *au*).

When we print initial *â*,	before sandhi that vowel was *a*
î or *ê*,	*i*
û or *ô*,	*u*
âi,	*e*
âu,	*o*
ā,	*ā*
ī,	*ī*
ū,	*ū*
ē,	*ī*
ō,	*ū*
ai,	*ai*
āu,	*au*
',	before sandhi there was a vowel *a*

When a final short vowel (*a*, *i*, or *u*) has merged into a following vowel, we print ' at the end of the word, and when a final long vowel (*ā*, *ī*, or *ū*) has merged into a following vowel we print " at the end of the word. The vast majority of these cases will concern a final *a* or *ā*. See, for instance, the following examples:

What before sandhi was	is represented as
atra asti	*atr' âsti*
atra āste	*atr' āste*
kanyā asti	*kany" âsti*
kanyā āste	*kany" āste*
atra iti	*atr' êti*
kanyā iti	*kany" êti*
kanyā īpsitā	*kany" ēpsitā*

Finally, three other points concerning the initial letter of the second word:

(1) A word that before sandhi begins with *ṛ* (vowel), after sandhi begins with *r* followed by a consonant: *yatha" rtu* represents pre-sandhi *yathā ṛtu*.

(2) When before sandhi the previous word ends in *t* and the following word begins with *ś*, after sandhi the last letter of the previous word is *c*

and the following word begins with *ch*: *syāc chāstravit* represents pre-sandhi *syāt śāstravit*.

(3) Where a word begins with *h* and the previous word ends with a double consonant, this is our simplified spelling to show the pre-sandhi form: *tad hasati* is commonly written as *tad dhasati*, but we write *tadd hasati* so that the original initial letter is obvious.

COMPOUNDS

We also punctuate the division of compounds (*samāsa*), simply by inserting a thin vertical line between words. There are words where the decision whether to regard them as compounds is arbitrary. Our principle has been to try to guide readers to the correct dictionary entries.

Exemplar of CSL Style

Where the Devanagari script reads:

कुम्भस्थली रक्षतु वो विकीर्णसिन्धूररेणुर्द्विरदाननस्य ।
प्रशान्तये विघ्नतमश्छटानां निष्ठ्यूतबालातपपल्लवेव ॥

Others would print:

kumbhasthalī rakṣatu vo vikīrṇasindūrareṇur dviradānanasya /
praśāntaye vighnatamaśchaṭānāṃ niṣṭhyūtabālātapapallaveva //

We print:

kumbha|sthalī rakṣatu vo vikīrṇa|sindūra|reṇur dvirad'|ānanasya
praśāntaye vighna|tamaś|chaṭānāṃ niṣṭhyūta|bāl'|ātapa|pallav" êva.

And in English:

May Ganésha's domed forehead protect you! Streaked with vermilion dust, it seems to be emitting the spreading rays of the rising sun to pacify the teeming darkness of obstructions.

("Nava·sáhasanka and the Serpent Princess" 1.3)

Wordplay

Classical Sanskrit literature can abound in puns (*śleṣa*). Such paronomasia, or wordplay, is raised to a high art; rarely is it a *cliché*. Multiple meanings merge (*śliṣyanti*) into a single word or phrase. Most common are pairs of meanings, but as many as ten separate meanings are attested. To mark the parallel senses in the English, as well as the punning original in the Sanskrit, we use a *slanted* font (different from *italic*) and a triple colon (⁝) to separate the alternatives. E.g.

> yuktaṃ Kādambarīṃ śrutvā kavayo maunam āśritāḥ
> *Bāṇa/dhvanāv* an|adhyāyo bhavat' îti smṛtir yataḥ.
>
> It is right that poets should fall silent upon hearing the Kadámbari, for the sacred law rules that recitation must be suspended when *the sound of an arrow ⁝ the poetry of Bana* is heard.
>
> (Soméshvara·deva's "Moonlight of Glory" I.15)

For Lisette and Howard, *úttama náyika* and *náyaka*.

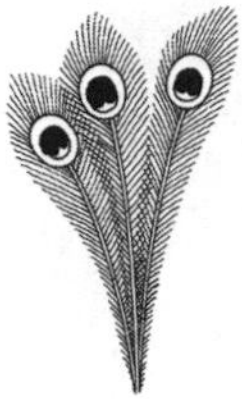

ACKNOWLEDGMENTS

I AM GRATEFUL to the following institutions and colleagues for their assistance:

The British Library, for providing copies of the *Nauka* of Gaṅgārāma Jaḍe, the *Rasikarañjanī* of Veṇīdatta Bhaṭṭācārya, and the *Rasikarañjanī* of Gopāla Bhaṭṭa;

Harvard University Library, for providing a copy of the *Kāvyasudhā* of Nemasāha;

Sitanshu Yashaschandra, for securing copies of the *Nūtanatarī* of Bhagavadbhaṭṭa and the *Rasikarañjanī* of Veṇīdatta Bhaṭṭācārya from the Oriental Institute, Baroda;

The University of Pennsylvania and Dr. David Nelson, for providing a copy of the *Kāvyasudhā* of Nemasāha;

Dr. Dalgeet, of the Painting Department, National Museum, New Delhi, for providing slides of the forty paintings of the Udaipur *Rasamañjarī* in the museum's holdings; Joachim Bautze, for securing slides of several unpublished folios of the same album in European private collections; and Laura Parsons, who as my research assistant at the University of Chicago helped assemble a number of additional images;

Guy Leavitt, for help in preparing the transliterated Sanskrit texts;

Dániel Balogh, for his punctilious editorial work on the final draft, and Stuart Brown for his constant care;

Hamsa Stainton and Arthur Dudney, for their research assistance.

New York City
January 20, 2008

INTRODUCTION

BHANU·DATTA IS PERHAPS the most famous Sanskrit poet —certainly the most famous Sanskrit poet of early modern India—whom no one today has heard of. Although accorded little more than a footnote in standard Indian literary histories, the two texts edited and translated in this edition, the "Bouquet of Rasa" (*Rasamañjarī*; on types of female and male characters in poetry) and the "River of Rasa" (*Rasataraṅgiṇī*; on Sanskrit aesthetics) attracted an astonishing amount of interpretive attention from the sixteenth to the eighteenth century, including commentaries from a dozen of the period's most celebrated scholar-exegetes. No other Sanskrit poet exercised anything remotely approaching Bhanu·datta's influence on the development of the Hindi literary tradition between 1600 and 1850, the "Epoch of High Style" (*riti/kal*). No literary work, at least of the non-religious, lyrical sort, made a bigger impact than the "Bouquet of Rasa" on the new art of miniature painting that burst onto the Indian scene in the late sixteenth century. When Abu al-Fazl, the leading intellectual at the court of Akbar, presented a review of the arts and sciences of the Hindus to the Mughal emperor in the 1590s, he turned in part to the work of Bhanu to describe the nature of literature. And two centuries later, when the first Europeans began to study Sanskrit, this poet's works, among others now more celebrated, were presented to them as exemplary by their Indian teachers.[1]

Bhanu·datta's extraordinary influence was not the result of any truly revolutionary break-through he achieved on the conceptual plane. It was due, rather, to his consummate skill in summarizing the thousand-year-long tradition of Indian aesthetic theory more clearly and engagingly than anyone had previously and, more important, to his talent for crafting illustrative verses of far higher literary caliber than anyone had offered before him. It will be helpful to review what we know about Bhanu himself and the genre of "science-poetry" he helped shape and to offer some assessment of his literary accomplishment in these two celebrated and charming works, before briefly describing their content—the nature of rasa and Sanskrit aesthetics, and the typology of literary characters—Bhanu's central place in the miniature painting tradition, and the principles adopted for this edition and accompanying commentary.

Who was Bhanu·datta?

As is commonly the case with Sanskrit poets, however great the literary influence they exerted (and Bhanu·datta's influence can be detected already within a few decades of his death), there is considerable uncertainty about Bhanu's time, place, and identity. One must start of course with what the poet-scholar himself tells us. He was from Vidéha (today's northern Bihar), a member of the highly learned Máithili brahmin community, and he was the son of a poet named Ganéshvara (or Gana·pati). He speaks of himself as Sanskrit poets usually do, in the third person:

His father was Ganéshvara,
brightest jewel in the crown of poetry,
his land, Vidéha country, where waves
of the holy river ripple.

With verse of his own making Shri Bhanu
the poet arranged this Bouquet
to rival the flower of the coral tree
at the ear of the Goddess of Language.
("Bouquet of Rasa" v. 138)

Unfortunately, given the reticence also typical of Sanskrit poets, this is all he says directly about himself. Bhanu provides only one other reference to his life—this time an indirect hint. In a poem in the "Bouquet of Rasa" illustrating the different "involuntary physical reactions," Bhanu offers the single historical allusion in the two works (and so far as I can tell in his entire oeuvre, aside from a brief genealogy in his *Kumārabhārgavīya* 1.16–28):

Her voice breaks, tears well up in her eyes,
her breast is beaded with sweat,
her lips tremble, her smooth cheeks grow pale,
goosebumps cover her body,
her mind absorbed, the light in her eyes dying,
her legs paralyzed—
did she, too, chance to glance at the royal highway
and see King Nijáma?
("Bouquet of Rasa" v. 121)

The very rarity of such references in his poetry makes this one a little suspect—if Sanskrit poets speak of their patrons at all, they usually do so in a far more copious if not fulsome way. On the other hand, it is hard to see why such a line should ever has been interpolated, and it alone, in the entire corpus (and in the middle, not at the beginning or end). One manuscript from Kerala and one commentator from

Tamil country make mention instead of the god Krishna, but that reading seems spurious. Moreover, Veni·datta, the most learned commentator on the "River of Rasa," who is a very careful reader of Bhanu, cites the verse with the Nijáma reference.[2]

On the assumption, then, that the dominant manuscript and commentarial tradition is credible in connecting Bhanu to a King Nijáma, to whom could this refer? One commentator on the poem, Anánta·pándita, who lived in the early seventeenth century and hailed from Punya·stambha (Puntambem, near Ahmadnagar) in Maharashtra, identifies Nijáma as the "king of Deva·giri." Deva·giri was the town, not far from Punya·stambha, that after the defeat of the Yádavas around the beginning of the fourteenth century was renamed Daulatabad (and later Aurangabad). And it was this celebrated stronghold that, after repeated attempts, Ahmad Nizam Shah, founder of the Nizam Shahi dynasty of Ahmadnagar in 1490, finally captured in 1499. The works of Bhanu cannot have been written much after this date, since one of them, the "Bouquet of Rasa," was adapted in a Hindi text of 1541.[3]

It seems probable, then, that the Maharashtrian commentator Anánta·pándita, who was more likely to have had access to authentic tradition about his region than a copyist from Kerala or a commentator from Tamil country, has preserved the truth here.[4] But does it seem credible that a brahmin poet from the far northeast area of Míthila should have made his way to a southern, Muslim court at that period? We know of many Sanskrit poets over the centuries who traveled vast distances in search of royal patronage:

Bílhana, one of the great poets of the twelfth century, journeyed from Kashmir to the Deccan, and four centuries later the Andhra poet-scholar Jagan·natha sojourned in Delhi, Assam, and Udaipur. Why should Bhanu not have sought patronage in the south, especially in a new and ascendant political context where other Sanskrit intellectuals, such as Dala·pati·raja, author of a great work on law (c. 1500) and who describes himself as "minister and record-keeper of Nijáma Saha, overlord of all Yávanas [Muslims]," were enjoying royal support?[5] Moreover, a Deccani provenance for at least the "Bouquet of Rasa" would go some way in explaining the impact of the work on poets at other southern sultanates, such as Golconda in the mid-seventeenth century, where the work was deeply studied (a fact also reflected in the large number of manuscripts of the work in Telugu script), as well as the presence of a relatively early painting tradition at Aurangabad, where an illustrated "Bouquet of Rasa" was prepared for a Sisodia Rajput in 1650.[6]

In addition to the two texts edited and translated here, Bhanu produced at least one other treatise on rhetoric, the "Forehead Ornament of Figures" (*Alaṅkāratilaka*); the *Gītāgaurīpatikāvya*, a short poem on Shiva and Gauri modeled on the "Gita·govínda"; a mixed prose-verse work, the *Kumārabhārgavīyacampū*, narrating the story of the deity Kartikéya; and an anthology of his own and his father's poetry called the "Heavenly Tree of Rasa" (*Rasapārijāta*). Several other attributed works have not survived. The "Bouquet of Rasa" is an early composition; it certainly precedes the "River of Rasa," which refers to it (6.14), and hence the two texts are presented in that order here.

Bhanu·datta and the Blurred Genre of Science-Poetry

The two works of Bhanu·datta presented here are representatives of a somewhat blurred genre in Sanskrit literary history. Although Indian thinkers always viewed science (*śāstra*) as fundamentally distinct from literature (*kāvya*), at a relatively early date poets began experimenting with a form of text that mixed the two categories. One variety, science-poetry (*śāstra/kāvya*), as the genre came to be called, makes use of a well-known narrative, say the story of Rama, to illustrate the rules of grammar or rhetoric; "Bhatti's Poem" (*Bhaṭṭikāvya*) from the early eighth century is a good example.[7] Another is the purely scientific treatise that aspires to the condition of poetry, such as Varáha·míhira's mid-sixth-century astronomical work, the "Great Compendium" (*Bṛhatsaṃhitā*). Yet a third type is constituted by treatises of literary theory or rhetoric (*alaṅkāra/śāstra*), where the rules of literary art are set out and illustrated with poems.[8] Or more justly put, this third variety, which we might call "rhetorical science-poetry," became a new genre in its own right thanks to the efforts of poet-scholars like Bhanu·datta, who achieved a degree of literary excellence in the form that few earlier authors equaled. A brief review of the formal history of Sanskrit rhetoric will show this and at the same time permit me to say a word about its conceptual history.

In texts on Sanskrit rhetoric from the earliest period, such as Dandin's late seventh-century "Mirror of Literature" (*Kāvyādarśa*), the illustrative poems were of the author's own making, written *ad hoc* and entirely pedestrian.

Within two centuries, poeticians had begun to draw illustrations from their own literary works; Údbhata (c. 800), for instance, took all his examples from his own courtly epic (the *Kumārasambhava*, no longer extant). When, however, in a momentous transformation that took place in mid-ninth-century Kashmir, the focus of literary theory suddenly shifted from how to write poetry to how to read it, scholars began to use citations from existing literature, almost exclusively, in making their theoretical arguments. Bhanu thus represents something of a throwback—though also a harbinger, since many later Sanskrit writers were to follow his example—in producing new poetry of a very high order to illustrate the aesthetic and rhetorical practices of Sanskrit literature.[9] He thereby fired the imagination of vernacular poets who were seeking—as Joachim du Bellay, a contemporary vernacular writer half a world away, wrote in 1549—at once to "defend and illustrate [i.e., ennoble]" their emergent literary languages. For them the science-poetry of Bhanu's sort offered the perfect vehicle. The poetic oeuvre of many Old Hindi poets in particular came to include what they called a "definition work" (*lakṣaṇa/grantha*)—often marked by extraordinary literary finesse—based on Bhanu's "Bouquet" or "River."[10]

These two works, viewed from one angle, function something like user manuals for Sanskrit literature, of a sort essential for readers of the CLAY SANSKRIT LIBRARY. As we will see momentarily, understanding the characterology, so to call it, of Sanskrit literature, to say nothing of rasa, or the emotion produced through the literary work, is crucial to our capacity to appreciate the presuppositions and goals of

Sanskrit writers. Viewed from another angle, Bhanu's texts provide a glimpse into the workshop of the Sanskrit poet, his tools and materials and ways of composition. There are other types of Sanskrit texts that bring us even deeper into that workshop—the so-called "instruction manuals for poets" (*kavi/śikṣā*), which set forth, for example, how to choose the best Sanskrit word for "king" from among the scores of synonyms to fit a certain complex Sanskrit metrical pattern. But Bhanu not only informs, he delights with far more accomplished poetry than that which we find in instruction manuals.

Even a few examples suffice to show this. Take the poem that Abu al-Fazl found worthy of translating into Persian (it was also known to and imitated by the great Telugu poet Kshetrayya a century and a half later):

You stayed awake all night, and yet
it's my eyes that are throbbing;
you were the one who drank the rum,
and yet it's my head that's splitting;
and in the bower buzzing with bees
it was you who stole beauty's fruit,
yet I'm the one the Love God wounds
with his arrows that burn like fire.
("Bouquet of Rasa" v. 13)

The poem illustrates the *nāyikā*, literally the "leading lady" or heroine, who is "average unsteady," whose desire and modesty are in balance and who, when confronted with infidelity on the part of her lover, does not mince her words. Bhanu deftly reveals the sorrow her lover has caused by showing how each of what are fleeting pleasures for him transforms into enduring pains for her.[11] Another poem, about the same "average" *nāyikā*, perfectly embodies her definition as one whose desire and modesty are in precise and, as the poet shows, impossible balance:

She thought, "If I fall asleep right now
I'll lose the chance to see
my love's face; and if I stay awake,
his hands might start to roam."
Over and over she thought it through,
that girl with lotus eyes,
and finally decided to go to sleep
and to stay awake.

("Bouquet of Rasa" v. 9)

Yet a third poem, showing the same average *nāyikā* confronted by "lipstick on his collar," expresses her constitutive ambivalence by reflecting on the ambivalence, so to put it, of the material world itself:

When she saw her husband's chest
stained with cream from another's breasts,
she didn't heave a long, deep sigh
and didn't say a single word;
she only began to wash her face
just as she did every morning
and with the water hid the water
that came pouring from her eyes.

("Bouquet of Rasa" v. 45)

Contemporary readers who might be disappointed by the conventional nature of these poems do well to understand that such is in fact their whole point. Bhanu's purpose is to show what poets can do when working within the tightest of constraints. He uses *śāstra* both to explain and to defend this tradition of voluntary self-limitation while exemplifying the especially intense pleasure that can come from inventiveness within narrow boundaries. This is not to say that Bhanu cannot produce something entirely new, either in pure play, as when he manufactures Sanskrit words in a way that some of his more fastidiously grammatical commentators found scandalous:

My figure shows no curvitude,
my breasts no altitude,
my body has no pulchritude,
my hips no amplitude,
my walk suggests no gravitude,
my eyes no magnitude,
my charm reveals no plenitude,
my speech no aptitude,
and my laugh no latitude—
why in the world has my lover given
his heart to me and me alone?

madhye na kraśimā stane na garimā
dehe na vā kāntimā
śroṇau na prathimā gatau na jaḍimā
netre na vā vakrimā
lāsye na draḍhimā na vāci paṭimā
hāsye na vā sphītimā

prāṇ'|ēśasya tath" âpi majjati mano
mayy eva kiṃ kāraṇam?
("Bouquet of Rasa" v. 70)

Or in aspiring almost to the condition of music, with something like the rhymes so characteristic of the new vernaculars:

tamo|jaṭāle harid|antarāle
kāle niśāyās tava nirgatāyāḥ
taṭe nadīnāṃ nikaṭe vanānāṃ
ghaṭeta śāt'|ôdari kaḥ sahāyaḥ?

When nighttime lets down its thick black hair
all around and you leave your house, slender girl,
who will be there to stand by your side
on the riverbank at the edge of the forest?
("Bouquet of Rasa" v. 111)

All in all, Bhanu·datta does represent something of the return *ad fontes* that is characteristic of much early modern Sanskrit culture. He does so not only in the formal dimension of his work as described earlier, but also in the ideas that inform it. I examine first the broad theory of literary art in the "River of Rasa," before going on to discuss the subset of that theory constituted by the characterology of the "Bouquet of Rasa."

Rasa, or How Literature Creates Emotion

From the beginning of their systematic reflection on literature, Indian thinkers were preoccupied by the question of how human emotion comes to be produced by words inscribed on a page or recited on stage accompanied by gestures and other physical expressions—and not just how emotion was produced, but what kinds of emotion, and why those kinds. The foundational work in this domain is the "Science of Drama" (*Nāṭyaśāstra*) of Bhárata (perhaps composed in the third or fourth century, but subject to substantial revision up to the ninth century), and the analysis it set out was never fundamentally contested.

In accordance with the widespread tendency in Sanskrit culture toward schematic thinking and the simplification of complexity in the interests of orderly analysis, Bhárata and all later Indian aestheticians promoted a theory of literary representation that reduced the vast welter of human emotions to a set of eight (a ninth would be added in later centuries). These eight aesthetic emotions they called rasas, "tastes," analogizing from the sense of taste on the grounds both of the physicality of emotion—it is something we feel, not something we think—and of the blending of ingredients that complex tastes and aesthetic moods both evince. The basic ingredient is called a "stable" or primary emotion (*sthāyi/bhāvas*), such as desire in the case of the erotic rasa, to which are added "underlying factors" (*ālambana/vibhāvas*) such as the beloved, "stimulant factors" (*uddīpana/vibhāvas*) such as a moonlit night or swinging earrings, "transitory feelings" (*vyabhicāri/bhāvas*) such as longing or worry or shame, and "physical reactions" (*anubhāvas*) such as perspiring or weeping. A stable emotion, when fully "developed" or "matured" by these factors, transforms into a rasa. Such a transformation was originally thought to be something that comes about in the main character of a poem or drama; it is Rama who feels the stable emotion of desire for Sita (not you or I) and who eventually relishes the erotic rasa that develops out of this desire. On this view, the reader's or viewer's response to the emotion is of little or no concern. On the contrary, rasa theory arose to enable literary analysis to grasp, as the American New Critics WIMSATT and BEARDSLEY put it in their famous 1949 essay "The Affective Fallacy," how poetry "fix[es] emotions, making them more permanently perceptible." And this purpose would reign unchallenged for six or more centuries after Bhárata.

The sudden shift of perspective that led Kashmiri thinkers such as Ánanda·várdhana (*fl.* 850) to focus on reading rather than writing (and therefore to cite already existent poetry rather than to create it *ad hoc*), concomitantly led them, less than a century later, to turn their attention away from how the literary text or the dramatic performance produces emotion and toward how readers and viewers respond to that emotion. Why do we not leap from our seats in the theater and rush the stage the moment Rávana reveals himself and prepares to abduct Sita? Why do we not shun sad stories like the "Ramáyana," as we shun sorrow in everyday life? In other words, how precisely does literary emotion differ from the non-literary? I say "from the non-literary" rather than "from real emotion," since the emotions of fear, sadness, and so on that we experience when watching a "Ramáyana" play are certainly real. After all we do feel them; they are just different from the emotions we experience outside the theater. Clearly, these are core questions not just of literature but of human existence: the very capacity to distinguish aesthetic from pragmatic emotion, even to respond to aesthetic emotion, is one of the things that make people cultured, perhaps even human. And they are questions that took Indian scholarship by storm in the late tenth century, transforming Indian aesthetic thought once and for all time.

At least this is what most scholars believe. In fact—and to register this fact is to record a historical truth, and not of course to denigrate the profound insights of the innovators—many later Indian literary theorists appear to have been entirely indifferent to the new ideas originating in Kashmir. Bhanu·datta is most certainly one of them throughout his exposition in the "River of Rasa." His are largely the old concerns of how literature creates emotion, the concerns of, say, King Bhoja, the great encyclopedist who synthesized the "normal science" of aesthetics in the mid-eleventh century.[12] Only rarely does Bhanu depart from the classical doctrine—hence his close dependence on the *Nāṭyaśāstra*—and the few times he does so, he reveals that he is far more a poet than a thinker. (His distinction between "ordinary" and "extraordinary" rasa—which differentiates between a rasa that arises for a character from normal contact with the underlying object and a rasa that arises for a character in dreaming, imagining, or witnessing a mimetic representation—does mark a noteworthy if undeveloped advance.)[13] It is for the poetry we should enter into the "River of Rasa," not the science—though of course having the science clearly in our heads, as Bhanu makes it very convenient to do, is the only way to fully engage wth the poetry.

Casting according to Type

As with his "River of Rasa," it is above all for the poetry that we enjoy Bhanu's "Bouquet of Rasa," though the doctrine of the work and its systematicity and (if such is conceivable) completeness were found impressive in their own right and were everywhere imitated.

The catalogue of character types with which the "Bouquet" is concerned fits, of course, perfectly into the thought world of rasa; indeed, it is its necessary complement. Rasa is all about typicality: A young man's desire, upon seeing a beautiful young woman with swinging earrings on a moonlit evening, will typically develop or mature into the erotic rasa—or to put this more strictly, for the erotic rasa to develop in literature, the *nāyaka*, literally the "leading man" or hero, must be young, the *nāyikā* must be beautiful, and so on. Atypicality—an old woman in love with a young man, for example—would have been considered *vi/rasa*, or "tasteless." Such themes would not become the stuff of literature until modernity; one can even say that what makes a literary text modern is precisely its violation of the expectations of the traditional social text. (Thus, in the iconic drama of early modernity, Corneille's *Le Cid*, one of the things that enraged critics in 1637 was the marriage of the heroine to her father's assassin, in violation of what the French critics, in an idiom remarkably similar to that of their Indian counterparts, called "propriety and probability"). Sanskrit poets were interested in exploring typicality and, accordingly, needed to master it across the whole universe of emotion. How were women expected to act when first falling in love, when confronted by an act of infidelity on the part of their lovers, when desiring someone other than their husband? To answer such questions a discourse arose that aimed to construct a typology of characters.

Again, Bhanu enters this discourse after a millennium or more of its cultivation by dozens of writers. Bhárata had already discussed eight types of women (and five types of men) in the erotic setting. An important late-tenth-century treatise on dramaturgy, the "The Ten Dramatic Genres" (*Daśarūpaka*) elaborated further, as did Bhoja half a century later in his "Light on Desire" (*Śṛṅgāraprakāśa*). In the same epoch, it seems, a writer named Rudra (or Rudra Bhaṭṭa) composed the "Forehead Ornament of the Erotic" (*Śṛṅgāratilaka*), the first systematic account of the subject prior to Bhanu, who knew the work well and adapted it to his purposes, which were, however, far more ambitious.[14]

Just as in the case with his rasa theory, Bhanu's own contribution to the discourse on character types, aside from being the first entirely independent treatise on the subject, is relatively modest and consists largely in identifying new subtypes of heroines. Yet the work was viewed as original enough to provoke serious critical comment in the following centuries. At the court of Abul Hasan Qutb Shah of Golconda in the last quarter of the seventeenth century, the "Bouquet of Rasa" was answered by the "Bouquet of the Erotic Rasa" (*Śṛṅgāramañjarī*), composed (or commissioned) by Akbar Shah, one of the intellectuals who formed the sultan's remarkable literary circle.[15]

Readers of the "Bouquet" will again be struck in the first instance by what will appear to be Bhanu's taxonomic obsessions. When he concludes his overview of female characters by stating, "This makes 128 types. All these can be further distinguished as 'excellent,' 'average,' and 'low,' which thus gives 384 types," our jaws are likely to fall slack at the hypertrophy of categories. We certainly feel a sense of relief when he spares us further elaboration, saying, "I reject the argument that there can be a further subdivision according to whether the *nāyikā* is divine, not divine, or semidivine—which would give us 1,152 types" ("Bouquet of Rasa" 81). Newcomers to such a style of analysis are likely to react with the same incomprehension and impatience of the colonial officer surveying "native education" in 1830s Bengal, who rebuked Indian scholars for "wasting their learning and their powers in … recompounding absurd and vicious fictions, and revolving in perpetual circles of metaphysical abstractions never ending still beginning" (Basu 1941: 276–77).

Yet as I have tried to suggest, Bhanu's typological thinking is an essential adjunct to the aesthetic theory in which it is embedded, and that theory does a better job of dissecting literary emotion than any other on offer. Its fault, if fault it is, lies in the excess of detail in the attempt to follow out every possible permutation to its logical conclusion. What ancient Indian scholars realized, and most of us moderns—to our surprise and sometimes repulsion—have not, is that we can bring analytical order even into realms that seem constitutively anarchic, the world of human feeling, for instance, or the apparently infinite ways, ways of pleasure and of pain, in which men and women interact with each other.

Bhanu·datta's Words Painted

Another indication of the importance of Bhanu·datta's work is the impact it made on the emergent painting traditions of early modern India. The "Bouquet of Rasa" was one of the best-loved poems in the sub-imperial realm of miniature painting that arose with the consolidation of Mughal rule at the end of the sixteenth century. The poem was illustrated in Mewar perhaps as early as the 1630s, in the Deccan in the 1650s, in Basohli between 1660 and 1690, in Chamba about 1690, in Nurpur in the 1710s, and elsewhere. The earliest album, from Udaipur, is an uneven assemblage from various artists (or, in some cases, evidently art students), but a number of paintings strongly suggest, to an inexpert viewer such as myself, the atelier if not the hand of the celebrated painter Sāhibdīn.[16] The commentary provided in this Clay Sanskrit Library edition refers to surviving folios of this early and largely hitherto unpublished album.[17]

What accounts for the remarkable appeal the "Bouquet of Rasa" held for early modern artists? Its attractiveness may partially lie in the new and intriguing challenges of capturing complex and subtle verbal narratives in visual imagery. In the preceding century and a half (little Indian painting is extant prior to 1500), the almost exclusive objects of painterly attention were narratively uncomplicated religious or epic texts such as Jain sutras, the "Maha·bhárata," and the *Harivaṃśa*. As Sanskrit poetry began to be illustrated, the texts chosen were also largely straightforward in their narrative—poems like the "The Fifty Stanzas of a Thief" (*Caurapañcāśikā*) or the "Gita·govínda."[18]

The "Bouquet of Rasa," by contrast, offers the fascination of what's difficult in representing in the medium of line and color the subtle emotional situations that Bhanu depicts in sophisticated and often oblique or indirect language. (The same is true of the *Rasikapriyā*, Keshavdas's great Hindi poem of 1591, which presents some of the same kinds of interpretive challenges and was painted in Udaipur between 1630 and 1640.) The creators of the Udaipur album certainly took the challenges of Bhanu's text seriously. The poems themselves appear on the front of the painting, not, as in later periods (Basohli, for example), on the back, and were accompanied by an Old Gujarati translation (on the verso). If it is true that later artists often painted what they wished to paint regardless of the text of the poem they were illustrating, this was decidedly not the case in the early Udaipur album. How the artists met the narrative challenge still has the power to charm, as well as to instruct as if they were commentaries in paint.[19]

Text and Annotation

The texts that form the basis for my editions of the *Rasamañjarī* and the *Rasataraṅgiṇī* are found in the collected works of Bhānudatta published by TRILOKANATHA JHA in 1988. JHA in fact only reprints already published texts for the two works, and I chose his edition merely as the most recent and convenient starting point for my own work. In the case of the *Rasamañjarī*, nothing approaching a critical edition has ever been produced. I was able to make use of collations from two manuscripts in Malayalam script (Triv. A and B) and, occasionally, the Old

Gujarati translation on the back of the Udaipur album. For the *Rasataraṅgiṇī* it was possible to supplement Jha with the edition of Urmila Sharma. Sharma assembles a good deal of additional textual material (on the basis of ten manuscripts), though some editorial judgments are decidedly odd and the number of misleading typographical errors surprisingly large.

The transmission of the two poems has in fact been highly stable, with no substantial variation, let alone the development of regionalized recensions that characterize so many Sanskrit literary texts. When I depart from Jha and Sharma, I do so on the evidence of readings offered by one or another of the dozen commentators I consulted. Many of these commentators were also editors and frequently comment on and weigh variants, and I have taken their arguments into account. I supply the evidence for my editorial decisions in the critical apparatus to the text; however, I refrain from reporting information already available in earlier editions and also omit variants that have no real bearing on the sense. Occasionally, even if I do not accept the commentators' readings, I record them if they seem worthy of further consideration, especially if they are not noticed in either Jha or Sharma, neither of whom made use of several of the still-unpublished commentaries to which I have had access.

Even a truly critical edition of Bhānu's works, however rigorously prepared, would never enable us to make editorial choices with anything approaching the ideal of stemmatic necessity. We would still be exposed to the potential delusions of our own subjectivity, assuming, of course, we are aiming for something approaching authorial intention, an aim that no contemporary theory leads me to entirely devalue. But this subjectivity becomes somewhat less unreliable to the degree it is disciplined by the commentators, ideal readers if there ever were ones. Their commentaries offer some of the most learned reflections on any Sanskrit literary text from the early modern period—some approximate veritable treatises on aesthetics in their own right—even as they provide further evidence of Bhānudatta's astonishing popularity. A few of the more accomplished exegetes and poeticians I draw upon, among the ten who wrote on the *Rasataraṅgiṇī* and the fifteen on the *Rasamañjarī*, include (in chronological order): Śeṣa Cintāmaṇi, younger brother of Śeṣa Kṛṣṇa, the most celebrated grammarian of the late sixteenth century (Kanpur/Varanasi, 1553—this is within a generation or two of Bhānu); Gopāla Bhaṭṭa (son of Harivaṃśa Bhaṭṭa), a direct disciple of Caitanya and teacher of the renowned Bangla poet Kṛṣṇadāsa Kavirāja (place unknown, 1572); Anantapaṇḍita, grandfather of the logician Mahādeva, and commentator on the *Āryāsaptaśatī* and *Mudrārākṣasa* (Ahmadnagar/Varanasi, 1636); Veṇīdatta Bhaṭṭācārya, author of the *Alaṅkāracandrodaya* (Bareilly, c. 1700); Nāgeśa Bhaṭṭa, the most remarkable polymath of the early eighteenth century (Varanasi, 1713); Gaṅgārāma Jaḍe, pupil of the *Mahābhārata* commentator Nīlakaṇṭha Caturdhara, and a scholar learned in both *alaṅkāra/śāstra* and logic (Varanasi, 1742); and Viśveśvara, author of the *Alaṅkārakaustubha*, the last of the important independent works on *alaṅkāra/śāstra* (Almora, d. 1750).[20]

The most insightful of these commentaries for the *Rasamañjarī* is without question Viśveśvara, probing the poems as he does with a very learned eye. In a category by himself is Anantapaṇḍita, who clearly has pretensions to be more than mere commentator: he appears to want to claim for his exegesis a status of expressivity almost equal to that of the poet himself, producing what at times approaches art-prose, though often with more heat than light. The most knowledgeable of *Rasataraṅgiṇī* commentaries is undoubtedly the still-unpublished work of Veṇīdatta, and I have frequently profited from his deep knowledge of Sanskrit poetry.[21] Space is available in the annotations to record only significant commentarial alternatives to the preferred translation.

There are several earlier translations of these two works of Bhānudatta. The *Rasamañjarī*, or at least its verses, has been rendered several times by Indian translators; a recent Italian dissertation offers a version as well.[22] The *Rasataraṅgiṇī* was translated only once, and only partially, into French by Paul Regnaud in 1884, as part of a study of the *Nāṭyaśāstra*. The present volume represents the first complete translation of both works to be published together and on the basis of texts established and interpreted with the help of the most important extant commentaries.

Notes

1 See discussion of the commentators, Hindi *rīti* literature, and the painting traditions that follows. 6 [3] (missed by the translator), 28 [13], and 47 [22] are cited in the *Ain-i Akbari* (vol. 3, pp.

256–58; Bhānudatta is not named but the verses are unmistakably his). The European mentioned is SIR WILLIAM JONES, who wrote in reference to the RM, "I have read this delightful book four times at least" (1807: vol. 13: 409); he attractively translated the title as "The Analysis of Love."

2 V cites the verse in RT 4.22 (f. 25v).

3 Kṛpārām's *Hittaraṅgiṇī*, the first work on the typology of heroines in Brajbhasha, is dated 1541 (the interpretation of the chronogram has been questioned, but unpersuasively), borrows from the RM, and thus supplies a definite *terminus ante quem* (ALLISON BUSCH, personal communication). This would be corroborated by the date of Śeṣa Cintāmaṇi's commentary on the RM, 1553, assuming that early date is indeed correct.

4 See also DE 1959 and KANE 1991: 304–09. An argument for a *terminus ante quem* of 1428 is based on a false dating of a commentary on the RM (DASGUPTA and DE 1962: 561; the *Rasamañjarīprakāśa*, which exists in a single MS., seems in fact to be the *Rasikarañjanī* of Gopāla Bhaṭṭa, which was also composed in 1572). An argument for a *terminus ante quem* of 1314 is based on the false attribution to Bhānu of a lawbook called *Parijāta* cited in another text dated 1315 (Bhānudatta's literary anthology *Rasapārijāta* is confused with the *dharmaśāstra Pārijāta* by GODE 1953: 444–51 (the verses cited are actually from the former) who is also unaware of the verse on Nijāma).

5 KANE 1997: 860–68; MINKOWSKI 2004: 331. We cannot be certain that the Nizam in question was not Burhan Nizam Shah (r. 1508–53) rather than Ahmad Nizam Shah, as some assert. I pass over here arguments identifying Bhānudatta and a much anthologized poet named Bhānukara, whose references would link Bhānudatta with other Muslim rulers such as Shershah. (The evidence is collected in CHAUDHURI 1942: 3–32, though not sifted critically; see also DE 1959: 147.)

6 On Golconda, see the remarks on Akbar Shah that follow; Sanskrit manuscript catalogues list a large number of Telugu MSS. of the RM, with only two (incomplete) MSS. in Mithilā and very scanty holdings elsewhere in the northeast. DOSHI 1972: 25–26 discusses the Aurangabad RM.

7 Forthcoming in the CSL, translated by OLIVER FALLON.

8 For the changeability of the category "literature" in Sanskrit literary history, see POLLOCK 2003: 55–60.

9 His only real peer is Jagannātha (*fl.* 1650). Southern writers used their own poetry for illustrations at least from the time of Vidyānātha (c. 1300).

10 The list of such works is long and their authors distinguished. It includes, in addition to Kṛpārām's *Hittaraṅgiṇī* (based on the RT), Nanddās' *Rasmañjarī* (c. 1585, based on the RM); Rahim's *Barvai Nāyikābhed* (c. 1600, based on the RM); Sundar's *Sundarśṛṅgār* (1631, based on the RM); Mahākavi Dev's *Bhāvvilās* (1689, based on the RT). Bhānu's influence continued well into the eighteenth century. (I owe this list to ALLISON BUSCH.)

11 Note the echo in Kshetrayya (RAMANUJAN et al. 1994: 65), though the Telugu poet emends to beautiful ironic effect: the lover used to tell her that their bodies were one—and now she knows why. Kshetrayya was patronized by the same Golconda court at which the *Śṛṅgāramañjarī* was later produced (RAGHAVAN 1951: 8).

12 See POLLOCK 1998.

13 See RT 6.2. Another significant if under-argued innovation concerns the possibility of *śānta* constituting a ninth rasa (RT 7.63).

14 For the earlier history see NŚ ch. 24; DR ch. 2; ŚP ch. 15.

15 The work itself has an interesting history, being first written in Telugu and then translated into Sanskrit (the latter version being adopted into Hindi by the celebrated poet Cintāmaṇi Tripāṭhī). See RAGHAVAN 1951: 73–90 for a detailed review of Akbar Shah's

critique of the RM. This critique is itself answered by one of Bhānu's later commentators, Trivikrama Miśra.

16 The paintings are themselves undated and have been placed everywhere between 1625 and 1660. The best of them strongly resemble the *rāgamālā* works of Sahibdin of 1630–40, perhaps even anticipating him. Compare, for example, BARRETT and GRAY 1963: 135–39; KHANDALAVALA and DOSHI 1987: 126; WILLIAMS 2007: pl. 6 (with which compare RM pl. 21). On the Basohli paintings, see RANDHAWA and BAMBHRI 1981, BEACH 1992: 171; for Nurpur, ARCHER 1976: plates 71–72.

17 The original album has been dispersed. Some seventeen images have been published, while more than forty remain unpublished in a variety of private collections and museums. A number of the latter have been made available on the CSL website.

18 See CSL editions prepared by RICHARD GOMBRICH and LEE SIEGEL, respectively.

19 For discussions of particular paintings, see the notes to 19 [9], 47 [22], 53 [25], 65 [32], 125 [58], 134 [62], 154 [71], and 156 [72].

20 There are thorny problems of dating that I must ignore in this brief notice; I offer best guesses.

21 A copy of his unpublished commentary, the *Rasikarañjanī*, has been made available on the CSL website, with the kind permission of the British Library.

22 For the former, see, e.g., RANDHAWA and BHAMBRI 1981; for the latter, ROSSELLA 2000 (unavailable to me).

Abbreviations

GENERAL

DR = *Daśarūpaka*
J = Trilokanatha Jha, ed. *Kavirājabhānudattagranthāvalī*
KS = *Kāmasūtra*
NŚ = *Nāṭyaśāstra*
RM = *Rasamañjarī*
RT = *Rasataraṅgiṇī*
SD = *Sāhityadarpaṇa*
ŚM = *Śṛṅgāramañjarī* of Akbar Shah
ŚT = *Śṛṅgāratilaka* of Rudra Bhaṭṭa
a, *b*, *c*, *d* = first, second, third, fourth quarter verse respectively
pl. = plate
v. = verse
v.l. = varia lectio
References in the notes are to CSL paragraphs, unless accompanied by "v."

RASAMAÑJARĪ

A = Commentary of Anantapaṇḍita (*Vyaṅgārthakaumudī*)
B = Bangla recension of Vidyāsāgara (in *Kāvyasaṃgraha*)
G = Commentary of Gopāla Bhaṭṭa (*Rasikarañjanī*)
J = Jha edition (*Kavirājabhānudattagranthāvalī*)
N = Commentary of Nāgeśa (*Prakāśa*)
OG = Old Gujarati translation (on verso, Udaipur album)
R = Commentary of Raṅgaśāyin (*Āmoda*) (extracts printed in Tripathi 1981)
Ś = Commentary of Śeṣa Cintāmaṇi (*Parimala*)
Jha = Commentary of Bhadrinath Jha (or Sharma) (*Surabhi*)
T = Commentary of Trivikrama Miśra (*Rasāmoda*)
U = Udaipur album
Triv. A = Trivandrum MS. no. 2656

Triv. B = Trivandrum MS. no 6986 (breaks off in the middle of v. 52)
V = Commentary of Viśveśvara (*Samañjasā*)

RASATARAṄGIṆĪ

B = Commentary of Bhagavadbhaṭṭa (*Nūtanatarī*)
G = Commentary of Gaṅgārāma Jaḍe (*Nauka*)
J = Jha edition (*Kavirājabhānudattagranthāvalī*)
N = Commentary of Nemasāha (sometimes Nemiśāha) (*Kāvyasudhā*)
O = Commentary of Jivanathaji Ojha
Ś = Sharma edition
V = Commentary of Veṇīdatta Bhaṭṭācārya (*Rasikarañjanī*)

Bibliography

SANSKRIT TEXTS

Amaruśataka of Amaruka. 1889. Edited by DURGAPRASAD and KASHINATH PANDURANG PARAB. Bombay: Nirnaya Sagar Press. Kāvyamālā 18.

Daśarūpaka of Dhanaṃjaya with the Āloka of Dhanika. Edited by T. VENKATACHARYA. Madras: Adyar Library and Research Centre, 1969.

Kāmasūtra of Vātsyāyana. Edited by DEVADATTA SHASTRI. Varanasi: Chowkhamba Sanskrit Series Office, 1964.

Kavirājabhānudattagranthāvalī. Edited by TRILOKANATHA JHA. Darbhanga: Mithila Institute, 1988.

Kāvyasaṃgraha, vol 2. Edited by JIVANANDA VIDYASAGARA BHATTACARYA. Calcutta: Sarasvatiyantra, 1888.

Kāvyasudhā (commentary on the Rasataraṅgiṇī) of Nemasāha. University of Pennsylvania Indic MS. 510; Harvard Indic MS. 1285.

Nāṭyaśāstra of Bharata. Edited by M.R. KAVI et al. Baroda: Oriental Institute, 1926–1992

Nauka (commentary on the Rasataraṅgiṇī) of Gaṅgārāma Jaḍe. Varanasi: Kashi Samskrita Press, Benares 1886; Bhandarkar Oriental Research Institute MS. no 113/1919–24.

Nūtanatarī (commentary on the Rasataraṅgiṇī) of Bhagavadbhaṭṭa. Oriental Institute, Baroda, MS. no. 10842.

Parimala (commentary on the Rasamañjarī) of Śeṣa Cintāmaṇi. Edited by RAM SURESH TRIPATHI. Aligarh: Viveka Publications, 1981.

Prakāśa (commentary on the Rasamañjarī) of Nāgeśa Bhaṭṭa. Edited by RAMA SHASTRI TAILANGA. Benares: Vidya Vilas Press, 1904. Benares Sanskrit Series vol. 21.

Rasamañjarī of Bhānudatta. Government Oriental Manuscripts Library, Kariavattom (Trivandrum), MSS. nos. 2656 and 6986.

Rasamañjarī with the commentary Surabhi of Bhadrinath Jha. Edited by NARAHARI SASTRI. Varanasi: Shri Hari Krishna Nibandha Bhawan, 1929.

Rasāmoda (commentary on the Rasamañjarī) of Trivikrama Miśra. Edited by Ram Suresh Tripathi. Aligarh: Viveka Publications, 1981.

Rasaratnapradīpikā of Allarāja. Edited by R.N. Dandekar. Bombay: Bharatiya Vidyabhavan, 1945.

Rasataraṅgiṇī [with bhāṣāṭīkā]. Edited by Jivanathaji Ojha. Bombay: Venkatesvara Steam Press V.S. 1971 (1914).

Rasataraṅgiṇī. Edited by Urmila Sharma. Delhi: Parimala Publications, 1988.

Rasikarañjanī (commentary on the Rasamañjarī) of Gopāla Bhaṭṭa. British Library IO San 1228 (Eggeling 1228: I. C. 1941).

Rasikarañjanī (commentary on the Rasataraṅgiṇī) of Veṇīdatta Bhaṭṭācārya. British Library IO San 1703a; Oriental Institute, Baroda, MSS. nos. 839 (incomplete) and 10805.

Sāhityadarpaṇa of Viśvanātha Kavirāja. Edited by Durgaprasad. Bombay: Nirnaya Sagar Press, 1915; reprint New Delhi1982.

Samañjasā (commentary on the Rasamañjarī) of Viśveśvara. Edited by Janardan Pandeya. Varanasi: Sampurnanand Sanskrit University, 1991.

Śṛṅgāramañjarī of Akbar Shah. Edited by V. Raghavan. Hyderabad: Hyderabad Archaeological Department. 1951.

Śṛṅgāraprakāśa of Bhoja, Part 1. Edited by V. Raghavan. Cambridge: Harvard University Press, 1998.

Śṛṅgāratilaka of Rudraṭa Bhaṭṭa. Kavyamala gucchaka III, pp. 111–52 (also Richard Pischel, ed. *Rudraṭa's Çṛṅgāratilaka and Ruyyaka's Sahṛdayalīlā* [Kiel: Haeseler, 1886]).

Vyaṅgārthakaumudī (commentary on the Rasamañjarī) of Anantapaṇḍita. Edited by Rama Shastri Tailanga. Benares: Vidya Vilas Press, 1904. Benares Sanskrit Series vol. 21. Also (no ed.) Bombay: Gopal Narayana and Company, 1926.

OTHER TEXTS AND SECONDARY WORKS

Ain-i Akbari of Abu al-Fazl, vol. 3. 1978, Trans. H.S. Jarrett; reprint New Delhi: Munshiram Manoharlal.

Archer, W.G. 1976. *Visions of Courtly India: The Archer Collection of Pahari Miniatures*. Washington, D.C.: The Foundation.

Barrett, Doulgas E., and Basil Gray. 1963. *Painting of India*. Geneva: Skira.

Basu, A. (ed.) 1941. *Reports on the State of Education in Bengal (1835 and 1838) by William Adam*. Calcutta: University of Calcutta.

Bautze, Joachim. 1991. *Lotosmond und Löwenritt*. Indische Miniaturmalerei. Stuttgart: Linden-Museum Stuttgart.

Beach, Milo Cleveland. 1992. *Mughal and Rajput Painting*. Cambridge: Cambridge University Press. The New Cambridge History of India 1.3.

Binney, Edwin, 3rd, and Archer, W.G. 1968. *Rajput Miniatures from the Collection of Edwin Binney, III*. Portland: Portland Art Museum.

Chaudhuri, Jatindra Bimal. 1942. *Muslim Patronage to Sanskrit Learning*, part 1. Delhi: Idarah-i Adabiyat-i Delli.

Dasgupta, S.N., and S.K. De. 1962. *A History of Sanskrit Literature: Classical Period*. Calcutta: University of Calcutta Press.

De, S.K. 1959. *Some Problems of Sanskrit Poetics*. Calcutta: Firma K.L. Mukhopadhyaya.

Dindayal, ed. 2004. *Dev aur unkā Bhāv Vilās*. Delhi: Navalok Prashan.

Doshi, Saryu. 1972. "An Illustrated Manuscript from Aurangabad, dated 1650 A.D." *Lalit Kala* 15: 19–28.

Eaton, Richard M. 2005. *A Social History of the Deccan 1300–1761: Eight Indian Lives*. The New Cambridge History of India 1:8. Cambridge: Cambridge University Press.

Ehnbom, Daniel. 1985. *Indian Miniatures: The Ehrenfeld Collection*. New York: Hudson Hills.

Gode, P.K. 1953. *Studies in Indian Literary History*, vol. 1. Bombay: Bharatiya Vidya Bhavan.

Indian Miniature Paintings. Tenth Annual Exhibition, November 16 to December 31, 1974. Doris Wiener Gallery, New York.

Indian Paintings from Rajasthan, from the Collection of Sri Gopi Krishna Kanoria of Calcutta. 1958. Circulated by the Smithsonian Institution.

JONES, SIR WILLIAM. 1807. *The Works of Sir William Jones*. London: Stockdale and Walker.

KANE, P.V. 1991. *History of Sanskrit Poetics*. 4th ed. Delhi: Motilal Banarsidass.

———. 1997. *History of Dharmaśāstra*, vol. 2:1, 3rd ed. Pune: Bhandarkar Oriental Research Insitute.

KHANDALAVALA, KARL, and SARYU DOSHI. 1987. *A Collector's Dream: Indian Art in the Collections of Basant Kumar and Saraladevi Birla and the Birla Academy of Art and Culture*. Bombay: Marg.

Lalitkalā portfolio 23. 1981. New Delhi: Lalitkala Akademi.

MINKOWSKI, CHRISTOPHER. 2004. "On Sūryadāsa and the Invention of Bidirectional Poetry." *Journal of the American Oriental Society* 124, 2: 325–33.

PAL, PRATAPADITYA. 1978. *The Classical Tradition in Rajput Painting from the Paul F. Walker Collection*. New York: Pierpont Morgan Library.

POLLOCK, SHELDON. 1998. "Bhoja's Śṛṅgāraprakāśa and the Problem of Rasa: A Historical Introduction and Translation." *Asiatische Studien/Études asiatiques* 70:1 (1998): 117–92.

———. 2003. "Sanskrit Literary Culture from the Inside Out." In *Literary Cultures in History: Reconstructions from South Asia*, ed. SHELDON POLLOCK. Berkeley: University of California Press.

——— (trans). 2007. *Rama's Last Act* (*Uttararāmacarita*). New York: New York University Press and the JJC Foundation.

RAGHAVAN, V., ed. 1951. *Srngaramanjari of Saint Akbar Shah*. [Hyderabad]: Hyderabad Government.

RAMANUJAN, A.K., et al. 1994. *When God Is a Customer: Telugu Courtesan Songs by Kshetrayya and Others*. Berkeley: University of California Press.

Randhawa, M.S., and S.D. Bhambri. 1981. *Basohli Paintings of the Rasamanjari*. New Delhi: Abhinav Publications.

Regnaud, Paul. 1884. *La rhétorique sanskrite exposée dans son développement historique et ses rapports avec la rhétorique classique*. Paris: E. Leroux.

Rossella, Daniela. 2000. *I personaggi femminili (nayika) nella lirica indiana classica*, tesi di Dottorato di Ricerca in "Studi Indologici (Classici e Medioevali)" approvata presso l'Universita degli Studi di Roma "La Sapienza."

Williams, Joanna, et al. 2007. *Kingdom of the Sun: Indian Court and Village Art from the Princely State of Mewar*. San Francisco: Asian Art Museum, Chong-Moon Lee Center for Asian Art and Culture.

Wimsatt, W.K., and M. Beardsley. 1954. "The Affective Fallacy." In *The Verbal Icon*. Lexington: University of Kentucky Press.

Appendix on Literary Allusions

Bhanu·datta's original audience would have been familiar with a wide range of stories that most contemporary readers are unlikely to know.

He makes frequent allusions to the avatars or embodiments of the god Vishnu. These include: the Fish, whereby he saved the Vedas; the Tortoise, upon which Mount Mándara rested when it was used as the stick to churn the primal milk ocean (which produced the goddess Lakshmi, Vishnu's wife, and his cosmic jewel, the Káustubha); the Boar, on whose tusk he hooked the Earth and raised it from the ocean; the Dwarf (in this form Vishnu received from the demon king Bali as much territory as he could cover in three strides, and he crossed all earth, the atmosphere, and heaven); the Man-Lion, a form half man, half lion, whereby Vishnu killed the demon Hiránya·káshipu, who could not be slain by god or man or beast; Párashu·rama, or Rama with the Axe, a brahmin who slaughtered the kshatriya clans twenty-one times; and Krishna, who as a child lived among the cowherds (the majority of the allusions here concern Krishna's beloved, Radha, and his other amorous exploits).

The avatar to which Bhanu·datta most frequently refers is Rama, son of Dasha·ratha, immortalized in the epic poem, the "Ramáyana." Rama was set to become king but was sent into exile with his wife Sita (also known as Jánaki [daughter of King Jánaka], Vaidéhi [princess of Vidéha], and Máithili [princess of Míthila]) and his younger brother Lákshmana. During his sojourn in the forest his wife was abducted by

Rávana, the ten-headed king of the *rákshasa*s, who took her back to Lanka, his island fortress. Rama made an alliance with the monkeys, chief of whom was Hanumán, and having found his way to Rávana's kingdom killed the *rákshasa*s and their king. Vibhíshana, Rávana's brother, lent his support to Rama and was crowned king of Lanka.

Reference is also often made to the second great Indian epic, the "Maha·bhárata," above all as a repository of heroic deeds. The warring factions were the sons of Pandu and the sons of Dhrita·rashtra. Among the former were the great warriors Árjuna and Bhima, among the latter, their half-brother Karna, who was also a paragon of generosity.

The stories associated with the Great God Shiva (also known as Hara and Shambhu) supply material for many allusions as well. Central to his biography is his marriage with Párvati ("Daughter of the [Himálaya] Mountain," also known here as Bhaváni). Shiva fell in love with Párvati thanks to the efforts of the god of love Kama (literally, "desire"), but in the process Kama was incinerated by a flame from Shiva's third eye, and was mourned by his wife Rati ("passion"). Shiva's accoutrements include a snake necklace and a tall headdress in which the crescent moon is fixed.

BOUQUET OF RASA

DESCRIPTION OF THE NÁYIKA

1 ŚRĪ|SARASVATYAI namaḥ

ātmīyaṃ caraṇaṃ dadhāti purato
nimn'|ônnatāyāṃ bhuvi,
svīyen' âiva kareṇa karṣati taroḥ
puṣpaṃ śram'|āśaṅkayā,
talpe kiṃ ca mṛga|tvacā viracite
nidrāti bhāgair nijair
antaḥ|prema|bhar'|ālasāṃ priyatamām
aṅge dadhāno Haraḥ.* [1]

vidvat|kula|mano|bhṛṅga|*rasa*|vyāsaṅga|hetave
eṣā *prakāśyate* śrīmad|*Bhānunā Rasa*|mañjarī. [2]

tatra raseṣu śṛṅgārasy' âbhyarhitatvena tad|ālambana|vibhāvatvena nāyikā tāvan nirūpyate. sā ca tri|vidhā svīyā parakīyā sāmānya|vanitā c' êti. tatra svāminy ev' ânuraktā svīyā. na ca pariṇītāyāṃ para|gāminyām ativyāptiḥ.† atra pati|vratāyā eva lakṣyatvāt. tasyāś ca para|gāmitayā parakīyātvam api samāyāti.

5 asyāś ceṣṭā bhartuḥ† śuśrūṣā śīla|saṃrakṣaṇam ārjavaṃ kṣamā c' êti. yathā:

---

4 *ativyāptiḥ* Ś T V : *avyāptiḥ* J A 5 *bhartuḥ* A N Ś T V : om. J

---

i Shiva ii "Leading lady," or principal female character

Homage to Sarásvati, Goddess of Language 1

Lest she feel fatigue, Hara[i] plants his foot,
his own foot, first on the rocky ground,
and with his own right hand he plucks a flower
from the tree, and on the couch
spread with his rough garment, an antelope skin,
falls asleep on his right side,
within his body bearing his beloved,
fatigued from her deep inner love.*

Glorious *Bhanu : the sun* here *publishes :*
opens to view
this sweet "Bouquet of *Rasa : nectar*"
where bees—the minds of swarms of learned
readers—may acquire *rasa : nectar.*

Now, among these rasas the most prized is the erotic. Insofar as the *náyika*[ii] is the underlying factor of the erotic rasa, she will be described first. She is of three sorts: one's own wife, another man's wife, or a courtesan. Among these, "one's own" implies a woman in love exclusively with her husband.* This definition of the category is thus not so wide as to include* a married woman in love with another man. In the case of the category one's own, fidelity is the constitutive feature, whereas it is the very fact of a married woman's being in love with another man that causes her to be classified as "another's."

The characteristic behavior of one's own *náyika* con- 5
sists of obedience to her husband, modesty, sincerity, and forgiveness.* For example:

gat'|āgata|kutūhalaṃ
nayanayor apāṅg'|âvadhi;
smitaṃ kula|nata|bhruvām
adhara eva viśrāmyati.
vacaḥ priyatama|śruter
atithir eva; kopa|kramaḥ
kadā cid api cet, tadā
manasi kevalaṃ majjati. [3]

svīyā tu tri|vidhā. mugdhā madhyā pragalbhā c' êti. tatr' âṅkurita|yauvanā mugdhā. sā c' â|jñāta|yauvanā jñāta|yauvanā ca. s" âiva kramaśo lajjā|bhaya|parādhīna|ratir nav'|ōḍhā. s" âiva kramaśaḥ sa|praśrayā viśrabdha|nav'|ōḍhā. asyāś ceṣṭā kriyā|hriyā mano|harā, kope mārdavaṃ, nava|bhūṣaṇe samīhā ca.

mugdhā yathā:

ājñaptaṃ kila Kāma|deva|dharaṇī|
pālena kāle śubhe
vastuṃ vāstu|vidhiṃ vidhāsyati tanau
tāruṇyam eṇī|dṛśaḥ:
dṛṣṭyā khañjana|cāturī, mukha|rucā
saudhādharī mādhurī,
vācā kiṃ ca sudhā|samudra|laharī|
lāvaṇyam āmantryate. [4]

Highborn women with curving brows
don't care to look this way or that.
Instead, they keep their eyes downcast,
their smiles coming to rest on their lips.
To their lovers' ears alone
their talk arrives as a welcome guest.
And if highborn women get angry
they bury their anger within their hearts.*

One's own *náyika* is herself of three types: the naïve, the average, and the sophisticated. The naïve is a girl who is just reaching puberty, and she may or may not understand its manifestations.* The same naïve *náyika* is in due course a "newly married" woman, who is bashful and timid in her desire; and, in due course, a "confident newly married" woman, who is more compliant. Her characteristic behavior is as follows: she enchants with the modesty of her actions,* she is mild in her love-anger, and eager for new ornaments.

An example of the naïve *náyika*:

Womanhood, ordered by the monarch himself,
the God of love, to take up its dwelling
in a young girl's body, performs the housewarming
rite
at the auspicious hour: her glancing eye
is directed to start to dance like the wagtail bird,
her complexion to shed a glow like the full moon's
light,
her speech to sound like waves on the nectar ocean.*

a|jñāta|yauvanā yathā:

nīrāt tīram upāgatā śravaṇayoḥ
sīmni sphuran|netrayoḥ
«śrotre lagnam idaṃ kim utpalam?» iti
jñātuṃ karaṃ nyasyati.
śaivāl'|âṅkura|śaṅkayā śaśi|mukhī
rom'|āvalīṃ proñchati.
«śrānt" âsm'» îti muhuḥ sakhīm a|vidita|
śroṇī|bharā pṛcchati. [5]

jñāta|yauvanā yathā:

Svayam/bhūḥ Śambhur, ambhoja|
locane, tvat|*payo/dharaḥ*
nakhena kasya dhanyasya
candra|cūḍo bhaviṣyati? [6]

nav'|ōḍhā yathā:

haste dhṛt" âpi, śayane viniveśit" âpi,
kroḍe kṛt" âpi yatate bahir eva gantum.
jānīmahe nava|vadhūr atha tasya vaśyā
yaḥ pāratam sthirayituṃ kṣamate kareṇa. [7]

An example of a girl who does not understand the manifestations of puberty: 10

Leaving the water for the bank, she thought
she saw a lotus petal caught at her ear,
and to be sure reached out her hand—only to touch
the corner where her eye was flashing bright.
Then the moonfaced girl tried to wipe away
the line of hair by her navel, thinking it seaweed,
and repeatedly asked her friend why she felt
so tired, unaware that her hips were filling out.*

An example of a girl who does understand the signs:

Lotus-eyed girl, these *breasts* of yours
are *growing on their own* so *graciously*
Self-existent, *All-gracious*, *Ganga-bearing*.
What lucky man will get to crown them
with a moon scratched on them with his nails?*

An example of the first type of newly married naïve *náyika*:

Although I took her by the hand 15
and set her on the bed
and held her tight in my arms, she never
stopped struggling to get out.
Now I understand why they say
the man who can control
a newlywed girl is the man who can hold
mercury in his palm.

viśrabdha|nav'|ōḍhā yathā:

dara|mukulita|netra|pāli, nīvī|
niyamita|bāhu, kṛt'|ōru|yugma|bandham,
kara|kalita|kuca|sthalaṃ nav'|ōḍhā
svapiti samīpam upetya kasya yūnaḥ? [8]

samāna|lajjā|madanā madhyā. eṣ" āiv' âtipraśrayād ativiśrabdha|nav'|ōḍhā. asyāś ceṣṭā s'|āgasi preyasi dhairye vakr'|ôktir, a|dhairye paruṣa|vāk. yathā:

«svāpe priy'|ānana|vilokana|hānir eva;
svāpa|cyutau priya|kara|grahaṇa|prasaṅgaḥ.»
itthaṃ saroruha|mukhī paricintayantī
svāpaṃ vidhātum api hātum api prapede. [9]

pati|mātra|viṣayaka|keli|kalāpa|kovidā pragalbhā. veśyāyāṃ kulaṭāyāṃ pati|mātra|viṣayatv'|â|bhāvān na tatr'† âtivyāptiḥ. asyāś* ceṣṭā rati|prītir, ānandāt saṃmohaḥ. prathamā yathā:

---

20 *tatr'* : om. J

An example of the newly married naïve *náyika* who is becoming more confident:

> Lucky the fellow whose new bride steals
> beside him to sleep, her eyes half closed,
> one hand on her belt, one covering her breasts,
> and her thighs locked tight together.*

A *náyika* is average if her desire and modesty are in balance. Because of her extreme compliance in lovemaking, the same woman is sometimes also classified as a very confident new bride.* Her characteristic behavior is as follows: if she is steady in her composure, she reacts with clever sarcasm when her lover has been unfaithful; if she is not, she reacts with insults.* An example:

> She thought, "If I fall asleep right now
> I'll lose the chance to see
> my love's face; and if I stay awake,
> his hands might start to roam."
> Over and over she thought it through,
> that girl with lotus eyes,
> and finally decided to go to sleep
> and to stay awake.*

The experienced *náyika* is skilled in all the arts of love- 20
making, which takes place solely with her husband. Again, since this takes place only with her husband, the definition is not so wide as to include courtesans or promiscuous women (that is, another's *náyika*). Her characteristic behavior is as follows:* she enjoys sexual intercourse, and she can lose all awareness in the bliss of lovemaking. An example of the first:

saṃspṛśya stanam, ākalayya vadanaṃ,
saṃślisya kaṇṭha|sthalaṃ,
niṣpīy' âdhara|bimbam, ambaram apā-
kṛṣya, vyudasy' âlakam,
devasy' âmbujinī|pateḥ samudayaṃ
jijñāsamāne priye
vām'|âkṣī vasan'|âñculaiḥ śravaṇayor
nīl'|ôtpalaṃ nihnute. [10]

dvitīyā yathā:

nakha|kṣatam uraḥ|sthale,
'dhara|tale* radasya vraṇaṃ,
cyutā bakula|mālikā,
vigalitā ca mukt"|āvaliḥ.
rat'|ânta|samaye mayā
sakalam etad ālokitaṃ.
smṛtiḥ kva* ca ratiḥ kva ca,
kva ca tav', āli, śikṣā|vidhiḥ? [11]

madhyā|pragalbhe praty|ekaṃ mān'|âvasthāyāṃ tri|vidhe. dhīr", â|dhīrā, dhīr'|â|dhīrā c' êti. vyaṅgya|kopa|prakāśā dhīrā. a|vyaṅgya|kopa|prakāś" â|dhīrā. vyaṅgy'|â|vyaṅgya|kopa|prakāśā dhīr'|â|dhīrā. iyāṃs tu viśeṣaḥ. madhyā|dhīrāyāḥ kopasya gīr vyañjikā. a|dhīrāyāḥ paruṣa|vāk. dhīr'|â|dhīrāyāś ca vacana|rudite kopasya prakāśake. prauḍhā†|dhīrāyās tu rat'|āudāsyam, a|dhīrāyās tarjana|tāḍan'|ādi, dhīr'|â|dhīrāyā rat'|āudāsyaṃ tarjana|tāḍan'|ādi

24 *prauḍhā-* Ś A T N : *pragalbhā-* (passim) J

He fondled her breasts and drew her face to his
and held her tight around the neck;
he drank deep at her full lips and pulled
her wrap away and mussed her hair.
But as he wondered aloud if the god, the king
who rules day-blooming flowers, had risen,
the woman took the hems of her sari and covered
the blue lotus at her ears.*

An example of the second:

His nails had scratched my chest, his teeth
had bitten deep into my soft lips,
my *bákula* wreath had fallen,
my necklace had broken
and pearls were everywhere.
But it was only when lovemaking had ended
that I noticed all this.
What have passion and mindfulness, my friend—
let alone your advice—to do with each other?

The average and the experienced *náyikas* each have three subtypes with respect to states of anger: steady, unsteady, and mixed (that is, both steady and unsteady). In the steady *náyika*, anger is made manifest by implication; in the unsteady, anger is made manifest explicitly; in the mixed, it can be both implied and explicit. The distinctions between the average and experienced angry *náyikas* are these: the average steady *náyika* uses subtle language to suggest her anger; the average unsteady *náyika* makes direct use of verbal abuse (and tears and the like); the average mixed

ca kopasya prakāśakam. dhīr"|ādi|bhedāḥ svīyāyā eva, na parakīyāyā iti prācīna|likhanam ājñā|mātram. dhīratvam a|dhīratvaṃ tad|ubhayaṃ vā māna|niyataṃ; parakīyāyāṃ mānaś cet, tadā teṣām apy† āvaśyakatvāt. mānaś ca svakīyāyā eva,† na parakīyāyā iti vaktum a|śakyatvāt.

madhyā dhīrā yathā:

lol'|âli|puñje vrajato nikuñje
  sphārā babhūvuḥ śrama|vāri|dhārāḥ?
dehe samīhe bhavato vidhātuṃ
  dhīraṃ samīraṃ nalinī|dalena. [12]

madhy" â|dhīrā yathā:

jātas te niśi jāgaro, mama punar
  netr'|âmbuje śoṇimā;
 niṣpītaṃ bhavatā madhu pravitataṃ,
  vyāghūrṇitaṃ me manaḥ;
bhrāmyad|bhṛṅga|ghane nikuñja|bhavane
  labdhaṃ tvayā śrī|phalaṃ,
 Pañceṣuḥ punar eṣa† māṃ hutavaha|
  krūraiḥ śaraiḥ kṛntati.* [13]

---

24 *apy* om. J 24 *svakīyāyā eva* om. J V 28 *eṣa* Ś A N T : *eva* J

náyika both suggests her anger by subtle words and expresses it in tears and verbal abuse. The experienced steady *náyika* shows indifference to lovemaking; the experienced unsteady *náyika* does such things as threatening and striking her lover; and the experienced mixed *náyika* implies her anger by indifference to lovemaking and expresses it by threatening and striking her lover. The view of older writers, that these subclasses ("steady" and the rest) apply only to one's own *náyika* and not to another's, is an empty assertion. For being steady or unsteady or a combination of the two is a function of anger alone, and if we admit that another's *náyika* is subject to anger, then she, too, must be susceptible to these subtypes. And who could maintain that it is only one's own and not another's *náyika* who is subject to anger?*

An example of the average steady *náyika*: 25

Oh, so you're only soaked with sweat from rushing
Shall I try to cool you down a little
to the bower where the bees are buzzing?
with a steady breeze from this lotus petal?*

An example of the average unsteady *náyika*:

You stayed awake all night, and yet
it's my eyes that are reddened;
you were the one who drank all that rum,
and yet it's my head that's splitting;
and in the bower buzzing with bees
it was you who stole beauty's fruit,
yet I'm the one the Love God wounds
with his arrows that burn like fire.*

madhyā dhīr'|â|dhīrā yathā:

30 «kānt"|ânurāga|caturo 'si, manoharo 'si;
nātho* 'si, kiṃ ca nava|yauvana|bhūṣito 'si.»
itthaṃ nigadya sudṛśā vadane priyasya
niḥśvasya bāṣpa|lulitā nihitā dṛg|antāḥ. [14]

prauḍhā dhīrā yathā:

no talpaṃ bhajase, na jalpasi sudhā|
dhār"|ânukārā giro,
dṛk|pātaṃ kuruṣe na vā, parijane
kopa|prakāśa|cchalāt.
itthaṃ, ketaka|garbha|gauri, dayite
kopasya saṅgopanaṃ;
tat syād eva, na cet punaḥ sahacarī
kurvīta sāci smitam. [15]

prauḍh" â|dhīrā yathā:

pratiphalam avalokya svīyam indoḥ kalāyāṃ,
Hara|śirasi parasyā vāsam āśaṅkamānā,
Giriśam Acala|kanyā tarjayām āsa kampa|
pracala|valaya|cañcat|kānti|bhājā kareṇa. [16]

An example of the average mixed *náyika*:

“You really know how to make a woman love you; 30
you’re handsome, adorned with the bloom of youth,
and my husband,”
the lovely woman said, and with tear-filled eyes
she gazed upon her lover’s face and sighed.*

An example of an experienced steady *náyika*:

You won’t come to bed and won’t release
the nectar that flows when you speak,
not even cast a glance, staring
at your girlfriends in a show of anger.
In this way you try to hide your anger
at the man who loves you, woman pale
as a *kétaka* bud. It might have worked
had your confidante not slyly smiled.*

An example of an experienced unsteady *náyika*:

The daughter of the holy Mountain
caught her own face reflected
in the digit of the moon
on Hara’s crown of hair. She thought,
“So he’s keeping another woman!”
and she began to slap Shiva,
and her hand shimmered with the glow
of bracelets shaken in a rage.*

prauḍhā dhīr'|â|dhīrā yathā:

talp'|ôpāntam upeyuṣi priyatame
vakrī|kṛta|grīvayā,
kāku|vyākula|vāci sāci|hasita|
sphūrjat|kapola|śriyā,
hasta|nyasta|kare punar mṛga|dṛśā
lākṣā|rasa|kṣālita|
proṣṭhī|pṛṣṭha|mayūkha|māṃsala|ruco
visphāritā dṛṣṭayaḥ. [17]

ete ca dhīr"|ādi|ṣaḍ|bhedā dvi|vidhāḥ, jyeṣṭhā kaniṣṭhā ca.† dhīrā jyeṣṭhā kaniṣṭhā ca. a|dhīrā jyeṣṭhā kaniṣṭhā ca. dhīr'|â|dhīrā jyeṣṭhā kaniṣṭhā ca. pariṇītatve sati bhartur adhika|snehā jyeṣṭhā. pariṇītatve sati bhartur nyūna|snehā kaniṣṭhā. adhika|snehāsu nyūna|snehāsu parakīyāsu† sāmānya|vanitāsu n' âtivyāptiḥ, pariṇīta|padena vyāvartanāt.

dhīrā jyeṣṭhā kaniṣṭhā ca yathā:

---

37 *jyeṣṭhā kaniṣṭhā ca* om. J *parakīyāsu* om. J

An example of an experienced mixed *náyika*: 35

When her lover stole close to the bed,
she turned her head away; when she heard
his strained and wheedling tone of voice,
her cheeks flushed with a dismissive laugh;
but when he tried to pat her hand,
the eyes of the doe-eyed girl gave off
a glow as rich as the beams that would flash
from the back of a darting fish
were it stained with the reddest lac.*

These six types of angry women are again divisible into two subtypes, depending on whether the *náyika* is more loved or less loved. We thus have a "steady more loved" and a "steady less loved" average *náyika*; an "unsteady more loved" and an "unsteady less loved" average *náyika* ; and a "mixed more loved" and a "mixed less loved" average *náyika*.* The woman who, being married, enjoys a greater share of her husband's affection is "more loved," whereas the "less loved" is the woman who, again, being married, enjoys a lesser share. The definition is not so wide as to include another's *náyika* or a "common" *náyika* who happens to enjoy a greater or lesser share of her lover's affection, since that is ruled out by the condition of being married.

An example of both the more loved and the less loved steady *náyikas*:

ekasmin śayane saroruha|dṛśor
vijñāya nidrāṃ tayor,
ekāṃ pallavit'|âvaguṇṭhana|paṭām
utkandharo dṛṣṭavān;
anyasyāḥ savidhaṃ sametya nibhṛta|
vyālola|hast'|âṅguli|
vyāpārair vasan'|âñcalaṃ capalayan
svāpa|cyutiṃ kḷptavān. [18]

a|dhīrā jyeṣṭhā kaniṣṭhā ca yathā:

antaḥ|kopa|kaṣāyite priyatame
paśyan, ghane kānane
puṣpasy' âvacayāya namra|vadanām
ekāṃ samāyojayat.
ardh'|ônmīlita|locan'|âñcala|camat|
kār'|âbhirām'|ānanāṃ
smer'|ârdh'†|âdhara|pallavāṃ nava|vadhūm
anyāṃ samāliṅgati. [19]

dhīr'|â|dhīrā jyeṣṭhā kaniṣṭhā ca yathā:

dhairy'|â|dhairya|parigraha|grahilayor
eṇī|dṛśoḥ prītaye†
ratna|dvandvam an|anta|kānti|ruciraṃ
muṣṭi|dvaye nyastavān
ekasyāḥ kalayan kare prathamato
ratnaṃ,† parasyāḥ priyo
hastāhasti|miṣāt spṛśan kuca|taṭīm
ānandam āvindati. [20]

---

41 *-ardha-* Ś A N T : *-ārdra-* J V 43 *prītaye* Ś A N : *prītayoḥ* J
43 *ratnam* Ś A N T : *dhūrtaḥ* J

Finding his two women to be asleep
on a single bed, he craned his neck
and saw that one lay wrapped up tight
within the cocoon of her veil.
And so he stole close to the other girl
and, with oft-repeated movements
of his trembling fingers, rustled the edge
of her garment and woke her up.*

An example of both the more loved and the less loved 40
unsteady *náyika*s:

He could tell that his two wives were almost
livid with rage, so he entreated the one
to go off into the thick woods
to gather flowers, and as she bowed
her head to the task he embraced the other,
his new wife, and her face began to glow
with eyes half-open and glancing
and lips half-formed in a smile.

An example of both the more loved and the less loved mixed *náyika*s:

His two wives were being now hard, now soft
in their anger, and so to win them over
he brought them two sparkling gems
held tight within his fisted hands.
One he placed straightway in one wife's palm,
but he made the second fight for hers
in hand-to-hand combat and had the joy
of feeling her full and heavy breasts.*

a|prakaṭa|para|puruṣ'|ânurāgā parakīyā. sā ca dvi|vidhā. par'|ōḍhā kanyakā ca. kanyakāyāḥ pitr|ādy|adhīnatayā parakīyatā. asyā gupt" âiva sakalā ceṣṭā. par'|ōḍhā yathā:

45 ayaṃ Revā|kuñjaḥ
Kusumaśara|sevā|samucitaḥ;
samīro 'yaṃ velā|
dara|vidalad|elā|parimalaḥ;
iyaṃ prāvṛḍ dhanyā
nava|jalada|vinyāsa|caturā—
par'|âdhīnaṃ cetaḥ,
sakhi, kim api kartuṃ mṛgayate. [21]

guptā|vidagdhā|lakṣitā|kulaṭ"|ânuśayānā|muditā|prabhṛtīnāṃ parakīyāyām ev' ântar|bhāvaḥ. guptā tridhā. vṛtta|surata|gopanā, vartiṣyamāṇa|surata|gopanā, vṛtta|vartiṣyamāṇa|surata|gopanā ca. tritayam api yathā:

A *náyika* that is another's is in love with another man, but her love is kept hidden.* This *náyika* is of two sorts, either married to another man or not yet married. The latter is another's insofar as she is under the power of her father and other males. The characteristic behavior of this *náyika* is total secretiveness.* An example of another's *náyika* who is married to another man:

This grove by the Reva is just the place to worship 45
the flower-arrowed God of love;
the wind is fragrant with cardamom now bursting
into blossom by the shore;
the blessed rainy season has arrived
with its skilled arrangement of fresh clouds—
my heart is no longer my own and now is looking
to do I don't know what.

Within the class of another's *náyika* various subtypes are included: the secretive, the cunning, the discovered, the promiscuous, the anxious, the joyfully expectant. The secretive girl is of three sorts, according to whether she conceals an episode of sexual intercourse that has taken place, or one that is about to take place, or one that already has taken place and will again. An example of all three types:*

śvaśrūḥ krudhyatu, vidviṣantu suhṛdo,
nindantu vā yātaras.
tasmin kiṃ tu na mandire, sakhi, punaḥ
svāpo vidheyo mayā.
ākhor ākramaṇāya koṇa|kuharād
utphālam ātanvatī
mārjārī nakharaiḥ kharaiḥ kṛtavatī
kāṃ kāṃ na me durdaśām! [22]

vidagdhā ca dvi|vidhā. vāg|vidagdhā kriyā|vidagdhā ca. tatra vāg|vidagdhā yathā:

nibiḍatama|tamāla|valli|vallī|
vicakila|rāji|virājit'|ôpakaṇṭhe,
pathika, samucitas tav' âdya tīvre
savitari tatra sarit|taṭe nivāsaḥ. [23]

50 kriyā|vidagdhā yathā:

dāsāya bhavana|nāthe
badarīm apanetum ādiśati
hemante hariṇ'|âkṣī
payasi kuṭhāraṃ vinikṣipati. [24]

lakṣitā yathā:

yad bhūtaṃ tad bhūtaṃ;
yad bhūyāt tad api vā bhūyāt;
yad bhavati tad bhavati vā;
viphalas tava ko 'pi gopan'|āyāsaḥ. [25]

Mother-in-law can rant, and friends
condemn, and sisters-in-law reprove.
How am I possibly to sleep
another night in that house?
That cat of theirs is forever
springing out of a corner niche
to catch a mouse, and you see what all
she's done to me with her sharp claws!*

The cunning one is of two sorts, with respect either to what she says or what she does. An example of the former:

Traveler, it's wise to rest now—the sun's
so hot—by the river where the jasmine blooms
and the vines twine tightly around
dense thickets of *tamála* trees.

An example of the latter: 50

When the slave was told by his master
to go cut down the jujube tree,
the doe-eyed girl stole the axe
and threw it deep in the ice-cold lake.*

An example of the discovered girl:

What's past is past; whatever will be
will be; and as for what is now
happening, it's happening, and the most valiant
effort to hide it will be in vain.*

kulaṭā yathā:

55 ete vāri|kaṇān kiranti, puruṣān
varṣanti n' âmbho|dharāḥ;
śailāḥ śādvalam udvamanti, na sṛjanty
ete punar nāyakān;
trailokye taravaḥ phalāni suvate,
n' âiv' ārabhante janān—
Dhātaḥ, kātaram ālapāmi, kulaṭā|
hetos tvayā kiṃ kṛtam? [26]

anuśayānā yathā. vartamāna|sthāna|vighaṭanena bhāvi|sthān'|â|bhāva|śaṅkayā sv'|ân|adhiṣṭhita|saṅketa|sthalaṃ prati bhartur gaman'|ânumānen'† ânuśayānā tridhā. praty|ekam udāharaṇāni.

samupāgatavati caitre
nipatita|patre* lavaṅga|latikāyāḥ,
sudṛśaḥ kapola|pālī,
Śiva Śiva, tālī|dala|dyutiṃ lebhe. [27]

nidrālu|keki|mithunāni, kapota|pota|
vyādhūta|nūtana|mahīruha|pallavāni
tatr' âpi, tanvi, na vanāni kiyanti santi.
khidyasva na, priyatamasya gṛhaṃ prayāhi. [28]

---

56 *ca* add J V

An example of the promiscuous girl:

The clouds in the sky rain down drops of rain, 55
not torrents of boyfriends;
the only thing the green hills produce is grass,
not crops of noble lovers;
and in all the universe the fruit of trees
is simply fruit, not men—
I've a bone to pick, dear Lord, about
        the arrangements
you've made for girls like me.*

The anxious another's *náyika* is of three sorts, depending on whether she is anxious over a disturbance to her normal meeting place; from concern whether any meeting place will be available; or from inferring that her lover went to the meeting place when she wasn't there.* Here follow examples of each:

When the cold month of spring came
and the poor clove tree vines lost their leaves,
the lovely woman's cheeks turned paler,
dear God, than the palest palm tree leaves.

Don't worry, girl, go off to your lover's house.
There are dense groves without number there,
filled with peacocks sleepy after mating
and baby doves rustling the fresh dense foliage.*

karṇa|kalpita|rasāla|mañjarī|
piñjarīkṛta|kapola|maṇḍalaḥ
niṣpatan|nayana|vāri|dhārayā
Rādhayā Madhu|ripur nirīkṣyate. [29]

60 muditā yathā:

«goṣṭheṣu tiṣṭhati patir, badhirā nanāndā,
netra|dvayasya ca na pāṭavam asti yātuḥ,»†
ittham niśamya taruṇī kuca|kumbha|sīmni
rom'|âñca|kañcukam udañcitam ātatāna. [30]

kanyakā yathā:

kiñcit|kuñcita|hāra|yaṣṭi, sarala|
bhrū|valli, sāci|smitam,
prānta|bhrānta|vilocana|dyuti, bhujā|
paryasta|karṇ'|ôtpalam
aṅgulyā sphurad|aṅgulīyaka|rucā
gaṇḍasya* kaṇḍūyanaṃ
kurvāṇā nṛpa|kanyakā sukṛtinaṃ
sa|vyājam ālokate. [31]

---

61 *yātuḥ* Ś A N T V : *mātuḥ* J

Krishna was coming, and he had by his ear
a mango twig that yellowed his cheeks,
and Radha saw him and no sooner saw the twig
than tears came streaming from her eyes.*

An example of the joyfully expectant another's *náyika*: 60

"The husband's always off in the cowshed,
the sister's a deaf mute,
and the wife of her brother-in-law
is blinder than a bat,"
she heard her girlfriend saying to him,
and felt the goosebumps spread
across her high firm breasts like armor
for the battle to come.*

An example of another's *náyika* who is not yet married:

Idly playing with her necklace, her brows
not archly raised, her smile half hidden,
glances flashing as she looks askance
and the lily dropping from ear to arm
as she scratches her cheek with fingers sparkling
with rich gems, the princess looks,
but barely looks, pretending not to look,
at the luckiest man in the world.*

vitta | mātr' | ôpādhika | sakala | puruṣ' | ânurāgā sāmānya | vanitā. na c' Âgnimitre kṣiti|patāv anuraktāyām Airāvatyām a|vyāptiḥ. tatra vitta|mātr' | ôpādher a|bhāvād iti cen—m" âivam. s" âpi kāśmīra|hīr' |ādi|dātari mahā|rāje 'nuraktā na tu maha" | rṣau ten' âvagamyate tatr' âpi vitta | mātram ev' ôpādhir iti. sāmānya|vanitā yathā:

dṛṣṭvā prāṅgaṇa|sannidhau bahu|dhanaṃ
dātāram abhyāgataṃ,
vakṣojau tanutaḥ parasparam iv' ā-
śleṣaṃ kuraṅgī|dṛśaḥ,
ānand'|âśru|payāṃsi muñcati muhur
mālā|miṣāt kuntalo,
dṛṣṭiḥ kiṃ ca dhan'|āgamaṃ kathayituṃ
karṇ'|ântikaṃ gacchati. [32]

etā anya | sambhoga | duḥkhitā vakr' | ôkti | garvitā māna-vatyaś c' êti tisro bhavanti.

tatr' ânya|sambhoga|duḥkhitā yathā:

A common *náyika* is one whose passion is directed toward all men, the only necessary condition being their money. It would be erroneous to argue that such a definition is too narrow to include Airávati's passion for King Agni·mitra, on the grounds that the condition—the payment of money—is absent. Her passion was directed toward a king, after all, capable of giving her saffron, diamonds, and so on, and not toward, say, an indigent holy man; and this leads us to affirm that the necessary condition, money, was indeed present.* An example of the common *náyika*:

From across the wide forecourt 65
the doe-eyed courtesan caught sight
of a rich big spender on the way,
and it was as if her high, full breasts
were giving each other a great big hug,
and in the guise of flowers dropping from her hair
when she motioned, tears of joy streamed down
and her eye slipped back to her ear
as if to report on the profits to come.*

All three of these *náyika*s are subject to three further states: they can be unhappy at their lover's infidelity; they can be proud, their pride being expressed by clever indirectness in speech; or they can be filled with love-anger.*

An example of the *náyika* who is unhappy at her lover's infidelity:

tvaṃ, dūti, niragāḥ kuñjaṃ,
na tu pāpīyaso gṛham?
kiṃśuk'|ābharaṇaṃ dehe
dṛśyate katham anyathā? [33]

vakr'|ôkti|garvitā dvi|vidhā, prema|garvitā saundarya|garvitā ca.

tatra prema|garvitā yathā:

vapuṣi tava tanoti ratna|bhūṣāṃ
prabhur, iti dhanyatamā 'si. kiṃ bravīmi,
sakhi? tanu|nayan'|ântarāla|bhīruḥ
kalayati me na vibhūṣaṇāni kāntaḥ. [34]

saundarya|garvitā yathā:

kalayati kamal'|ôpamānam akṣṇoḥ,
prathayati vāci sudhā|rasasya sāmyam.
sakhi, kathaya, kim ācarāmi kānte?
samajani tatra sahiṣṇut" âiva doṣaḥ. [35]

mānavatī yathā.† priy'|âparādha|sūcikā ceṣṭā mānaḥ. sa ca laghur madhyamo guruś ca. alp'|âpaneyo laghuḥ. kaṣṭatar'|âpaneyo madhyamaḥ. kaṣṭatam'|âpaneyo guruḥ. a|sādhyas tu ras'|ābhāsaḥ. apara|strī|darśan'|ādi|janmā laghuḥ. gotra|skhalan'|ādi|janmā madhyamaḥ. apara|strī|saṅga|janmā guruḥ. anyathā|siddha|kutūhal'|ādy|apaneyo

74 *mānavatī yathā* Ś A N Triv. A : om. J V

You didn't go to that scoundrel's house,
you went to the woods, didn't you, go-between?
How else could you have gotten that garland
of flame-tree flowers you're wearing?*

The proud *náyika* who expresses her pride by clever indirectness in speech is of two sorts: she can be proud on account of being loved or on account of her beauty.

An example of the *náyika* who is proud on account of 70
being loved:

Lucky girl to have a lover who covers
your body with precious jewels. What's there to say,
dear friend? Mine won't put any jewelry on me
for fear some part might be concealed.

An example of the *náyika* who is proud on account of her beauty:

What am I to do, my friend, with a lover
who claims my eyes compare with lotuses
and insists my voice is almost as sweet as nectar?
Tolerating his insults is my one shortcoming.*

Now the angry *náyika*. Anger is a type of behavior indicative of a transgression on the part of her lover.* It can be mild, average, or intense, that is to say, being appeased with no difficulty, some difficulty, or extreme difficulty, respectively. Anger represented as completely unappeasable creates a "semblance of rasa."* Mild anger arises from his looking at another woman and so on; average anger from his calling her by another woman's name, and so on; and intense anger from his having sexual relations with another

laghuḥ. anyathā | vāda | śapath' | ādy | apaneyo madhyamaḥ. caraṇa|patana†|bhūṣaṇa|dān'|ādy|apaneyo guruḥ. apara|strī|darśan'|ādi|janmā yathā:

sved'|âmbubhiḥ kva cana picchilam aṅgam etat,
  śāt'|ôdari, kva cana kaṇṭakitaṃ cakāsti,
anyāṃ vilokayati bhāṣayati†* priye 'pi.
  mānaḥ kva dāsyati padaṃ tava, tan na vidmaḥ.
[36]

gotra|skhalan'|ādi|janmā yathā:

yad gotra|skhalanaṃ, tatra
  bhramo†*—yadi na manyase,
rom'|āli|vyāla|saṃsparśaṃ
  śapathaṃ, tanvi, kāraya. [37]

apara|strī|saṅga|janmā yathā:

dayitasya nirīkṣya bhāla|deśaṃ
  caraṇ'|âlaktaka|piñjaraṃ sa|patnyāḥ,
sudṛśo nayanasya koṇa|bhāsā†
  śruti|muktāḥ śikhar'|ôpamā babhūvuḥ.* [38]

---

74 *-patana-* J Triv. A : *-pāta-* Ś A V 75 *bhāṣayati* Ś R N B : *bhūṣayati* G A V U J 77 *bhramaḥ* A N : *bhramam* J 79 *koṇabhāsā* G V R : *koṇabhāsaḥ* J A N

woman. The first is appeased by her naturally rekindled interest; the second by the lover's denials, oaths, and so on; the third by his falling at her feet, giving her jewelry, etc. An example of a *náyika*'s anger arising from his looking at another woman and the like:

He looked at another woman 75
and even spoke with her,
but your body, slender girl,
became so slick with sweat
and dense with goosebumps sharp as thorns,
there's nowhere I can see
that your love-anger with him
could hope to find a foothold.*

An example of her anger arising from his calling her by another woman's name:

It was just a simple mistake, my stumbling
over your name—if you don't believe me
then make me swear an oath by touching a snake,
that thin black snake just below your waist.*

An example of her anger arising from his having sexual relations with another woman:

When the woman saw her husband's forehead
stained by tawny lac from a rival's foot,
the pearls at her ear were turned redder than rubies
by the flash of anger from the corner of her eye.*

80 etāḥ ṣoḍaś' âpy aṣṭābhir avasthābhiḥ praty|ekam aṣṭa|vidhāḥ: proṣita|bhartṛkā, khaṇḍitā, kalah'|ântaritā, vipralabdh", ôtkā, vāsaka|sajjā, sv'|âdhīna|patik", âbhisārikā c' êti gaṇanād etāsām aṣṭā|viṃśaty|adhikaṃ śataṃ bhedā bhavanti. tāsām apy uttama|madhyam'|âdhama|bheda|gaṇanayā catur|adhik'|âśīti|yutaṃ śata|trayaṃ bhedā bhavanti.

yat tv etāsāṃ divy'|â|divy'|ôbhaya|bhedena gaṇanayā dvi|pañcāśad|adhika|śata|yutaṃ sahasraṃ bhedā bhavanti—divyā Indrāṇy|ādayaḥ, a|divyā Mālaty|ādayaḥ, divy'|â|divyāḥ Sīt"|ādaya iti—tan na. avasthā|bheden' âiva nāyikānāṃ bhedāt. jāti|bhedena bheda|svīkāre nāyakānām apy evam ānantyaṃ syāt. tathā bhedā nāyakānām api santi. divyā Indr'|ādayo. a|divyā Mādhav'|ādayaḥ. divy'|â|divyā Rām'†|ādaya iti. yady api mugdhāyā yathā dhīr'|ādi|bhed'|â|bhāvas tathā|vidha|prajñā|sāmagry|a|bhāvāt, tath" âtr' âpy aṣṭa|vidhatv'|â|bhāvo bhavitum arhati; tathā 'pi prācīna|lekhan'|ânurodhena nav'|ōḍhām ālamby' âite bhedā avagantavyāḥ.

---

81 *rāma-* J : *arjuna-* Ś A N : *kṛṣṇa-* V

---

[i] "Leading man," or principal male character

Each of the sixteen types of *náyikas* described so far* can be further subdivided into eight sorts: the woman whose lover is away on travels, the woman whose lover has cheated on her, the woman separated from her lover by a quarrel, the jilted woman, the worried woman, the woman preparing for the occasion, the woman whose lover is under her thumb, and the woman who goes on a secret rendezvous. This makes 128 types. All these can be further distinguished as excellent, average, and low,* which thus gives 384 types. 80

I reject the argument that there can be a further subdivision according to whether the *náyika* is divine (e.g., Indráni), not divine (e.g., Málati), or semidivine (e.g., Sita)—which would give us 1,152 types. *Náyikas* differ only by reason of temporary condition. If we were to differentiate them on the basis of species, the same would have to apply to *náyakas*[i] as well, for they, too, can be differentiated into divine beings such as Indra, non-divine beings such as Mádhava, and semidivine beings such as Rama.* Insofar as the varieties "steady" and so on do not apply to the naïve *náyika*, since she lacks the requisite degree of intelligence, these eight varieties do not pertain to her. However, in deference to the writings of the older authorities, these types may be understood to apply, but only to the naïve *náyika* of the newly married type.

deś'|ântara|gate preyasi santāpa|vyākulā proṣita|bhartṛkā. utkā|kalah'|ântaritā|vipralabdhānāṃ patir deś'|ântara|gato na bhavat', îti na tatr' âtivyāptiḥ. asyāś ceṣṭā daś'|âvasthā, tās tv agre vakṣyante.

mugdhā proṣita|bhartṛkā yathā:

duḥkhaṃ dīrghataraṃ vahanty api sakhī|
vargāya no bhāṣate;
śaivālaiḥ śayanaṃ sṛjanty api punaḥ
śete na vā lajjayā;
kaṇṭhe gadgada|vācam añcati, dṛśā
dhatte na bāṣp'|ôdakaṃ.
santāpaṃ sahate yad ambuja|mukhī,
tad veda ceto|bhavaḥ. [39]

85 madhyā proṣita|bhartṛkā yathā:

vāsas tad eva vapuṣo, valayaṃ tad eva,
hastasya s" âiva jaghanasya ca ratna|kāñcī.
vācāla|bhṛṅga|subhage surabhau samastam
ady' âdhikaṃ bhavati te, sakhi, kiṃ nidānam? [40]

prauḍhā proṣita|bhartṛkā yathā:

---

[i] In 265 [ii] The God of love

A *náyika* whose lover is away on travels is a woman distraught with grief at her lover's absence in another land. The definition is not so wide as to include the worried *náyika*, the *náyika* separated by a quarrel, and the jilted *náyika*, for though in each case the lover is absent, he is not in another land. Her characteristic behavior consists of the ten conditions, to be defined at a later point.[i]

An example of a naïve *náyika* whose lover is away:

The young girl's been upset so long
but says nothing to her friends;
she spreads out a bed of cool water plants
but is too embarrassed to lie on it;
she holds her sobs deep in her throat
and won't let a tear into her eye.
How sick with grief she really is
none knows but the god born in the heart.[ii]

An example of an average *náyika* whose lover is away: 85

The dress is one you've worn before,
and the bracelet on your wrist
and the jeweled belt you carry on your hips.
So why does it all seem too big,
dear friend, on this lovely spring day
that buzzing bees make lovelier?*

An example of the experienced *náyika* whose lover is away:

mālā bāl'|âmbuja|dalamayī,
mauktikī hāra|yaṣṭiḥ,
kāñcī yāte prabhavati Harau
subhruvaḥ prasthit" âiva.*
anyad brūmaḥ: kim iha dhamanī
vartate vā na v" êti
jñātuṃ bāhor, ahaha, valayaṃ
pāṇi|mūlaṃ prayāti. [41]

parakīyā proṣita|bhartṛkā yathā:

śvaśrūḥ padma|dalaṃ dadāti, tad api
bhrū|saṃjñayā gṛhyate,
sadyo marmara|śaṅkayā na tu† tayā
saṃspṛśyate pāṇinā.
yātur vāci suhṛd|gaṇasya vacasi
praty|uttaraṃ dīyate,
śvāsaḥ kiṃ tu na mucyate huta|vaha|
krūraḥ kuraṅgī|dṛśā. [42]

sāmānya|vanitā proṣita|bhartṛkā yathā:

«viraha|viditam antaḥ|prema vijñāya kāntaḥ
punar api vasu tasmād etya me dāsyat'» îti
marica|nicayam akṣṇor nyasya bāṣp'|ôda|bindūn
visṛjati pura|yoṣid dvāra|deś'|ôpaviṣṭā. [43]

90 *tu* J : *ca* Ś A N V

Her garland made of fresh water lilies,
her necklace strung with pearls,
and the belt she wore—all left her the moment
her lover, Hari, left.
And there's one thing more to tell: her armlet
slipped down her thin arm
to the wrist, poor thing, as if to see
if any pulse was left.*

An example of another's *náyika* whose lover is away:

When her mother-in-law offered a lotus leaf, 90
she raised a brow in thanks
but wouldn't touch it with her hand for fear
it would dry to the point of kindling.
And while she answered her friends
when they spoke,
and her sister-in-law as well,
she never let out her breath, which was burning
hotter than a ritual fire.*

An example of a common *náyika* whose man (chief customer) is away:

"If he sees I love him—and my grief
at his absence will prove it—
I know that he'll come back and shower me
with presents." And with this thought
the courtesan took her place in the doorway
and began to cry
the big round tears some pepper in the eyes
can always summon forth.

any'|ôpabhoga|cihnitaḥ prātar āgacchati patir yasyāḥ sā khaṇḍitā. prātar ity upalakṣaṇam. asyāś ceṣṭā a|sphuṭ'|ālāpa| cintā|santāpa|niḥśvāsa|tūṣṇīmbhāv'|âśru|pāt'|ādayaḥ.

mugdhā khaṇḍitā yathā:

vakṣaḥ kimu kalaś'|âṅkitam?
iti kim api praṣṭum icchantyāḥ
nayanaṃ nav'|ôḍha|sudṛśaḥ
prāṇ'|ēśaḥ pāṇinā pidadhe. [44]

madhyā khaṇḍitā yathā:

vakṣoja|cihnitam uro dayitasya vīkṣya,
dīrghaṃ na niḥśvasiti, jalpati n' âiva kiṃ cit;
prātar jalena vadanaṃ parimārjayantī
bālā vilocana|jalāni tirodadhāti. [45]

prauḍhā khaṇḍitā yathā:

mām udvīkṣya vipakṣa|pakṣmala|dṛśaḥ
pād'|âmbuj'|âlaktakair
ālipt'|ānanam, ānatī|kṛta|mukhī
citr'|ârpit" êv' âbhavat.
rūkṣaṃ n' ôktavatī, na vā kṛtavatī

The "cheated on" *náyika* is one whose husband (or lover) returns at daybreak bearing the marks of having made love with another woman. "Daybreak" is meant to include other times as well. Her characteristic behavior consists of muttering, pensiveness, sadness, sighing, silence, weeping, and so on.

An example of a naïve *náyika* who has been cheated on:

The new bride seemed about to ask, "What are 95
those two large jug marks upon your chest?"
when her husband covered up
the lovely girl's eyes with his hand.*

An example of an average *náyika* who has been cheated on:

When she saw her husband's chest
stained with cream from another's breasts,
she didn't heave a long, deep sigh
and didn't say a single word;
she only began to wash her face
just as she did every morning
and with the water hid the water
that came pouring from her eyes.*

An example of an experienced *náyika* who has been cheated on:

When she saw my face smeared with lac
from the foot of her large-eyed rival,
she only lowered her face and fell as still
as if painted in a picture,
said nothing harsh nor warmed the air

niḥśvāsa|koṣṇe diśaḥ†—
prātar maṅgalam aṅganā kara|talād
ādarśam ādarśayat. [46]

100 parakīyā khaṇḍitā yathā:

kāntaṃ nirīkṣya valay'|âṅkita|kaṇṭha|deśaṃ,
muktās tayā para|bhiyā paruṣā na vācaḥ.
dūtī|mukhe mṛga|dṛśā skhalad|ambu|pūrā
dūrāt paraṃ nidadhire* nayan'|ânta|pātāḥ. [47]

sāmānya|vanitā khaṇḍitā yathā:

«uras tava payodhar'|âṅ-
kitam idaṃ—kuto me kṣamā?
tato mayi nidhīyatāṃ
vasu, purā yad aṅgīkṛtam.»
iti pracala|cetasaḥ
priyatamasya vāra|striyā
kvaṇat|kanaka|kaṅkaṇaṃ
kara|talāt samākṛṣyate. [48]

patim avamatya paścāt paritaptā kalah'|ântaritā. asyāś ceṣṭā bhrānti|santāpa|saṃmoha|niḥśvāsa|jvara|pralāp'|ādayaḥ.

---

99 *diśaḥ* Triv. A : *dṛśau* J

around her with her sighs—
she only had me look in the mirror
she carried mornings for good luck.*

An example of another's *náyika* who has been cheated on: 100

She looked at her lover, the marks of another's
bracelet on his neck,
but the doe-eyed woman used no cruel words,
afraid others might hear.
All she did was fix a sidelong glance
from afar upon the face
of her friend, her go-between,
tears welling in her eyes.*

An example of a common *náyika* who has been cheated on:

"This chest of yours is marked by another's breasts—
and you tell me to relax?
You will still have to pay me the amount
you earlier agreed to pay."
And with this, the courtesan approached
her gallivanting lover
and snatched away from his wrist a golden bracelet
that jingled as it went.

A woman who spurns her lover and later regrets it is "separated by a quarrel." Her characteristic behavior consists of confusion, remorse, mental disorder, sighs, fever, raving, and so on.

mugdhā kalah'|ântaritā yathā:

anunayati patiṃ na lajjamānā,
kathayati n' âpi sakhī|janāya kiṃ cit;
prasarati Malay'|ânile nav'|ōḍhā
vahati paraṃ tu cirāya śūnyam antaḥ. [49]

madhyā kalah'|ântaritā yathā:

«viramati kathanaṃ vinā na khedaḥ,
sati kathane samupaiti k" âpi lajjā.»
iti kalaham adho|mukhī sakhībhyo
lapitum an|ālapituṃ samācakāṅkṣa. [50]

prauḍhā kalah'|ântaritā yathā:

akaroḥ kimu, netra, śoṇimānaṃ?
kim akārṣīḥ, kara, padma|tarjanaṃ vā?†
kalahaṃ kim adhāḥ krudhā,† rasa|jñe?
hitam arthaṃ na vidanti daiva|daṣṭāḥ. [51]

---

110 *kara padma-* A N : *karapadma* J V : *karapadma-* Ś T : *karapallavā [sic] nirodham* R 110 *krudhā* Ś A N V : *mudhā* J

An example of a naïve *náyika* separated by a quarrel:

The new bride won't make up with her husband;
she's too ashamed, and won't tell her friends a thing;
but when the breeze from Malabar starts blowing,
she learns how heavy an empty heart can be.*

An example of an average *náyika* separated by a quarrel:

"The pain won't stop unless I tell,
but if I tell
I know I'll die of shame." The girl
was so embarrassed
that she wanted to tell her friends
about the quarrel
and at the same time wanted them
to never hear.

An example of an experienced *náyika* separated by a quarrel:

Why, my eye, did you have to become
so awfully red?
And my hand, why did you go and hit him
with the lotus?
And you, my tongue, why did you go
scold him in anger?
When fate's not on your side, everything
turns out wrong.*

parakīyā kalah'|ântaritā yathā:

bhartur yasya kṛte gurur laghur abhūd,
goṣṭhī kaniṣṭhī|kṛtā,
dhairyaṃ kośa|dhanaṃ gataṃ, saha|carī
nītiḥ kṛtā dūrataḥ,
nirmuktā tṛṇavat trapā, paricitā
srotasvinī binduvat—
sa krodhād avadhīrito hata|dhiyā.
mātar, balīyān vidhiḥ! [52]

sāmānya|vanitā kalah'|ântaritā yathā:

yat paṅkeruha|lakṣma pāṇi|kamalaṃ,
bhāgy'|ālaye yad Gurur,
nyastaṃ vā mama yal lalāṭa|phalake
bhāgy'|âkṣaraṃ Vedhasā—
tat sarvaṃ, sakhi, yo yath"|ârtham akarot,
tasmin prakopaḥ kṛto
dhiṅ māṃ, dhiṅ mama jīvitaṃ, dhig Atanuṃ,
dhik ceṣṭitaṃ, dhig vayaḥ. [53]

115 saṅketa|niketane priyam an|avalokya samākula|hṛdayā vipralabdhā. asyāś ceṣṭā nirveda|niḥśvāsa|santāp'|ālāpa|bhaya|sakhī|jan'|ôpālambha|cint"|âśru|pāta|mūrch"|ādayaḥ.

An example of another's *náyika* separated by a quarrel:

For my lover's sake I outlawed my in-laws,
I ignored my closest circle of friends,
squandered the poise that was money in the bank,
destroyed my close friendship with common sense,
didn't care a straw for modesty, and learned
to treat a raging river like a puddle—
and now, foolish me, I've thrown him out in anger.
Ah mother, what all can fate not make you do?*

An example of a common *náyika* separated by a quarrel:

My hand with a lotus birthmark, Jupiter in my
astral house,
the lucky letters on my forehead written by
the Creator—
the man who made it all come true I've spurned
because of anger.
A curse on me, youth, life, and Love,
a curse on all my ways.*

The jilted *náyika* is one who becomes distraught while 115
waiting at the rendezvous place and not seeing her lover. Her characteristic behavior consists of despair, sighing, remorse, complaining, fear, blaming her female friends, pensiveness, weeping, fainting, and so on.*

mugdhā vipralabdhā yathā:

ālībhiḥ śapathair aneka|kapaṭaiḥ
kuñj'|ôdaraṃ nītayā,
śūnyaṃ tac ca nirīkṣya vikṣubhitayā
na prasthitaṃ na sthitam.
nyastāḥ kiṃ tu nav'|ōḍha|nīraja|dṛśā
kuñj'|ôpakaṇṭhe tṛṣā†*
tāmyad|bhṛṅga|kadamba|ḍambara|camat|
kāra|spṛśo dṛṣṭayaḥ. [54]

madhyā vipralabdhā yathā:

saṅketa|keli|gṛham etya, nirīkṣya śūnyam,
eṇī|dṛśo nibhṛta|niḥśvasit'|âdharāyāḥ
ardh'|âkṣaraṃ vacanam, ardha|vikāśi netraṃ,
tāmbūlam ardha|kabalī|kṛtam eva tasthau. [55]

prauḍhā vipralabdhā yathā:

śūnyaṃ kuñja|gṛhaṃ nirīkṣya, kuṭilaṃ
vijñāya ceto|bhavaṃ,
dūtī n' âpi niveditā, saha|carī
pṛṣṭ" âpi no vā tayā.
«Śambho, Śaṅkara, Candraśekhara, Hara,
Śrīkaṇṭha, Śūliñ, Chiva,
trāyasv'!» êti paraṃ tu paṅkaja|dṛśā
Bhargasya cakre stutiḥ. [56]

117 *tṛṣā* G Ś V : *ruṣā* J A N

An example of a naïve *náyika* who is jilted:

Her friends swore up and down, made every excuse
to get her into the woods.
Seeing he wasn't there, she was too distraught
to go or yet to stay.
The lotus-eyed bride could only cast glances
of longing toward the grove,
glances like bees, just as wild and craving,
and swarming just as densely.*

An example of an average *náyika* who is jilted:

When she reached their meeting place
and saw that it was empty,
a hot but secret sigh began
to dry the woman's full lips,
she left half said what she was saying,
left the betel leaf half chewed,
and left her eyes, her doe-like eyes,
half closed—and half open.

An example of an experienced *náyika* who is jilted: 120

When she saw the grove was empty
and grasped how cruel love is,
she didn't tell the go-between
or ask her confidante.
She intoned—"Benefactor, Beneficent,
Moon-crested, Remover,
Shri·kantha, Trident-bearer, Bharga!
Save me!"—a hymn to Shiva.*

parakīyā vipralabdhā yathā:

dattvā dhairya|bhujaṅga|mūrdhni caraṇāv,
ullaṅghya lajjā|nadīm,
aṅgīkṛtya khal'†|ândhakāra|paṭalaṃ,*
tanvyā na dṛṣṭaḥ priyaḥ.
santāp'|ākulayā tayā ca paritaḥ
pāthodhare garjati
krodh'|ākrānta|Kṛtānta|matta|mahiṣa|
bhrāntyā dṛśau yojite. [57]

sāmānya|vanitā vipralabdhā yathā:

«kapaṭa|vacana|bhājā kena|cid vāra|yoṣā
sakala|rasika|goṣṭhī|vañcikā vañcit" âsau!»
iti vihasati riṅgad|bhṛṅga|vikṣipta|cakṣur
vikaca|kusuma|kānti|cchadmanā keli|kuñjaḥ. [58]

saṅketa|sthalaṃ prati bhartur an|āgamana|kāraṇaṃ yā cintayati sā utkā. avadhi|divas'|ân|āgata|preyasi proṣita|patikāyāṃ n' âtivyāptiḥ. tasyā bhartur avadhi|divase bhavan'|āgamana|niyama iti saṅketa|padena vyāvartanāt. asyāś ceṣṭā a|rati|santāpa|jṛmbh'|âṅg'|ākṛṣṭi|kapaṭa|rudita|sv'|âvasthā|kathan'|ādayaḥ.

---

123 *khala* A N V (v.l.) U : *ghana* J G

An example of another's *náyika* who is jilted:

She stomped the snake of self-control,
crossed the deep river of shame,
and befriended that shady character,
the cover of dense darkness.
When she didn't see her lover, her grief
turned the rumbling cloud before her eyes
into the wild bull of Death
bearing straight down on her.*

An example of a common *náyika* who is jilted:

"The courtesan deceives every man 125
who'll let himself be taken in
but has just found herself deceived
by some smooth-talking guy!"
or so the pleasure grove seems to snicker
with its bright laughter
of blooming white flowers and the darting
glances of quick black bees.*

The worried *náyika* is one who frets over why her lover has not come to their meeting place. This definition is not so wide as to include "one whose lover is away on travels" when he has not returned on the appointed day, for the latter is restricted to the case where it is to home the lover is expected to return on the appointed day, which I exclude by adding the condition "meeting place" here.* Her characteristic behavior consists of despondency, sadness, yawning, shrinking into herself, weeping on any pretext, and talking about her condition.

mugdhā utkā yathā:

«yan n' âdy' âpi samāgataḥ priya, iti
prāyaḥ prapede parām,»
itthaṃ cetasi cintayanty api sakhīṃ
na vrīḍayā pṛcchati,
dīrghaṃ na śvasitaṃ dadhāti, cakitaṃ
na prekṣate, kevalaṃ
kiṃ|cit|pakva|palāṇḍu|pāṇḍura|ruciṃ
dhatte kapola|sthalīm. [59]

madhyā utkā yathā:

130 «ānetuṃ na gatā kimu priya|sakhī,
bhīto bhujaṅgāt kimu,
kruddho vā pratiṣedha|vāci kim asau
prāṇ'|ēśvaro vartate?»
itthaṃ karṇa|suvarṇa|ketaka|rajaḥ|
pāt'|ôpaghāta|cchalād
akṣṇoḥ k" âpi nav'|ōḍha|nīraja|mukhī
bāṣp'|ôdakaṃ muñcati. [60]

prauḍhā utkā yathā:

bhrātar nikuñja, sakhi yūthi, rasāla bandho,
mātas tamasvini, pitas timira, prasīda!
pṛcchāmi kiṃ cid iti nīradhar'|âbhirāmo
Dāmodaraḥ, kathaya, kiṃ na samājagāma? [61]

[i] Krishna

An example of a naïve *náyika* who is worried:

> “It’s late and my love still hasn’t come,
> he must have gone to another,”
> she thought, but was too ashamed to ask
> her confidante about it
> or sigh a heavy sigh or watch
> anxiously—it was only
> her cheeks that were growing paler
> than a barely ripened onion.

An example of an average *náyika* who is worried:

> “Maybe my girlfriend didn’t go 130
> to bring him out of fear, or because
> of a snake, or maybe he’s angry
> with me for refusing him.”
> At this thought the lotus-faced
> new bride begins to cry, pretending
> it’s pollen in her eye from the golden
> *kḗtaka* flower by her ear.*

An example of an experienced *náyika* who is worried:

> Bower, my brother, and you,
> vine, my friend,
> cousin mango, mother night,
> father darkness, take pity!
> Can’t you tell me when I ask
> why he hasn’t come to meet me,
> Damódara,[i] who is as dark
> as a rain cloud in the rains?*

parakīyā utkā yathā:

snātaṃ vārida|vāribhir, viracito
vāso ghane kānane,
śītaiś† candana|bindubhir manasi|jo
devaḥ samārādhitaḥ,
nītā jāgaraṇa|vratena rajanī,
vrīḍā kṛtā dakṣiṇā—
taptaṃ kiṃ na tapas, tath" âpi sa kathaṃ
n' âdy' âpi netr'|âtithiḥ. [62]

135 sāmānya|vanitā utkā yathā:

«kathaṃ na kāntaḥ samupaiti kuñjam?»
itthaṃ ciraṃ cetasi cintayantī
asrāvayan niṣpatad|aśru|vārā†
vār'|âṅganā k" âpi dhan'|âbhilāṣān.†* [63]

adya me priya | vāsara iti niścitya yā surata | sāmagrīṃ sajjīkaroti sā vāsaka | sajjā. vāsako vāraḥ. asyāś ceṣṭā mano | ratha|sakhī|parihāsa|dūtī|praśna|sāmagrī|sampādana|mārga| vilokan'|ādayaḥ.

---

134 *śītaiś* Ś A N V : *puṣpaiś* J 136 *-vārā* Ś (G?) : *-dhārā* J
136 *-abhilāṣān* Ś V : *-abhilāṣāt* J G R A

An example of another's *náyika* who is worried:

I've dwelled in the deep forest, performed
ablutions in the pouring rain,
worshipped with cool sandalwood drops
the god born in the heart,
kept vigil all through the long dark night
and renounced all modesty—
every penance I've done, and still
he's not shown himself to me.*

An example of a common *náyika* who is worried: 135

"Why isn't my lover coming to the woods?"
the courtesan was thinking ceaselessly,
and with the tears pouring from her eyes
she washed all hope of money down the drain.

The woman who prepares all the accoutrements for love-making, thinking, "Today is the occasion of my beloved," is one who "prepares for the occasion." "Occasion" literally means day.* Her characteristic behavior consists of wishing, joking with her friends, questioning the go-between, preparing the accoutrements, looking out toward the road he would take, and so on.

mugdhā vāsaka|sajjā yathā:

hāraṃ gumphati tārak"|âtiruciraṃ,*
grathnāti kāñcī|latāṃ,
dīpaṃ nyasyati, kiṃ tu tatra bahulaṃ
snehaṃ na datte punaḥ—
ālīnām iti vāsakasya rajanau
kām'|ânurūpāṃ kriyāṃ
sāci|smera|mukhī nav'|ōḍha|sumukhī
dūrāt samudvīkṣate. [64]

140 madhyā vāsaka|sajjā yathā:

śilpaṃ darśayituṃ karoti kutukāt
kahlāra|hāra|srajaṃ;
citra|prekṣaṇa|kaitavena kim api
dvāraṃ samudvīkṣate;
gṛhṇāty ābharaṇaṃ navaṃ sahacarī|
bhūṣā|jigīṣā|miṣād.
itthaṃ padma|dṛśaḥ pratītya caritaṃ
smer'|ānano 'bhūt Smaraḥ. [65]

pragalbhā vāsaka|sajjā yathā:

kṛtaṃ vapuṣi bhūṣaṇaṃ,
cikura|dhoraṇī dhūpitā,
kṛtā śayana|sannidhau
kramuka|vīṭikā|sambhṛtiḥ.
akāri hariṇī|dṛśā
bhavanam etya deha|tviṣā

An example of a naïve *náyika* who prepares for the occasion:

One strings a necklace brighter than stars,
one weaves a vine-like belt,
one puts a lamp in place but puts
just a drop of oil in it—
while her friends prepare the love toys
as day turns into night
the new bride watches, but only from far off,
and smiles, but only faintly.*

An example of an average *náyika* who prepares for the occasion: 140

As if to show her skill, she tries
to plait a necklace of lilies;
she stares at the doorway on the pretext
of examining a painting;
she puts new jewelry on, pretending
to outdo her friends.
And Love understands the things the girl
with lotus eyes does, and smiles.*

An example of an experienced *náyika* who prepares for the occasion:

She put on all her jewelry,
perfumed her thick head of hair,
and at her bedside had them place
areca nut and betel leaf.
And the bedroom, when the woman
entered, her body all aglow,

sphurat|kanaka|ketakī|
kusuma|kāntibhir dur|dinam. [66]

mano|rathaś ca yathā:

145 āvayor aṅgayor dvaite
bhūyo viraha|viplavaḥ;
a|dvaite ca smitaṃ sphītaṃ
na syād anyonya|vīkṣaṇam.* [67]

parakīyā vāsaka|sajjā yathā:

śvaśrūṃ svāpayati, cchalena ca tiro-
dhatte pradīp'|âṅkuraṃ,
dhatte saudha|kapota|pota|ninadaiḥ
sāṅketikaṃ ceṣṭitam.
śaśvat|pārśva|vivartit'|âṅga|latikaṃ
lolat|kapola|dyuti
kv' âpi kv' âpi kar'|âmbujaṃ priya|dhiyā
talp'|ântike nyasyati. [68]

sāmānya|vanitā vāsaka|sajjā yathā:

«colaṃ nīla|nicola|karṣaṇa|vidhau,
cūḍā|maṇiṃ cumbane
yāciṣye, kucayoḥ kar'|ârpaṇa|vidhau
kāñcīṃ punaḥ kāñcanīṃ.»
itthaṃ candana|carcitair mṛga|madair
aṅgāni saṃskurvatī
tat kiṃ yan na mano|rathaṃ vitanute
vāreṣu vār'|âṅganā. [69]

was a darkened overcast day
set ablaze by golden *kétaki* flowers.*

An example of wishing:*

When our bodies are apart, 145
the separation is calamitous,
but when together, neither can see
how richly the other one is smiling.*

An example of another's *náyika* who prepares for the occasion:

She tricks her mother-in-law to go to sleep
and removes the shining lamp
and makes a sound like the dovecote chicks,
the signal for their meeting.
Tossing ceaselessly from side to side,
her cheeks beginning to flush,
she feels around the bed with her lotus-soft hand,
hoping to find her lover.

An example of a common woman who prepares for the occasion:

"I'll demand a new bodice
just for drawing back my dark veil,
a hairpin for a kiss, a belt of gold
for the chance to fondle my breasts"—
what dreams doesn't the courtesan
dream about her many lovers
as she carefully rubs her body
with creams of musk and sandalwood.

150 sadā s'|ākūt'|ājñā|kara|priyatamā sv'|âdhīna|patikā. nirantar'|ājñā|kara|priyatvam ity arthaḥ. asyāś ceṣṭā vana|vihār'|ādi|madana|mah"|ôtsava|mad'|âhaṅkāra|mano|rath'|āvāpti|prabhṛtayaḥ. mado harṣ'|ôtkarṣaḥ.

mugdhā sv'|âdhīna|patikā yathā:

madhye na kraśimā, stane na garimā,
dehe na vā kāntimā,
śroṇau na prathimā, gatau na jaḍimā,
netre na vā vakrimā,
lāsye na draḍhimā, na vāci paṭimā,
hāsye na vā sphītimā—
prāṇ'|ēśasya tath" âpi majjati mano
mayy eva kiṃ kāraṇam? [70]

madhyā sv'|âdhīna|patikā yathā:

yad api rati|mah"|ôtsave na|kāro,
yad api kareṇa ca nīvi|dhāraṇāni,
priya|sakhi, patir eṣa pārśva|deśaṃ
tad api na muñcati. tat kim ācarāmi? [71]

A woman whose lover always obeys her command at the 150
slightest prompting is one whose lover is under her thumb.* That is, he does what she wants without hesitation. Her characteristic behavior consists of such things as outings to the forest, worshipping the God of love, intoxication, pride, and getting her way. "Intoxication" here means extreme joy.*

An example of a naïve *náyika* whose lover is under her thumb:

My figure shows no curvitude,
my breasts no altitude,
my body has no pulchritude,
my hips no amplitude,
my walk suggests no gravitude,
my eyes no magnitude,
my charm reveals no plenitude,
my speech no aptitude,
and my laugh no latitude—
why in the world has my lover given
his heart to me and me alone?*

An example of an average *náyika* whose lover is under her thumb:

Although I say no to the festival of love
and keep my hand on my belt at all times,
still my lover refuses to leave my side.
What am I going to do with him, dear friend?*

prauḍhā sv'|âdhīna|patikā yathā:

vaktrasy', âdhara|pallavasya, vacaso,
hāsyasya lāsyasya vā
dhanyānām aravinda|sundara|dṛśāṃ
kāntas tanoti stutim.
svapnen' âpi na gacchati śruti|pathaṃ,
cetaḥ|pathaṃ, dṛk|pathaṃ,
k" âpy anyā dayitasya me. sakhi, kathaṃ
tasy' âstu bheda|grahaḥ? [72]

parakīyā sv'|âdhīna|patikā yathā:

svīyāḥ santi gṛhe saroruha|dṛśo†
yāsāṃ vilāsa|kvaṇat|
kāñcī|kuṇḍala|hema|kaṅkaṇa|jhaṇat|
kāro na viśrāmyati.
ko hetuḥ, sakhi, kānane, pura|pathe,
saudhe, sakhī|sannidhau
bhrāmyantīm api† vallabhasya parito
dṛṣṭir na māṃ muñcati?* [73]

sāmānya|vanitā sv'|âdhīna|patikā yathā:

---

158 *gṛhe saroruhadṛśo* A U G B Ś A V Triv. A : *gṛhe gṛhe mṛgadṛśo* J
158 *bhrāmyantīm api* B A V Triv. A : *bhrāmyantī mama* J G

An example of an experienced *náyika* whose lover is under her thumb: 155

> How lucky are those women whose lovers extol
> their mouth or lips, their talk or laugh or grace.
> My lover has never seen, heard, thought, or dreamed
> of another woman. What's he to compare me with?*

An example of another's *náyika* whose lover is under her thumb:

> At home he has his own lovely women
> whose bell-studded belts and earrings
> and golden bracelets never stop jingling
> with their graceful movements.
> So why, my friend, wherever I may go—
> forests, city streets, or rooftop
> terraces, or even among my friends—
> won't my lover take his eyes off me?*

An example of a common *náyika* whose lover is under her thumb:

160 santy eva prati|mandiraṃ yuvatayo
yāsāṃ sudhā|sāgara|
srotaḥ|syūta|saroja|sundara|camat|
kārā dṛśo vibhramāḥ.
citraṃ kiṃ tu, vicitra|manmatha|kalā|
vaiśadya|hetoḥ punar
vittaṃ citta|haraṃ prayacchati yuvā
mayy eva kiṃ kāraṇam? [74]

svayam abhisarati priyam abhisārayati vā yā s" âbhisārikā. asyāś ceṣṭā samay'|ânurūpa|veṣa|bhūṣaṇa|śaṅkā|prajñā|naipuṇya|kapaṭa|sāhas'|ādaya iti parakīyāyāḥ. svīyāyās tu prakṛta eva kramaḥ,* alakṣyatā|sampādakasya śvet'|ādy|ābharaṇasya svīy'|âbhisārikāyām a|sambhavāt.

mugdh" âbhisārikā yathā:

dūtī vidyud upāgatā, sahacarī
rātriḥ saha|sthāyinī,
daiva|jño diśati svanena jaladaḥ
prasthāna|velāṃ śubhām,
vācaṃ māṅgalikīṃ tanoti timira|
stomo 'pi jhillī|ravair.
jāto 'yaṃ dayit'|âbhisāra|samayo;
mugdhe, vimuñca trapām. [75]

In every single house you can find women 160
whose lovely eyes dart
like lotuses bobbing on a wave
of the nectar ocean.
Yet amazingly—I can't see why—the boy
pays me a small fortune
for the sake of seeing some refinement
in the complex arts of love.*

The woman who goes on a secret rendezvous either goes out herself to meet her lover or has him brought to her. When she is another's *náyika*, her characteristic behavior consists of wearing jewelry and clothing appropriate to the time of the month,* worry, intelligence, skill, deceptiveness, recklessness, and so on. In the case of one's own *náyika*, the procedures regarding dress and the like are her normal ones, since she has no need to wear special white clothing and jewelry to keep her from being noticed.

An example of a naïve woman who goes on a secret rendezvous:

The swift go-between, lightning, has arrived,
your fast friend, night, will go along,
the cloud, that wise astrologer, declares
with a rumble that this is the right time,
and the deep darkness is giving you his blessing
with the chirping of the cicadas.
It's now time to go meet him; enough
of your shyness, you silly girl.

madhy" âbhisārikā yathā:

165 bhīt" âsi n' âiva bhujagāt pathi, mad|bhujasya
saṅge punaḥ kim† api kampam urī|karoṣi.
ambhodhara|dhvanibhir a|kṣubhit" âsi, tanvi,
mad|vāci sāci|vadan" âsi. kim ācarāmi? [76]

prauḍh" âbhisārikā yathā:

sphurad|urasija|bhāra|bhaṅgur'|âṅgī
kisalaya|komala|kāntinā padena—
atha kathaya, kathaṃ saheta gantuṃ
yadi na niśāsu mano|ratho rathaḥ syāt. [77]

parakīy" âbhisārikā yathā:

rabhasād abhisartum udyatānāṃ
vanitānāṃ, sakhi, vārido vivasvān,
rajanī divaso, 'ndhakāram arcir,
vipinaṃ veśma, vimārga eva mārgaḥ. [78]

---

165 *kim* Ś A N V T : *kam* J

An example of an average woman who goes on a secret rendezvous:

What am I to do with you? You're completely 165
unafraid
of snakes on the way, but at my very touch
you tremble
like a leaf. And the rumble of storm clouds
leaves you
unshaken, but one word from me and your face
goes taut.*

An example of an experienced woman who goes on a secret rendezvous:

With a body like hers—almost bent double
from the weight of full breasts, and with feet soft
as petals—don't tell me she'd ever come out
in the night
if her desire weren't transporting her.

An example of another's woman who goes on a secret rendezvous:

To women impassioned for an assignation,
night is day, clouds sun, and darkness light,
the forest home, and the longest way around,
my friend, is the shortest way of all.

jyotsn"|âbhisārikā yathā:

candr'|ôdaye candanam aṅgakeṣu
vihasya vinyasya vinirgatāyāḥ
mano nihantuṃ Madano 'pi bāṇān
kareṇa kaundān bibharāṃ babhūva. [79]

tamisr'|âbhisārikā yathā:

n' âmbujair na kumudair upameyaṃ
svairiṇī|jana|vilocana|yugmam—
n' ôdaye dinakarasya na v" êndoḥ,
kevale tamasi tasya vikāsaḥ. [80]

divas'|âbhisārikā yathā:

pallīnām adhipasya paṅkaja|dṛśāṃ
parv'|ôtsav'|āmantraṇe
jāte, sadma|janā mithaḥ kṛta|mah"|ôt-
sāhaṃ puraḥ prasthitāḥ.
sa|vyājaṃ sthitayor vihasya gatayoḥ
śuddh'|ântam atr'|ântare
yūnoḥ svinna|kapolayor vijayate
ko 'py eṣa kaṇṭha|grahaḥ. [81]

An example of a woman who goes on a secret rendezvous in moonlight: 170

At moonrise she left with a sly smile on her face,
having rubbed her pale limbs with white
sandalwood cream.
But the God of love, to cut her down to size,
drew out his white night-blooming jasmine arrows.*

An example of a woman who goes on a secret rendezvous in darkness:

You can't compare to day lilies or night lotuses
the eyes of women who do just what they please—
for their eyes don't blossom at sunrise or moonrise
but only in the deepest dark of night.*

An example of a woman who goes on a secret rendezvous by day:

At the invitation from the village headman 175
to his wives' new-moon fête
the whole household went rushing off together,
bursting with excitement.
But the young couple made some excuse
to stay back,
and laughing they went off
to the bedroom—and how they held each other
tight,
cheek by sweating cheek.*

sāmānya|vanit" âbhisārikā yathā:

lola|ccela†|camatkṛti, pravilasat|
kāñcī|latā|jhaṅkṛti,
nyañcat|kañcuka|bandha|bandhura|calad|
vakṣoja|kumbh'|ônnati,
sphūrjad|dīdhiti, visphurad|gati, calac|
cāmīkar'|âlaṃkṛti—
krīḍā|kuñja|gṛhaṃ prayāti kṛtinaḥ
kasy' âpi vār'|âṅganā. [82]

mugdhāyā lajjā|prādhānyena; madhyāyā lajjā|madana|sāmyena; pragalbhāyāḥ prākāśya|prādhānyena; dhīrāyā dhairya|prādhānyen'; â|dhīrāyā a|dhairya|prādhānyena; dhīr'|â|dhīrāyā dhairy'|â|dhairya|prādhānyena; jyeṣṭhāyāḥ sneh'|ādhikya|prādhānyena; kaniṣṭhāyāḥ sneha|nyūnatva|prādhānyena; par'|ōḍhāyāḥ saṃgupti|prādhānyena; mugdhāyā iva kanyakāyāś ca; sāmānya|vanitāyā dhana|prāpti|prādhānyen'; âṣṭa|vidha|nāyikā|varṇanam iti viśeṣaḥ.

---

177 *-cela-* V T : *-cola-* J G

An example of a common woman who goes on a secret rendezvous:

> Charm of fluttering cloak, shining belt
> jingling, undulation
> of breasts bulging in a tight bodice
> and heaving almost out,
> brilliant sparkle, gold jewelry jangling,
> quick step—the courtesan
> sets off to the garden house
> of some lucky man.*

Thus the eight-fold typology of *náyikas* ("the woman whose lover is away on travels" and so on) can be differentiated for the naïve *náyika* with her predominant characteristic of shame; the average, with her predominant characteristic of shame balanced by desire; the experienced, with her predominant characteristic of directness; the steady, unsteady, and steady-unsteady with their varying degrees of steadiness; the better loved with her greater degree of affection, and the less loved with her lesser degree; the *náyika* married to another with her secretiveness; the unmarried girl, who is like the naïve *náyika* (as far as shamefulness is concerned); and the common *náyika*, with her predominant characteristic of money-making. In view of such ancient compositions as the following:

prasthānaṃ valayaiḥ kṛtaṃ; priya|sakhair
asrair a|jasraṃ gataṃ;
dhṛtyā na kṣaṇam āsitaṃ; vyavasitaṃ
cittena gantuṃ puraḥ.
yātuṃ niścita|cetasi priyatame
sarve samaṃ prasthitā.
gantavye sati, jīvita, priya|suhṛt|
sārthaḥ kimu tyajyate? [83]

180 ity|ādi|prācīna|grantha|lekhanād agrima|kṣaṇe deś'|ântara| niścita|gamane preyasi proṣyat|patik" âpi navamī nāyikā bhavitum arhati. tathā hi, tasyāḥ proṣita†|patikā|vipralabdh'| ôtkāsu n' ântarbhāvaḥ. bhartuḥ sannidhi|vartitvāt. na kalah'| ântaritāyām antarbhāvaḥ. kalah'|â|bhāvād an|avamānita| patitvāc ca. n' âpi khaṇḍitāyām antarbhāvaḥ. priyasy' âny'| ôpabhoga|cihnitasy' āgaman'|â|bhāvāt. priyāyāḥ kop'|â| bhāva|darśanāt kāku|vacana|kātara|prekṣaṇ'|ādi|pakṣa|pāta| darśanāc† ca. na vāsaka|sajjāyām antarbhāvaḥ. vāra|niyam'| â|bhāvāt. sajjīkaraṇ'|â|bhāva|nirved'|ādi|darśanāc ca. na sv'| âdhīna|patikāyām antarbhāvaḥ. agrima|kṣaṇa eva saṅgasya viccheda|darśanāt. na hi sv'|âdhīna| patikāyāḥ kadā

---

180 *proṣyat-* Ś A N V : *pravatsyat-* (passim) J 180 *ādipakṣapātadarśanāc* V : *ādisañcintāntaḥpakṣapātitvadarśanāc* J A N : *ādisūcitāntaḥpakṣapātadarśanāc* Ś B

My bracelets have left; my tears, those
beloved friends,
have been streaming away;
my fortitude couldn't stay a moment; my mind
was the first to choose to go.
They departed all at once when the man I love
decided to leave. It's time
to go, my life, for how can you abandon
the troop of your dear friends?*

it would seem that there should be a ninth type of *náyika*, 180
one whose lover is about to go away on travels*—given that her lover has decided to leave for another country and might depart at any moment. That is to say, this type cannot be included in the category of "the woman whose lover is away on travels" or the "jilted woman" or the "worried woman," since her lover is still present. She cannot be included in the category of "the woman who is separated from her lover by a quarrel," since there has been no quarrel and she has not spurned her lover. Nor can she be included in the category of the "angry" *náyika*, since her lover has not appeared with telltale marks of lovemaking with another woman, and accordingly she does not show any anger with him but on the contrary shows a predilection for sarcasm, anxious glances, and so on. She cannot be included in the category of "the woman preparing for the occasion," for there is no restriction in this case as to occasion, and she shows, not the preparing of her bedchamber, but rather despair, and so on. She cannot be included in the category of "the woman whose lover is under her thumb," because here their relationship will be interrupted the very next moment,

cid api saṅga|viccheda, iti saṃpradāyaḥ. vrajann api patiḥ sv'|âdhīna|patikayā nirudhyate, 'nyathā bhartari svādhīnatvam eva bhajyeta. n' êha tathā. sarvathā bhartur videśa|gamanāt. kiṃ ca nirved'|âśru|pāta|niḥśvāsa|vana|vihār'|ādi|madana|mah"|ôtsava|vyatireka|darśanāc ca. n' âpy abhisārikāyām antarbhāvaḥ. abhisār'|ôtsav'|â|bhāvāt. antas|tāpa|darśanāc c'; êti yuktam utpaśyāmaḥ.

lakṣaṇaṃ tu: yasyāḥ patir agrima|kṣaṇe deś'|ântaraṃ yāsyaty eva sā proṣyat|patikā. asyāś ceṣṭā kāku|vacana|kātara|prekṣaṇa|gamana|vighn'|ôpadarśana|nirveda|santāpa|saṃmoha|niḥśvāsa|bāṣp'|ādayaḥ.

mugdhā proṣyad|bhartṛkā yathā:

prāṇ'|ēśvare kim api jalpati nirgamāya
    kṣām'|ôdarī vadanam ānamayāṃ cakāra.
ālī punar nibhṛtam etya latā|nikuñjam
    unmatta|kokila|kala|dhvanim ātatāna. [84]

and it is conventional in that category for the relationship never to be shown as interrupted: a woman whose lover is under her thumb can prevent him from going even when he is on the point of setting out—otherwise the very fact of the lover's being under her power would dissolve—and that is clearly not the case here, where the lover goes on foreign travel despite her. In the present case we also find sighing, weeping, depression—the very opposite of outings to the forest, worshipping the God of love, and so on. Nor, finally, can she be included in the category of "the woman who goes on a secret rendezvous," because there is no joyous undertaking of a rendezvous; on the contrary, she shows anguish. It is therefore appropriate that we anticipate this category.

She is defined as a woman whose lover is about to leave for another country at any moment. Her characteristic behavior includes sarcasm, anxious glances, providing reasons to stop him from going, despair, sorrow, bewilderment, sighing, tears, and so on.

An example of a naïve *náyika* whose lover is about to go away on travels:

> As the lord of her life began to mumble
> something about setting out, the slender woman
> only hung her head, but her friend stole off
>   to the bower
> and made the long sweet call of the maddened cuckoo.*

madhyā proṣyat|patikā yathā:

gantuṃ priye vadati niḥśvasitaṃ na dīrgham
āsīn, na vā nayanayor jalam āvir|āsīt.
āyur|lipiṃ paṭhitum eṇa|dṛśaḥ paraṃ tu
bhāla|sthalīṃ kimu kacaḥ samupājagāma? [85]

prauḍhā proṣyat|patikā yathā:

n' âyaṃ muñcati subhruvām api tanu|
tyāge viyoga|jvaras.
ten' âhaṃ vihit'|âñjalir, Yadu|pate,
pṛcchāmi, satyaṃ vada:
tāmbūlaṃ, kusumaṃ, paṭīram, udakaṃ
yad|bandhubhir dīyate,
syād atr' êva* paratra tat kimu viṣa|
jvāl'|āvalī|duḥsaham? [86]

parakīyā proṣyat|patikā yathā:

nyastaṃ pannaga|mūrdhni pāda|yugalaṃ,
bhaktir vimuktā guros,
tyaktā nītir—akāri kiṃ na bhavato
hetor mayā duṣkṛtam?
aṅgānāṃ śata|yātanā, nayanayoḥ
ko 'pi kramo rauravaḥ,
Kumbhīpāka|parābhavaś ca manaso
yuktaṃ tvayi prasthite. [87]

---

[i] Krishna

An example of an average *náyika* whose lover is about to go away on travels:

When her lover said he would be leaving, 185
she didn't heave a deep sigh, not one round tear
formed in her eyes; just a strand of hair fell down
to her forehead—to read how short her lifeline was?*

An example of an experienced *náyika* whose lover is about to go away on travels:

I'm not sure even death can release a woman
from this pain of love's loss.
So I ask in all sincerity, Yadu lord,[i]
tell me the truth: do the betel leaf,
the flowers, the sandalwood cream, and
 the cool water
that kinsmen offer to the dead
burn in the other world as they burn here,
with the unbearable flames of fever's poison?*

An example of another's *náyika* whose lover is about to go away on travels:

I trod barefoot on snakes and disrespected
my elders, renounced all modesty—
I committed every wrong and all because
of you. And now that you're leaving,
it's only right the infernal pain in my eyes
should begin, the thousand tortures
in every limb, the torment of my heart
baking in the hell called Potter's Kiln.*

190 sāmānya|vanitā proṣyat|patikā yathā:

«mudrāṃ pradehi valayāya: bhavad|viyogam
āsādya yāsyati bahiḥ sahasā yad etat.»
itthaṃ nigadya vigalan|nayan'|âmbu|dhārā
vār'|âṅganā priyatamaṃ karayor babhāra. [88]

a|hita|kāriṇy api priyatame hita|kāriṇy uttamā. asyā uttam" âiva ceṣṭā. yathā:

patiḥ śayanam āgataḥ kuca|vicitrit'|ôraḥ|sthalaḥ;
prasanna|vacan'|âmṛtair ayam atarpi vāma|bhruvā,
acarci subhaga|smita|dyuti|paṭīra|paṅka|dravair,
apūji vilasad|vilocana|camatkṛtair ambujaiḥ. [89]

hit'|â|hita|kāriṇi priyatame hit'|â|hita|ceṣṭāvatī madhyamā. asyās tu vyavahār'|ânusāriṇī ceṣṭā. yathā:

An example of a common *náyika* whose lover is about to go away on travels: 190

"Give me a ring for a bracelet, since this one
is sure to slip right off the moment you leave,"
the courtesan insisted, her eyes streaming tears
while holding her lover tightly by the hands.*

The *náyika* who is kind to her lover even though he is unkind to her is termed "excellent," for her characteristic behavior is of this sort.* For example:

When he came to bed she saw his chest
dappled with cream from another's breasts,
and still his wife offered him the ambrosia
of sweet words for his refreshment
and rubbed him with the rich sandalwood cream
of her lovely shining smile,
and paid him worship with open lotuses,
her beautiful, her sparkling eyes.

A *náyika* whose characteristic behavior is kind or otherwise as her lover is kind or otherwise is termed average; her characteristic behavior is simply a response to his conduct. For example:

195 kānte s'|āgasi kañcuka|spṛśi tayā
sāci|kṛta|grīvayā
muktāḥ kopa|kaṣāya|Manmatha|śara|
krūrāḥ kaṭ'|âkṣ'|âṅkurāḥ.
s'|ākūte dara|hāsa|kesara|vaco|
mādhvīka|dhār"|âlasā*
prītiḥ kalpa|lat" êva kā cana mahā|
dānī|kṛtā su|bhruvā. [90]

hita|kāriṇy api priyatame '|hita|kāriṇy adhamā. eṣ" âiva nirnimitta|kopanā caṇḍ" îty abhidhīyate. asyā niṣkāraṇa|kopatvād adham" âiva ceṣṭā. yathā:

prasthāne tava yaḥ karoti kamala|
cchāyāṃ mukh'|âmbhoruhe,*
śrī|khaṇḍa|drava|dhārayā śiśirayā
mārgaṃ puraḥ siñcati,
tasmin preyasi vidruma|drava|nadī|
riṅgat|taraṅga|bhrami|
bhrānta|klānta|saroja|patra|sadṛśā
bhūyo dṛśā krudhyasi. [91]

vistara|bhiyā praty|ekam etāsām uttama|madhyam'|âdhama|bhedā n' ôdāhṛtā iti.

viśvāsa|viśrāma|kāriṇī pārśva|cāriṇī sakhī. asyā maṇḍan'|ôpālambha|śikṣā|parihāsa|prabhṛtīni karmāṇi. tatra maṇḍanaṃ yathā:

When her cheating lover reached for her blouse 195
she turned her face away,
unleashing a storm of looks sharp as Love's arrows
when he grows purple with anger.
But when he showed contrition, what cheerfulness
she bestowed—a wish-granting vine,
laden with shoots, her half smile, and
a steady stream
of nectar, her expressions of love.*

A *náyika* who is mean to her lover even when he is kind is termed "low." She is also called "irascible" because her anger is wholly groundless.* And it is precisely because her anger is groundless that her behavior is considered low. For example:

When you step out, your lover will shade
your face with a lotus
and besprinkle the path before you
with cool sandalwood essence,
and yet you show him unrelenting
anger with those glances,
petals wilting in swirling pools
of a coral tree's red sap.*

For fear of prolixity I will not cite examples of the excellent, average, and low categories into which each of the various types of *náyika* can be subdivided.*

A friend is a companion who gives comfort and consolation. Her actions consist in such things as adorning, reproving, instructing, teasing the *náyika*, and so on. An example of adorning:

200 stana|kanaka|mahīdhar'|ôpakaṇṭhe
priya|kara|pallavam ullasat|pramodam
rahasi makarikā|miṣāl likhantīṃ†*
kamala|mukhī kamalaiḥ sakhīṃ jaghāna. [92]

upālambho yathā:

sāndra|dhvānair mukharita|diśaḥ
śreṇayas toya|dānāṃ
dhār"|āsārair dharaṇi|valayaṃ
sarvataḥ plāvayanti.
tena *snehaṃ vahati vipulaṃ*
mat|sakhī yuktam eva;
tvaṃ *niḥsneho* yad asi, tad idaṃ,
nātha, me vismayāya. [93]

śikṣā yathā:

s'|ānandam, āli, vana|māli|vilokanāya
nirgaccha kuñjam; iti kiṃ tu vicārayethāḥ:
jhaṅkāriṇo madhuliho divase bhramanti,
rātrau punaś capala|cañcu|puṭāś cakorāḥ. [94]

---

200 *likhantīṃ* G Ś : *likhantī* J A N V

In private her girlfriend pretended to draw 200
upon her breasts—
two golden hillocks—the usual design,
but drew instead
the quivering hand of her lover.
And the lotus-faced girl
beat her as hard as she could
with lotus flowers.*

An example of reproving:

Massed clouds roaring incessantly
make every horizon resound,
and the whole wide world is swimming
in streams of steady rain.
It's only right my friend should fall
more deeply in love : become wetter,
but I'm amazed, my lord, that you
*should feel no love : be not wet at all.**

An example of instructing:

Go off in joy to the grove, my friend, to see
your lover
decked in his wildflower garland, but don't forget:
by day bees buzz about, eager for honey,
by night *chakóras* fly, beaks pecking for
moonbeams.*

parihāso yathā:

«āgāra|bhitti|likhitāsu nivedayasva,
kaḥ saptamo daśasu mūrtiṣu loka|bhartuḥ?»
itthaṃ sakhī|jana|vacaḥ pratipadya sadyaḥ
Sītā smita|dyutibhir uttarayāṃ cakāra. [95]

sakhyāḥ parihāsavat priyasy' âpi parihāsaḥ. yathā:

«bhrū|saṃjñay" ādiśasi, tanvi, sakhīṃ, na vāgbhir?»
itthaṃ vihasya Mura|vairiṇi bhāṣamāṇe
Rādhā cirāya daśana|vraṇa|dūyamāna|
bimb'|âdharā vadanam ānamayāṃ cakāra. [96]

priyasya parihāsavat priyāyā api parihāsaḥ. yathā:

«divyaṃ vāri kathaṃ? yataḥ Suradhunī
maulau. kathaṃ pāvako
divyaṃ? tadd hi vilocanaṃ. katham ahir
divyaṃ? sa c' âṅge tava.
tasmād dyūta|vidhau tvay" âdya muṣito
hāraḥ parityajyatām.»
itthaṃ Śaila|bhuvā vihasya lapitaḥ
Śambhuḥ śivāy' âstu vaḥ. [97]

An example of teasing: 205

"Here on the wall of the house are drawn
ten incarnations of God.
Now tell us, what is the name
of the seventh one among them?"
her girlfriends asked, and the answer
they got came straight away
in the flashing of the smile
that Sita flashed at them.*

A lover can tease his beloved no less than her friend can. For example:

Krishna was laughing as he said,
"Why do you signal your girlfriend
with your brows instead of simply
telling her what to do?"
And for a long time Radha stood there,
her face lowered in shame,
while her full lips were throbbing
where Krishna had bitten them.

The beloved can tease her lover just as he teases her, for example:

"You carry the Ganga on your head, 210
so what good is an oath by water?
Or by fire—it's your third eye?
Or by snakes—your ornaments?
You stole my necklace at dice so give it back!"
said the Mountain's daughter with a laugh
to Shiva—and may he show you his grace.*

dūtya | vyāpāra | pāraṅgamā dūtī. tasyāḥ saṃghaṭṭana | viraha|nivedan'|ādīni karmāṇi. saṃghaṭṭanaṃ yathā:

añcati rajanir, udañcati
  timiram idaṃ, cañcati Manobhūḥ:
uktaṃ na tyaja yuktaṃ,
  viracaya raktaṃ manas tasmin. [98]

viraha|nivedanaṃ yathā:

cakre candra|mukhī pradīpa|kalikā
  dhātrā dharā|maṇḍale.
tasyā daiva|vaśād daś" âpi caramā
  prāyaḥ samunmīlati.
tad brūmaḥ śirasā natena, sahasā,
  śrī|Kṛṣṇa, nikṣipyatāṃ
snehas tatra tathā, yathā na bhavati
  trailokyam andhaṃ tamaḥ. [99]

215 iti nāyikā|nirūpaṇam

A go-between is an expert in the business of mediation. Her characteristic behavior consists of arranging the lovers' meeting, informing them of the other's loneliness, and so on. An example of her arranging their meeting is as follows:

Night is coming, darkness is closing in,
and Love begins his dance:
Don't break your solemn promise, but put
your heart and soul into it.*

The go-between also can inform the lover of the beloved's loneliness. For example:

God made the moon-faced girl the single lamp
of beauty on earth,
and Fate would have it that her final hour
is nearly upon her.
I bow my head and beg you, dear Krishna, hurry
and pour a drop of *love : oil*
in her, to keep deep darkness from engulfing
the entire universe.*

The end of the Description of the *Náyika* 215

DESCRIPTION OF THE NÁYAKA AND RELATED MATTERS

Śṛṅgārasy' ôbhaya|nirūpyatvān nāyako 'pi nirūpyate. sa ca tri|vidhaḥ: patir, upapatir, vaiśeṣikaś c' êti. vidhivat| pāṇi|grāhakaḥ patiḥ. yathā:

tvaṃ, pīyūṣa|mayūkha, muñca śiśira|
snigdhān sudhā|śīkarān.
tvaṃ, bhog'|îndra, vilambase kimu? phaṇ"|ā-
bhogaiḥ śanair vījaya.
tvaṃ, svar|vāhini, kiṃ ca siñca salilair.
aṅgaiḥ śirīṣ'|ôpamaiḥ
s" êyaṃ Śaila|sutā kaṭhora|mahasaḥ
kāntyā pathi klāmyati. [100]

anukūla | dakṣiṇa | dhṛṣṭa | śaṭha | bhedāt patiś caturdhā. sārvakālika | par' | âṅganā | parāṅ | mukhatve sati sarva | kālam anurakto 'nukūlaḥ. yathā:

pṛthvi, tvaṃ bhava komalā; dina|maṇe,
tvaṃ śaityam aṅgī|kuru;
tvaṃ, vartman, laghutāṃ prayāhi; pavana,
tvaṃ khedam utsāraya.
sānnidhyaṃ śraya, Daṇḍakā|vana; gire,
nirgaccha mārgād bahiḥ:
Sīt" âsau vipinaṃ mayā saha yato
nirgantum utkaṇṭhate. [101]

---

[i] Shiva speaks. [ii] Rama speaks.

SINCE THE EROTIC rasa requires a description of both partners, the *náyaka*, too, will now be described. There are three kinds of *náyaka*s: "husband," "paramour," and "libertine." A "husband" is married to a woman according to the proper rites. For example:[i]

You there, moon with nectar rays,
shower your cool moist drops of ambrosia.
Why so slow here, serpent king?
Start fanning gently with your coils.
You, river of heaven, sprinkle water.
The Mountain's daughter, with limbs soft
as flowers, is tiring on her way
under the fierce glare of the sun.*

There are four types of husbands: faithful, gallant, brazen, and deceptive.* A husband is faithful if he is constant in affection toward his wife while constant in his lack of interest in the wives of other men. For example:[ii]

You, earth, be soft, and you, sun, now cool down,
grow short, you, road, and you, wind, remove
her sweat.
Come close, Dándaka forest, and mountain,
begone:
My Sita is eager to leave with me for the forest.*

sakala | nāyikā | viṣayaka | sama | sahaj' | ânurāgo dakṣiṇaḥ. yathā:

«etat puraḥ sphurati padma|dṛśāṃ sahasram.
aksi|dvayaṃ, kathaya, kutra niveśayāmi?»
ity ākalayya nayan'|âmburuhe nimīlya
rom'|âñcitena vapuṣā sthitam Acyutena. [102]

bhūyo niḥśaṅka|kṛta|doṣo 'pi bhūyo nivārito 'pi bhūyaḥ praśraya|parāyaṇo dhṛṣṭaḥ. yathā:

baddho hāraiḥ kara|kamalayor,
dvārato vārito 'pi,
svāpaṃ jñātvā punar upagato
dūrato datta|dṛṣṭiḥ.
talp'|ôpānte kanaka|valayaṃ
muktam† anveṣayantyā
dṛṣṭo dhṛṣṭaḥ punar api mayā
pārśva eva prasuptaḥ. [103]

---

223 *muktam* Ś A N V : *bhraṣṭam* J

He is gallant when he is naturally and equally affectionate 220
toward all women:

> "Before me flash a myriad eyes
> of lotus-eyed women.
> So tell me, where am I supposed
> to rest this pair of mine?"
> With this, Krishna simply closed
> his lotus eyes and stood stock still
> while the goosebumps slowly spread
> over his whole body.*

He is brazen when, although not hesitating to commit repeated infidelities while being repeatedly reproved, he repeatedly ends up groveling before the *náyika*. For example:

> They bound his hands with necklaces
> and kept him away from the door
> but peering in at a distance
> he saw that I was fast asleep.
> And when I woke and searched the bed
> for the bracelet that had come undone,
> what did I see but the brazen fellow
> once more asleep right by my side!*

kāminī|viṣayaka|kapaṭa|paṭuḥ śaṭhaḥ. yathā:

maulau dāma vidhāya, bhāla|phalake
vyālikhya patr'|āvalīṃ,
keyūraṃ bhujayor nidhāya, kucayor
vinyasya muktā|srajam,
viśvāsaṃ samupārjayan mṛga|dṛśaḥ
kāñcī|niveśa|cchalān
nīvī|granthim apākaroti mṛdunā
hastena vāma|bhruvaḥ. [104]

ācāra|hāni|hetuḥ patir upapatiḥ. yathā:

śaṅkā|śṛṅkhalitena yatra nayana|
prāntena na prekṣyate,
keyūra|dhvani|bhūri|bhīti|cakitaṃ
no yatra v" āśliṣyate,
no vā yatra śanair a|lagna|daśanaṃ
bimb'|âdharaḥ pīyate,
no vā yatra pidhīyate† ca maṇitaṃ—
tat kiṃ rataṃ kāminoḥ? [105]

upapatir api caturdhā. paraṃ tu śaṭhatvaṃ tatra niyatam. a|niyatāḥ pare.

227 *pidhīyate* V : *vidhīyate* J

He is deceptive if he is clever in deceiving his mistress.* For example:

He placed a tiara on her head, 225
painted a dot of musk on her brow,
set bangles on her arms, and draped
a pearl necklace over her breasts.
Thus gaining her confidence,
and pretending to adorn her with a belt,
he untied the skirt of the doe-eyed girl
with a very careful hand.*

A man who causes a woman to forsake her virtue is a paramour.* For example:

Where you don't have to look at one another
with glances checked by anxiety,
don't have to embrace with obsessive care
lest her bracelets make a noise,
don't have to keep your teeth from sinking deep
as you sip the ripe fruit of her lips,
and she needn't hide the moan a woman will moan—
what kind of lovers' love is that?*

The paramour is subdivided into the same four types as the husband.* All necessarily comprise qualities of the deceptive *náyaka*; the qualities of the others may, but do not necessarily, pertain to him.

bahula|veśy"|ôpabhoga|rasiko vaiśikaḥ. yathā:

kāñcī|kala|kvaṇita|komala|nābhi|kāntiṃ,
pārāvata|dhvanita|citrita|kaṇṭha|pālim,
udbhrānta|locana|cakoram an|aṅga|raṅgam
āśāsmahe kam api vāra|vilāsavatyāḥ. [106]

vaiśikas t' ûttama|madhyam'|âdhama|bhedāt tridhā. dayitāyā bhūyaḥ prakope 'py upacāra|parāyaṇa uttamaḥ. yathā:

cakṣuḥ|prāntam udīkṣya pakṣmala|dṛśaḥ
śoṇ'|âravinda|śriyaṃ,
n' ôccair jalpati, na smitaṃ vitanute,
gṛhṇāti vīṭīṃ na vā.
talp'|ôpāntam upetya kiṃ tu pulaka|
bhrājat†|kapola|dyutiḥ
kāntaḥ kevalam ānatena śirasā
muktā|srajaṃ gumphati. [107]

---

232 *-bhrājat-* Ś A N V : *-sphūrjat-* J

A libertine is a man who has a great taste for affairs with courtesans, for example:

A midriff made more lovely by bells ringing 230
gently on the belt,
a throat magnificently full with sounds
like the cooing of doves
and eyes as wild as thirsty *chakóra* birds—
how I long to visit
Love's grand playhouse when a courtesan
with real grace is starring.*

Libertines are classified as excellent, average, and low. The libertine who shows great indulgence despite the beloved's intense anger is termed excellent. For example:

He spied the corner of her long-lashed eye,
and it was red as a lotus.
He didn't raise his voice or smile
or reach for the betelnut.
The lover just came to the edge of the bed,
cheeks flushed with excitement,
and only lowered his head and began
restringing her necklace of pearls.*

priyāyāḥ prakopam anurāgaṃ vā na prakaṭayati, ceṣṭayā mano|bhāvaṃ gṛhṇāti sa madhyamaḥ. yathā:

āsyaṃ yady api hāsya|varjitam idaṃ,
lāsyena vītaṃ vaco,
netraṃ śoṇa|saroja|kānti, tad api
kv' âpi kṣaṇaṃ sthīyatām.
mālāyāḥ karaṇ'|ôdyamo, makarik"|ā-
rambhaḥ kuc'|âmbhojayor,
dhūpaḥ kuntala|dhoraṇīṣu su|dṛśaḥ
sāyantano dṛśyate. [108]

235 bhaya|kṛpā|lajjā|śūnyaḥ kāma|krīḍāyām a|kṛta|kṛty'|â|kṛtya|vicāro 'dhamaḥ. yathā:

udayati hṛdi yasya n' âiva lajjā,
na ca karuṇā, na ca ko 'pi bhīti|leśaḥ,
bakula|mukula|kośa|komalāṃ māṃ
punar api tasya kare na yātayethāḥ. [109]

The libertine who takes no notice of his beloved's anger or passion but infers her affection from her private behavior is termed average. For example:

Laughter may have left her face,
singing may have left her tongue,
her eyes may be red as a red lotus,
but just be patient for a moment.
You'll see her working on her garlands,
painting her breasts with Love's emblems,
and scenting that thick mass of hair
with perfume for the evening hour.

The libertine who is devoid of fear, pity, or shame, and 235
who gives no thought to what he should and should not do in the game of love, is termed low. For example:

He feels no shame whatever in his heart,
no compassion, not a trace of fear.
Don't let him get his hands on me again
or I'll be crushed like a *bákula* bud.

mānī caturaś ca śaṭha ev' ântar|bhavati. mānī yathā:

«bāhy'|ākūta|parāyaṇaṃ tava vaco,
vajr'|ôpameyaṃ manaḥ.»
śrutvā vācam imām, apāsya vinayaṃ
vyājād bahiḥ prasthite,
prātar vīta|vilokane parihṛt'|ā-
lāpe vivṛtt'|ānane
prāṇ'|ēśe nipatanti hanta karuṇā†
vāma|bhruvo dṛṣṭayaḥ. [110]

vacana|ceṣṭā|vyaṅgya|samāgamaś caturaḥ. vacana|vyaṅgya|samāgamo yathā:

tamo|jaṭāle harid|antarāle
kāle niśāyās tava nirgatāyāḥ
taṭe nadīnāṃ nikaṭe vanānāṃ
ghaṭeta, śāt'|ôdari, kaḥ sahāyaḥ? [111]

ceṣṭā|vyaṅgya|samāgamo yathā:

kānte kanaka|jambīraṃ
kare kim api kurvati,
āgāra|likhite bhānau
bindum indu|mukhī dadhau. [112]

---

238 *karuṇā* Ś A N Triv. A : *kṛpaṇā* J V

The love-angry and the clever are classed under the deceiving *náyaka*. An example of the former:

When he heard her say, "You only talk
of love, your heart is hard as a diamond,"
he dropped all show of courtesy and went off,
or at least pretended to,
at dawn without a look or a single word,
just turning his back on her,
while her pitiful glances fell—as he knew
they would fall—on the lord of her life.*

The clever lover is able, even in a crowd, to intimate a rendezvous by a word or a gesture. An example of the former:

When nighttime lets down its thick black hair 240
all around and you leave your house, slender girl,
who will be there to stand by your side
on the riverbank at the edge of the forest?*

An example of the latter:

When her lover held up a lemon,
luscious and golden, the girl
with the full-moon face drew a circle
on the sun painted on the wall.*

proṣitaḥ patir upapatir vaiśikaś ca bhavati.† proṣita|patiḥ proṣit'|ôpapatiḥ proṣita|vaiśikaś c' êti trayaḥ. krameṇ' ôdāharaṇāni.

ūrū rambhā, dṛg api kamalaṃ,
 śaivalaṃ keśa|pāśo,
vaktraṃ candro, lapitam amṛtaṃ,
 madhya|deśo mṛṇālam,
nābhiḥ kūpo, valir api sarit,
 pallavaḥ kiṃ ca pāṇir
yasyāḥ, sā ced urasi, na kathaṃ
 hanta tāpasya śāntiḥ? [113]

yāntyāḥ saraḥ salila|keli|kutūhalāya,
 vyājād upetya mayi vartmani vartamāne,
antaḥ|smita|dyuti† camat|kṛta|dṛk|taraṅgair
 aṅgī|kṛtaṃ kim api vāma|dṛśaḥ smarāmi. [114]

a|dhṛta|paripatan|nicola|bandhaṃ,
 muṣita|na|kāram, a|vakra|dṛṣṭi|pātam,
prakaṭa|hasitam, unnat'|āsya|bimbaṃ
 pura|sudṛśaḥ smara|ceṣṭitaṃ smarāmi. [115]

---

243 *proṣitaḥ … bhavati* A N : om. J 245 *-dyuti* Ś A N : *-dyuti-* J V

The husband, the paramour, and the libertine can each be absent *náyaka*s, giving three more types. We will illustrate them in order:

Her thighs are palms, her eyes lotus leaves,
her hair a dark plant from the sea,
her face the moon, her voice pure ambrosia,
her midriff the breadth of a lily's stem,
her navel a deep well, her waist a flowing
river, her hand a tender frond ...
she's all this—and if she were in my arms,
wouldn't this burning fire be quenched?

How well I remember the day she went to the lake 245
to bathe; we met on the road, I approached on some
pretext,
and she said yes to me by waves in the clear
pools of her eyes and the faint flash of a smile.

When her garment slipped, she let it
fall away completely,
"no" was a word unknown to her,
she looked you in the eye
and her smile was broad, her face a bright
circle of light held high—
how well I remember the way
the city girl made love.

an|abhijño nāyako nāyak'|ābhāsa eva. yathā:

śūnye sadmani yojitā bahu|vidhā
bhaṅgī. vanaṃ nirjanaṃ
puṣpa|vyājam upetya nirgatam atha
sphārī|kṛtā dṛṣṭayaḥ,
tāmbūl'|āharaṇa|cchalena vihitau
vyaktau ca vakṣo|ruhāv.
eten' âpi na vetti! dūti, kiyatā
yatnena sa jñāsyati? [116]

na ca nāyikāyā iva nāyakasy' âpi te te bhedāḥ santv iti vācyam. tasyā avasthā|bhedena bhedāt† tasya ca sva|bhāvena bheda iti viśeṣāt. anukūlatvaṃ, dakṣiṇatvaṃ, dhṛṣṭatvaṃ, śaṭhatvam iti catvāra eva nāyakasya sva|bhāvā iti. anyac c'* âvasthā|bhedena bhedo yadi nāyakasya syāt, tad" ôtka|vipralabdha|khaṇḍit'|ādayo nāyakā api svī|kartavyāḥ. tathā ca saṅketa|vyavasthāyāṃ strīṇāṃ anāgamane† v" â|sampradāyād† anya|samāgama|śaṅkā. dhūrtatvaṃ v" ânya|sambhoga|cihnitatvaṃ vā nāyakānāṃ na tu nāyikānām.* tān prati tad|udbhāvane ras'|ābhās'|āpattir iti.

249 *bhedāt* Ś A N : *bhedaḥ* J V 249 *anāgamane* Ś V : *gamane* J
249 *asaṃpradāyād* G Ś V : *saṃpradāyād* J

An innocent *náyaka* is termed a "semblance of a *náyaka*," for example:

The house was empty, and I'd used every charm
I knew. So I took him to the woods
(not a soul was there) on the pretext of picking
flowers, and I looked at him
with longing, and pretending to offer him betel,
I let him see my breasts in full.
He still doesn't get the point! O go-between,
what must I do to make him get it?*

Now, one should not suppose that the *náyaka* has the same subclassifications as the *náyika*. An essential distinction lies in the fact that the *náyika*'s different classifications derive from her different temporary states, whereas the *náyaka*'s derive from his inherent character, and there are only four such sorts of character: the faithful, the gallant, the brazen, and the deceptive. Moreover, if the *náyaka* were subject to subclassification according to his different temporary states, then we should have also to recognize a type of *náyaka* who is worried, jilted, cheated on, etc.* And this means that we would have a "worried" *náyaka* at the time of a rendezvous if the woman did not come, though this is contrary to literary convention. And it is only the *náyaka*, and not the *náyika*, who can be a cad or actually bear the marks of having made love with someone else.* To impute those temporary states to the *náyaka* would produce a semblance of rasa.

teṣāṃ narma | sacivaḥ pīṭhamarda | viṭa | ceṭaka | vidūṣaka | bhedāc caturdhā. kupita | strī | prasādakaḥ pīṭha | mardaḥ. yathā:

ko 'yaṃ kopa|vidhiḥ? prayaccha karuṇā|
garbhaṃ vaco, jāyatāṃ
pīyūṣa|drava|dīrghikā|parimalair
āmodinī medinī.
āstāṃ vā. spṛhayālu locanam idaṃ
vyāvartayantī muhur
yasmai kupyasi, tasya, sundari, tapo|
vṛndāni vandāmahe. [117]

kāma|tantra|kalā|kovido viṭaḥ. yathā:

āyātaḥ kumud'|ēśvaro, vijayate
sarv'|ēśvaro māruto,
bhṛṅgaḥ sphūrjati bhairavo, na nikaṭaṃ
prāṇ'|ēśvaro muñcati—
ete *siddha|rasāḥ*, prasūna|viśikho
vaidyo 'n|a|vady'|ôtsavo:*
māna|vyādhir asau, kṛś'|ôdari, kathaṃ
tvac|cetasi sthāsyati? [118]

---

[i] The moon

The boon companion of the *náyaka* can be one of four types: mediator, rake, pander, and clown. The mediator mollifies his friend's angry mistress: 250

Why show such anger, lovely woman?
Speak just one word of compassion
and perfume the entire world with fragrance
from pools of your ambrosial sound.
Or let it be. For him to be fixed,
your anger's object, in your jealous gaze
must be the reward for ascetic acts,
hard acts devoutly to be admired.*

The rake is proficient in all the branches of the art of love, for example:

The lord of lotuses has risen,[i] the south wind,
the sovereign lord, is triumphant,
the bees are buzzing loudly, and the lord
of your life won't leave your side—
all proven potions : all things from which
*[the erotic] rasa arises,** these, and the doctor,
the God of love, is a sure bet:
How can this sickness—your anger—shapely lady,
hang on so tenaciously?

sandhāna|caturaś ceṭakaḥ:

sā candra|sundara|mukhī, sa ca nanda|sūnur
daivān nikuñja|bhavanaṃ samupājagāma.
atr'|ântare saha|caras taraṇau kaṭhore
pānīya|pāna|kapaṭena saraḥ pratasthe. [119]

aṅg'|ādi|vaikṛtyair hāsya|kārī vidūṣakaḥ. yathā:

ānīya nīraja|mukhīṃ śayan'|ôpakaṇṭham,
utkaṇṭhito 'smi kuca|kañcuka|mocanāya.
atr'|ântare muhur akāri vidūṣakeṇa
prātastanas taruṇa|kukkuṭa|kaṇṭha|nādaḥ. [120]

stambhaḥ, svedo, 'tha rom'|âñcaḥ,
svara|bhaṅgo, 'tha vepathuḥ,
vaivarṇyam, aśru, pralaya—
ity aṣṭau sāttvikāḥ smṛtāḥ.

yathā:

bhedo vāci, dṛśor jalaṃ, kuca|taṭe
svedaḥ, prakampo 'dhare,
pāṇḍur gaṇḍa|taṭī, vapuḥ pulakitaṃ,
līnaṃ manas tiṣṭhati,
ālasyaṃ nayana|śriyaś, caraṇayoḥ
stambhaḥ samujjṛmbhate—
tat kiṃ rāja|pathe Nijāma|dharaṇī|
pālo† 'yam ālokitaḥ. [121]

---

260 *nijāmadharaṇipālo* J : *vrajendratanayaḥ kṛṣṇas* G Triv. A

---

i Krishna

The pander is skillful in promoting the lovers' union, for example:

A girl fairer than the full moon
and the son of Nanda[i]
met one day by chance* in a bower,
and no sooner did they meet
than his companion set off to the pond,
offering as pretext
the heat of the summer sun
to slake a sudden thirst.

The clown amuses the lovers with different antics, such as pulling faces, and so on. For example:

I finally got the girl to the edge of the bed
and was aching to take off her bodice,
        when suddenly
the clown began imitating the cry
a young rooster makes at the break of dawn.*

There are eight involuntary physical reactions: paralysis, sweating, horripilation, a breaking voice, trembling, pallor, weeping, and absorption.

An example:

Her voice breaks, tears well up in her eyes,
her breast is beaded with sweat,
her lips tremble, her smooth cheeks grow pale,
goosebumps cover her body,
her mind absorbed, the light in her eyes dying,
her legs paralyzed—
did she, too, chance to glance at the royal highway
and see King Nijáma?*

rati|sthāyi|bhāvaḥ śṛṅgāraḥ. sa ca dvi|vidhaḥ, sambhogo vipralambhaś ca. saṃbhogo yathā:

viyati vilolati jaladaḥ,
skhalati vidhuś calati, kūjati kapotaḥ,
niṣpatati tārakā|tatir,
āndolati vīcir a|mara|vāhinyāḥ. [122]

vipralambho yathā:

prādur|bhūte nava|jala|dhare
tvat|pathaṃ draṣṭu|kāmāḥ
prāṇāḥ paṅke|ruha|dala|dṛśaḥ
kaṇṭha|deśaṃ prayānti,
anyat kiṃ vā tava mukha|vidhuṃ
draṣṭum uḍḍīya gantuṃ
vakṣaḥ pakṣaṃ sṛjati bisinī|
pallavasya cchalena. [123]

265 vipralambhe c' âbhilāṣa|cintā|smṛti|guṇa|kīrtan'|ôdvega|pralāp'|ônmāda|vyādhi|jaḍatā|nidhanāni daś'|âvasthā bhavanti.

tatra saṅgam'|êcch" âbhilāṣaḥ. yathā:

tasyāṃ sutanu|sarasyāṃ
ceto nayanaṃ ca niṣpatitam
ceto guru tu nimagnaṃ
laghu nayanaṃ sarvato bhramati. [124]

The rasa in which desire is the stable emotion is the erotic. It is of two sorts, enjoyment and frustration. An example of the former:

In the sky a dark cloud floats, the moon
swims in and out of view, a dove coos,
numberless stars are shooting, and on the river
of the gods the waves are dancing.*

An example of the latter:

When the lotus-eyed girl beheld
the first cloud of the rains,
her life leapt to her throat to watch
the road you might be taking,
and so that her breast might rise
to see your moon-like face
the cooling lotus stalks she wore
seemed to turn into wings.*

In the frustrated variety there are ten conditions: de- 265
sire, pensiveness, remembrance, glorification, distress, raving, madness, sickness, stupor, and death.*

Desire is the longing to be together, for example:

That woman is a flowing river,
my heart and eye fell in.
My heavy heart sank down, but my eye
is light and floats about.*

saṃdarśana|santoṣayoḥ prakāra|jijñāsā cintanam.† yathā:

maya vidheyo muhur adya tasmin
kuñj'|ôpakaṇṭhe kala|kaṇṭha|nādaḥ.
Rādhā madhor vibhramam āvahantī
kurvīta netr'|ôtpala|toraṇāni. [125]

priy'|āśrita|ceṣṭ"|ādy|udbodhita†|saṃskāra|janyaṃ jñānaṃ smṛtiḥ. yathā:

Rāmo Lakṣmaṇa|dīrgha|duḥkha|cakito
n' āviṣ|karoti vyathāṃ,
śvāsaṃ n' ôṣṇataraṃ jahāti, salilaṃ
dhatte na vā cakṣuṣi.
vāt'|āvarta|vivartamāna|dahana|
krūrair an|aṅga|jvaraiḥ*
kṣāmaḥ kiṃ tu Videha|rāja|tanayāṃ
bhūyaḥ smaran vartate. [126]

viraha | kālika | kāntā | viṣayaka | praśaṃsā | pratipādanaṃ guṇa|kīrtanam. yathā:

sparśaḥ stana|taṭa|sparśo,
vīkṣaṇaṃ vaktra|vīkṣaṇam,
tasyāḥ keli|kath"†|ālāpa|
samayaḥ samayaḥ, sakhe. [127]

268 *cintanam* Ś A N V : *cintā* J 270 *-ceṣṭādyudbodhita-* J Ś V : *-ceṣṭādyudvegabodhita-* A N 273 *-kathā-* Ś A N V : *-kalā-* J

[i] Krishna speaks.

Pensiveness is a desire for an encounter and its shared pleasures. For example:[i]

Today near the bower I should make the cry
the sweet cuckoo makes, again and again;
then Radha might think spring's come and
    welcome me
with a garland of dark lotuses—her glances.*

Remembering is a thought produced by a latent impres- 270
sion when stimulated by some action on the part of the beloved. For example:

For fear of adding to Lákshmana's grief
Rama would not show his pain,
the sighs he sighed were not too heavy,
no tears welled up in his eyes.
He just continued wasting ever away,
recalling the princess of Vidéha,
from a love fever hotter than a bonfire
whipped up by a whirlwind.

Glorification is an expression of praise with reference to an absent beloved. For example:

The only sight worth seeing is her face,
the only thing worth touching her breasts,
and the times she whispers sweet nothings
    in my ear,
my friend, are the only times for me.

kāma|kleśa|janita|sakala|viṣaya|heyatā|jñānam udvegaḥ. yathā:

275 garala|druma|kanda indu|bimbaṃ.
karuṇā|vārija|vāraṇo vasantaḥ.
rajanī dmara|bhū|pateḥ kṛpāṇī.
karaṇīyaṃ kim ataḥ paraṃ, vidhātaḥ? [128]

priy'|āśrita|kālpanika|vyavahāraḥ pralāpaḥ. kalpanāyāḥ kāraṇam antaḥ|karaṇa|vikṣepaḥ. tasya ca nidānam utkaṇṭhā. yathā:

a|dvi|saṃvīkṣaṇaṃ cakṣur,
a|dvi|saṃmīlanaṃ manaḥ,
a|dvi|saṃsparśanaḥ pāṇir
adya me kiṃ kariṣyati? [129]

autsukya|santāp'|ādi|kārita|mano|viparyāsa|samuttha| priy'|āśrita|vṛthā|vyāpāra unmādaḥ. viparyāso vyākula| vyāpāraḥ. sa ca kāyiko vācikaś ca. yathā:

pratiphalam amṛt'|âṃśor vīkṣya kānto, mṛg'|âkṣyā
mukham iti parihāsaṃ kartum abhyudyato 'bhūt.
atha śithilita|vāco mānam āśaṅkya tasyāḥ
spṛśati pulaka|bhājā pāṇi|paṅkeruheṇa. [130]

Distress is the feeling, produced by the sorrows of love, that everything is worthless. For example:

Full moon—root of the poison tree. 275
Springtime—elephant on the lotus of pity.
Evening—dagger of the king of love.
Dear god, what am I supposed to do now?*

Raving is a fantastic declaration referring to the beloved. The cause of the fantasy is a mental distraction produced by unfulfilled desire:

There's only one thing my eyes can see
and only one thing my mind can think,
and my hands can touch only one thing—
what's to become of me now?

Madness is irrational behavior with reference to the beloved, which comes from mental derangement produced by longing, anguish, and so on.* By "derangement" is meant confused behavior, either physical or verbal. An example of the former:

The lover saw the reflection
of the full moon and thought
it was his lady's face,
and he started joking with her.
But when he noticed the face
remained silent, he feared
she was angry and went to touch her
with a hand trembling with desire.

vāciko yathā:

kiṃ, re vidho? mṛga|dṛśo mukham a|dvitīyaṃ
Kandarpa, dṛpyasi! dṛg|ambujam anyad eva.
jhaṅkāram āvahasi, bhṛṅga! tanur na tādṛk.
karmāṇi dhiṅ! kva† punar īdṛśam īkṣaṇīyam?
[131]

madana|vedanā|samuttha|santāpa|kārśy'|ādi|doṣo vyādhiḥ. yathā:

kodaṇḍaṃ, viśikho, mano|nivasatiḥ
kāmasya. tasyā api
bhrū|vallī, nayan'|âñcalaṃ, manasi te
vāsaḥ samunmīlati.
itthaṃ sāmya|vidhau tayoḥ prabhavati,
svāmiṃs, tathā snihyatāṃ,
tanvānā tanutāṃ kramād a|tanutāṃ
n' âiṣā yathā gacchati. [132]

viraha|vyathā|vikāra|mātra|vedyaṃ† jīvan'|âvasthānaṃ jaḍatā. yathā:

pāṇir nīrava|kaṅkaṇaḥ, stana|taṭī
niṣkampamān'|âṃśukā,
dṛṣṭir niścala|tārakā samabhavan,
nistāṇḍavaṃ kuṇḍalam—
kaś citr'|ârpitayā samaṃ kṛśa|tanor
bhedo bhaven, no yadi

281 *kva* G V : *na* J Ś A 284 *vikāramātravedyam* Ś V : *āviṣkāramātravedyam* G : *āviṣkāramātram eva* J A N

[i] The God of love, whose body was destroyed by Shiva

An example of verbal derangement: 280

What, you bloody moon? There is nothing
like my woman's face.
And you, conceited God of love!
Her eyes are unique.
Buzz around all you want, black bee!
Her body is without compare.
Damn this work that takes me from home!
Where to find such a vision again?*

Sickness is a state in which the pain of infatuation brings about illness such as fever, weight loss, and so on. For example:

Kama[i] has a bow and arrows, and lives in the heart.
Her brows, too, are arched,
glances dart from the corners of her eyes,
and she lives within your heart.
The two are enough alike already. O master,
love her, lest her slender
body waste away and she gradually becomes,
like Kama, bodiless as well.*

Stupor is a state in which the only sign of life is a physical reaction produced by the pain of separation. For example:

No sound from the bracelet on her arm, 285
no flutter in the blouse on her breast,
the pupils of her eyes unmoving,
her earrings no longer dancing—
you couldn't tell the slender girl
from a painting of a woman

tvan|nāma|smaraṇeṇa† ko 'pi pulak'|ā-
rambhaḥ samujjṛmbhate. [133]

nidhanasy' â|maṅgalatvān n' ôdāhṛtir udāhṛtā.

svapna | citra | sākṣād | bhedena darśanaṃ tridhā. tatra svapna|darśanaṃ yathā:

muktā|hāraṃ na ca kuca|gireḥ,
kaṅkaṇaṃ n' âiva hastāt,
karṇāt svarṇ'|ābharaṇam api† vā
nītavān n' âiva tāvat?
adya svapne bakula|mukulaṃ
bhūṣaṇaṃ sandadhānaḥ
ko 'yaṃ cauro hṛdayam aharat,
tanvi, tan na pratīmaḥ. [134]

citra|darśanaṃ yathā:

«nīvīṃ hared, urasijaṃ vilikhen nakhena,
danta|cchadaṃ ca daśanena daśed akasmāt.»
itthaṃ paṭe vilikhitaṃ dayitaṃ vilokya
bālā pur" êva na jahāra vihāra|śaṅkām. [135]

285 *-smaraṇeṇa* Ś A N V : *-śravaṇena* J R   288 *api* Ś A N V : *ayi* J

were it not for the goosebumps rising
at the mention of your name.

As for "death," I forego citing an example, since it would be inauspicious to do so.

There are three different modes of seeing the beloved: in a dream, in an artistic representation (e.g., a painting), and in person.* An example of the first:

He didn't take the necklace of rich pearls
from your high breasts, my girl,
he didn't take the bracelet from your wrist,
or the gold earrings from your ears?
We cannot understand what kind of thief,
garlanded with *bákula*,
came to you last night as you lay dreaming
and stole your heart away.*

An example of the second:

"He might untie my skirt or scratch 290
my breast with his nails
or without warning sink his teeth
deep into my lips,"
the girl thought as she stared at her love
painted on canvas
and felt all the worries of making love
she ever felt in his presence.

sākṣād|darśanaṃ yathā:

cetaś, cañcalatāṃ tyaja; priya|sakhi
vrīḍe, na māṃ pīḍaya.
bhrātar, muñca dṛśau, nimeṣa; bhagavan
kāma, kṣaṇaṃ kṣamyatām:
barhaṃ mūrdhani, karṇayoḥ kuvalayaṃ,
vaṃśaṃ dadhānaḥ kare
so 'yaṃ locana|gocaro bhavati me
Dāmodaraḥ sundaraḥ. [136]

iti nāyak'|ādi|nirūpaṇam

An example of the last:

Heart, don't be unsteady, and modesty,
dear friend, don't go and bother me.
Blinking, my brother, leave my eyes alone,
and blessed love, be still a minute:
With a peacock feather on his head
and a lily at his ear
and a bamboo flute in hand, the lovely Krishna
has finally come into view.*

The end of the Description of the *Náyaka*
and Related Matters

MĀDHVĪKA|SYANDA|sandoha|
sundarīṃ Rasamañjarīm
kurvantu kavayaḥ karṇa|
bhūṣaṇam kṛpayā mama. [137]

295 tāto yasya Gaṇeśvaraḥ kavi|kul'|â-
laṃkāra|cūḍā|maṇir,
deśo yasya Videha|bhūḥ sura|sarit|
kallola|kirmīritā,
padyena sva|kṛtena tena kavinā
śrī|Bhānunā yojitā
vāg|devī|śruti|pārijāta|kusuma|
spardhā|karī mañjarī. [138]

iti Maithili|śrotriya|kula|tilaka|mahā|kavi|
Bhānudatta|viracitā Rasamañjarī sampūrṇā

Poets, take pity on me and deck your ears
with flowers from my Bouquet of Rasa,
for it is as sweet as such a bouquet can be
with the essence of its flowing nectar.*

His father was Ganéshvara, 295
brightest jewel in the crown of poetry,
his land, Vidéha country, where waves
of the holy river ripple.
With verse of his own making Shri Bhanu
the poet arranged this Bouquet
to rival the flower of the coral tree
at the ear of the Goddess of Language.

The end of the "Bouquet of Rasa" composed by
the great poet Bhanu·datta, forehead ornament
of the clan of learned brahmins of Míthila

RIVER OF RASA

THE FIRST WAVE
DESCRIPTION OF THE STABLE EMOTIONS

1.1 Lakṣmīm ālokya lubhyan,
nigamam upaharañ,†* chocayan yajña|jantūn,
kṣatraṃ śoṇ'|âkṣi paśyan,
samiti Daśa|mukhaṃ
vīkṣya rom'|âñcam añcan,
hṛtvā haiyaṅgavīnaṃ
cakitam apasaran, mleccha|raktair dig|antān
siñcan, dantena bhūmiṃ
tilam iva tulayan—pātu vaḥ pīta|vāsāḥ. [1]

Bhāratyāḥ śāstra|kāntāra|śrāntāyāḥ śānti|kāriṇī
kriyate Bhānunā bhūri|*rasā* Rasataraṅgiṇī. [2]

vāṇī kamalinī Bhānor
eṣā Rasataraṅginī;
haṃsāḥ kṛta|dhiyas tatra—
yuktam atra pratīyatām! [3]

girāṃ, devi, taraṅgiṇyāṃ vāraya krūra|vāraṇān,
yad bhaviṣyati lokānām āvilo vimalo* *rasaḥ*. [4]

1.1 *upaharan* N : *upahasan* J

---

[i] Vishnu

He looked at Lakshmi with longing, 1.1
retrieved the Vedas,
and grieved for the victims of sacrifice;
beheld the kshatriyas with his reddened eye,*
and spied
Rávana in battle with delight;
stole fresh butter and ran in fear, bedaubed
the horizon with barbarians' blood, and balanced
the earth like a sesame seed on his tusk—
may this God
of the yellow robe[i] protect you!*

To refresh the Goddess of Language, weary
from wandering the jungle of rhetoric,
Bhanu has made this "River of Rasa"
such that it overflows with *water : rasa.*

This "River of Rasa," the language of sun-like
Bhanu, is a pond of daylight lotuses,
and subtle readers are the geese upon it—
keep the logic of this in mind!

O Goddess of Language, keep away
all wild elephants from this River
so the turbid *water : rasa* may grow
crystal clear for everyone.

1.5 hetoḥ pūrva|vṛttitva|niyamād ataḥ pūrvam eva tasy' ôpanyāsaḥ samucitaḥ. rasasya hetavo bhāv'|ādayaḥ. tena rasebhyaḥ pūrvaṃ bhāv'|ādayo nirūpyante. ras'|ânukūlo vikāro bhāvaḥ. vikāraś c' ânyathā|bhāvaḥ. sa dvi|vidhaḥ. āntaraḥ, śārīraś ca. āntaro 'pi dvi|vidhaḥ. sthāyī bhāvo, vyabhicārī bhāvaś c' êti. śārīras tu sāttvikaḥ. yat tu mano|vikāro bhāvas, tathā ca deha|vikāre sved'|ādau bhāva|pada|prayogo gauṇa iti. tan na. tulyavad ubhayatra bhāva|pada|prayogeṇa vinigantum a|śakyatvāt. lakṣaṇ'|ânurodhena lakṣy'|â|vyavasthiteḥ.

itara|bhāvasy' ātma|bhāvatv'|ôpanāyakatve sati sajātīya|vijātīya|bhāv'|ân|abhibhāvyaḥ prathamaḥ. par'|ân|abhibhāvyo mano|vikāro vā. sakala|pradhāno mano|vikāra iti vā sthāyī bhāvaḥ. na ca vyabhicāriṇi sāttvika|bhāve v" âtivyāptiḥ. tasy' êtara|bhāvasy' ātma|bhāvatv'|ôpanāyakatv'|â|bhāvāt. carama|samaya|paryanta|sthāyitvād asya sthāyitva|vyapadeśaḥ. sa c' âṣṭadhā. tatra Bharataḥ:

Since the source of a thing must by definition precede it, we are right to deal first with the sources of rasa. These are the emotions and so on. Thus the emotions will be described prior to the rasas. An emotion is a transformation conducive to rasa. "Transformation" refers to a modification and is of two sorts: internal and bodily. The internal is also two-fold: stable and transitory. A bodily transformation is an involuntary physical reaction. We reject the argument that "emotion" refers exclusively to a mental transformation and therefore the use of the term in reference to bodily transformations such as sweating must be purely figurative. Since the word "emotion" is found in use equally in both cases, it is impossible to decide the matter one way or the other, since after all one does not determine the nature of things so they may accord with their definitions.* 1.5

The first, or stable, emotion is defined as one that is not displaced by other emotions whether similar (that is, stable) or dissimilar (that is, transitory), insofar as it has the capacity to subordinate other emotions to itself; or more simply, as a mental transformation that is not displaced by any other stable emotion; or better yet,* as a mental transformation dominant over all others. The definition is not so wide as to include either transitory emotions or physical reactions, because neither has the capacity to subordinate all other emotions to itself. This emotion is referred to as "stable" since it remains stable up to the climax.* It is eightfold, as Bhárata has declared:

«ratir, hāsaś ca, śokaś ca,
krodh'|ôtsāhau, bhayaṃ tathā,
jugupsā, vismayaś c' êti
sthāyi|bhāvāḥ prakīrtitāḥ.»

tatr' êṣṭa|vastu|samīhā|janita|mano|vikār'|ākṛtir a|paripūrṇā ratiḥ. sā kva cid darśanena, kva cic chravaṇena, kva cit smareṇena. yathā:

cakṣur yasya kṛṣīvalo, nigaditaṃ
pīyūṣa|pāthodharo,
bhrū|saṃjñā paricārikā samajani,
sphīta|smitaṃ dohadam;
santāpaṃ, taruṇ'|ârka|karkaśa|ruciṃ,
niḥśvāsa|vāt'|āhatiṃ
kasmād eva sahiṣyate, sakhi, ca me
prema|drumaḥ komalaḥ? [5]

1.10 komala|padād a|pūrṇatā.

kutūhala|kṛta|vacana|veṣa|vaisādṛśya|kṛto mano|vikāraḥ parimito hāsaḥ. vacana|bheda|veṣa|bheda|kṛte bhaye krodhe vā n' âtivyāptiḥ. tatra kutūhala|kṛtatv'|â|bhāvāt. yathā tāta|caraṇānām:

"Stable emotion comprises desire, humor, grief,
anger, energy, fear, revulsion, and wonder."

Among these, desire is a mental transformation not fully matured,* produced by longing for some wished-for object. It can arise from seeing, hearing, or remembering. An example:

It is planted by the eye and watered
by the ambrosial cloud of sweet words,
tended daily by eyebrows' play,
and fertilized by bright smiles.
The tree of love is delicate, my friend,
how can it withstand
the harsh sunlight of worry, the buffeting
from the high winds of sighs?*

The word "delicate" indicates that the emotion is not fully matured.* 1.10

Humor is an incomplete mental transformation produced by an incongruity of speech or dress that is meant for amusement. The definition is not so wide as to include fear or anger brought about by a peculiar type of speech or dress, since the element of amusement is absent there. An example from my honored father:*

āgacchan nagar'|ôpakaṇṭha|militair
āveṣṭito bālakaiḥ,
śuddh'|ânte paricārikābhir a|ciraṃ
s'|ôllāsam āveditaḥ,
s'|ākūtaṃ sa|kutūhalaṃ Bali|vadhū|
vṛnde puro dāpayaty
annaṃ kiṃ cid, udañcita|smita|lavo
pāyāt sa vo Vāmanaḥ. [6]

lava|padād a|pūrṇatā.

iṣṭa|viśleṣa|janito raty|an|āliṅgito parimito mano|vikāraḥ śokaḥ. na ceṣṭa|viśleṣa|janita|vipralambha|śṛṅgārasya karuṇa|rasatv'|āpattiḥ. tasya raty|āliṅgitatvāt. na ca ratiḥ prītis, tayā vinā śoko 'pi n' ôtpadyata, iti tathā c' â|sambhava iti vācyam. iṣṭa|samīhā|janita|mano|vikṛte rater uktatvāt. Kumāra|sambhave Ratyāḥ Kādambaryāṃ Mahāśvetāyā Raghu|kāvye 'jasya pralāpe karuṇa eva rasaḥ. tatra tatra bādha|niścayād iṣṭa|vastu|samīhāyā a|bhāvāt. yatra ca mṛte jīvit'|āśā tatra śṛṅgāra eva rasaḥ. bādha|sandehasya grāhya|sandeha|paryavasitatayā samīhāyām a|pratibandhakatvāt. tathā ca yūnor ekatarasmin mṛte pralāpaḥ karuṇa|rasaḥ. jīvitayor viśliṣṭayoḥ pralāpaḥ śṛṅgāraḥ. ata eva Rasa|ratna|dīpikāyāṃ karuṇa|ras'|ôdāharaṇam:

As he approached he was surrounded by lads
congregating near the town,
and before long he was being warmly welcomed
into the private quarters by servants,
and as the wives of Bali, amused and eager,
put a little food before him
he gave the bare hint of a smile—the Dwarf,
and may He ever protect you.*

The word "hint" indicates that the emotion is not fully matured.

Grief is an incomplete mental transformation produced by separation from a cherished object and emptied of all desire. Nor would such a definition entail that the rasa called the erotic frustrated, which is produced by separation from a desired object, turns out to be the same as the sorrowful rasa, since the former is alloyed with desire. Nor can one argue that "desire" really means "love" and that without love grief cannot come into existence, so that it cannot be as it has been described (unalloyed with desire). For we have defined desire as a mental transformation produced by longing for some wished-for object. In the case of Rati's raving in "The Birth of Kumára," that of Mahá·shveta in the "Princess Kadámbari," and that of Aja in "The Lineage of Raghu," the rasa can only be the sorrowful since in each of these cases there is no longing for some wished-for object because of the certitude that the object is no longer accessible. Where the love object is actually dead and yet there is still hope of life,* it remains the erotic rasa: since the uncertainty that the object is no longer accessible can issue

1.15 «ayi, jīvita|nātha, jīvas'?» îty
abhidhāy' ôtthitayā tayā puraḥ
dadṛśe puruṣ'|ākṛti kṣitau
hara|kop'|ânala|bhasma kevalam. [7]

iti. nanu vipralambha|śṛṅgārasya pūrv'|ânurāga|māna|pravāsa|karuṇ'|ātmakatvāj jīvator api vipralambhasya karuṇa|rasatvam āyātam iti cet—satyam. tatra karuṇa|rasasy' âṅgatvena bhāsamānatvāt tatra karuṇ'|ātmakatva|vyapadeśaḥ. yathā:

viraha|jvara|mūrchayā patantīṃ,
nayanen' âśru|jalena sicyamānām
samavekṣya Ratiṃ viniḥśvasantīṃ
karuṇā kuḍmalitā babhūva Śambhoḥ. [8]

kuḍmalit" êty a|paripūrṇatā.

---

[i] Rati laments the incineration of her husband, Kama, by Shiva.
[ii] Shiva

in the uncertainty that it may be recoverable, the former presents no hindrance to the desire. In short, when one of two young lovers is actually dead the lamentation constitutes the sorrowful rasa; when both are alive but separated, the lamentation constitutes the erotic rasa. Accordingly, the follow example of the sorrowful rasa is given in the "Jewel Lamp of Rasa":*

"Ah lord of my life, are you alive?" she cried, 1.15
and rising, she saw before her
on the ground the ash of Hara's anger
that had the shape of a man.[i]

One may object that even when both lovers are alive, the erotic frustrated, consisting as it does of the sorrow of unrequited love, or separation through jealous anger or travel, approaches the sorrowful rasa. And that is true: we may apply the designation "sorrowful" to frustrated love because the sorrowful rasa appears as one of its components. An example:

As Rati fell in a faint, overcome
by the fever of loss, and sighed a deep sigh
and was sprinkled with teardrops from her eyes
Shambhu[ii] looked at her, and his sorrow began
to bud.

"To bud" indicates that the emotion is not fully matured.

avajñ" | ādi | kṛtaḥ pramoda | pratikūlaḥ parimito mano | vikāraḥ krodhaḥ. pramoda | pratikūla iti viśeṣaṇād Daśa-mukha | durvacan' | âvamānitasya Rāmasya vīra | rase n' âti-vyāptiḥ. yathā Paraśurāma|vākyam:

1.20 n' âdy' ārabhya karomi kārmuka|latā|
vinyasta|hast'|âmbujaḥ
kiñcit|pāṭala|bhāsi locana|yuge
tāvan nimeṣ'|ôdayān,
yāvat sāyaka|koṭi|pāṭita|ripu|
kṣmā|pāla|mauli|skhalan|
mallī|mālya|patat|parāga|paṭalair
n' āmodinī medinī. [9]

kiñcit|pāṭalatvād apūrṇatā.

śaurya|dāna|day"|ânyatama|kṛtaḥ parimito mano|vikāra utsāhaḥ. vīras tu yuddhavīra|dānavīra|dayāvīra|bhedāt tri-dhā. yuddha|vīrasy' ôtsāho yathā:

Anger is an incomplete mental transformation produced by an act of disrespect or something similar that one finds disagreeable. The qualification "that one finds disagreeable" prevents the definition from being so wide as to include the heroic rasa, as in the case of Rama when shown disrespect by the Ten-headed Rávana.* An example is the following speech of Párashu·rama:

Having once commenced today, with my lotus hands 1.20
fixed on the pliant stalk that is my bow,
I shall not allow a blink to rise
in either of my pale red eyes
until the heaps of pollen falling
from the jasmine wreaths dislodged from the crowns
of enemy kings cut down by my myriad arrows
have ceased to perfume the earth.

Here the phrase "pale red" indicates that the emotion is not fully matured.

Energy is an incomplete mental transformation produced by any one of the following: valor, munificence, or compassion. The heroic,* for its part, can be one of three types: the heroic in war, in munificence, or in compassion. The energy pertaining to the heroic in war is illustrated in the following:

«senāṃ saṃghaṭayan, dyutiṃ dvi|guṇayañ,
cāpaṃ camatkārayan
netrasy' âbhimukho bhaviṣyati jagad|
vidrāvaṇo Rāvaṇaḥ.»
ity utsāha|vicāra|mūḍha|hṛdayo*
devo Raghūṇāṃ patir
jyā|vinyāsa|vidhiṃ vin" âiva viśikhaṃ
bāṇ'|âsane nyastavān. [10]

atra vicārād a|pūrṇatā.

1.25 dāna|vīrasy' ôtsāho yathā:

ādarśāya śaś'|âṅka|maṇḍalam idaṃ,
harmyāya Hem'|âcalaṃ,
dīpāya dyu|maṇiṃ mahīm iva kathaṃ
no bhikṣave dattavān?
ditsā|pallavita|pramoda|salila|
vyākīrṇa|netr'|âmbujo,
jānīmo, Bhṛgu|nandanas tad akhilaṃ
na prāyaśo dṛṣṭavān. [11]

pallavitaṃ na tu phalitam ity a|pūrṇatā.

dayā|vīrasy' ôtsāho yathā:

dustāra|saṃsāra|payodhi|pāra|
prakāram ālocayatāṃ janānām
samutthito vakṣasi Kaiṭabh|āreḥ
kṛp"|âṅkuraḥ Kaustubha|kaitavena. [12]

[i] Rama [ii] After his destruction of the kshatriyas, Párashu·rama gave the earth to the sage Káshyapa.

"Forming his battalion, redoubling his majesty,
setting his bow to twanging, he is about
to come before my eyes at last,
Rávana, ravisher of worlds!"—
with his mind thus frenzied in reflecting on how
to unleash his energy, the lord of the Raghus,[i]
the mighty king, placed his arrow
on his bow without even stringing it.

Here the word "reflecting" indicates that the emotion is not fully matured.

The energy pertaining to the heroic in munificence is illustrated in the following: 1.25

Why did he not give the mendicant
the moon for a mirror, the Himálaya for a house,
the sun for a lamp in just the way
he bestowed the earth itself? We know:
the desire to give had budded and produced
in Bhrigu's son such joy that his eyes
were blinded by tears that made it almost
impossible to see any of this at all.[ii]

Here the word "budded"—rather than "flowered"—indicates that the emotion is not fully matured.

The energy pertaining to the heroic in compassion is illustrated in the following:

For the people seeking some way to reach
the far shore of the vast ocean of rebirth
a sprout of pity appears on the chest
of Vishnu in the guise of the Káustubha jewel.*

1.30 aṅkur'|ôpanyāsād a|pūrṇatā.

aparādha|vikṛta|rava|vikṛta|sattv'|ādi|janito '|paripūrṇo mano|vikāro bhayam. yathā:

Tārkṣya|pakṣa|pavan'|ôpasevitaṃ
vīkṣya vīkṣya Yadu|nandanaṃ puraḥ
bhīta|bhīta iva tatra Kāliyo
manda|mandam apasartum udyataḥ. [13]

iv' ôpanyāsād a|pūrṇatā.

a|hṛdya|darśana|śravaṇa†|sparśaṇa|janitā* mano|vikṛtir a|paripūrṇā jugupsā. yathā:

1.35 śārdūla|śāvaka|caṭac|caṭa|pāṭyamāna|
sāraṅga|śṛṅgavati bhūbhṛti Rāma|bhadraḥ
vāsaṃ cakāra, na babhāra tathā jugupsāṃ:
duḥkheṣu duḥkha|matir eva na duḥkhitānām. [14]

na tath" êti padād a|pūrṇatā.

1.34 *-śravaṇa-* V : *-smaraṇa-* J Ś

Here the mention of "sprout" indicates that the emotion 1.30
is not fully matured.

Fear is a mental transformation, not fully matured, produced by such things as a transgression* or a gruesome sound or creature. For example:

The more he stared at the joy of the Yadus,
who stood before him, fanned by Gáruda's wings,
the more afraid Káliya* seemed to become
and the more he sought to slink away.

Here the mention of "seemed" indicates that the emotion is not fully matured.

Revulsion is a mental transformation, not fully matured, produced by a disgusting sight, sound, or memory. For example:

Good Rama made his dwelling on the mountain 1.35
where tiger cubs would munch with a crack
the horns of deer—and yet felt no great revulsion:
those in pain can feel no pain when new pains
come.*

From the phrase "no great" we understand that the emotion is not fully matured.

camatkāra|darśana|smaraṇa†|janito '|paripūrṇo mano|vikāro vismayaḥ. yathā:

yudhyantam Arjunaṃ vīkṣya
ke vā devā na vismitāḥ?
na mene bahu Govindo
dṛṣṭa|Karṇa|parākramaḥ. [15]

na mene bahv iti|padād a|pūrṇatā.

1.40 śṛṅgār'|ādau camatkāra|darśanād yatra mano|vikāro 'ṅgatayā bhāsate, tatra śṛṅgāra eva rasaḥ. prādhānyena yatra bhāsate, tatr' âdbhuta eva rasaḥ. aṅgatayā yathā:

vaiṣamyaṃ śruti|paṅkajāt prakaṭayaty
ānanda|nīraṃ dṛśoḥ;
svarṇ'|âlaṅkaraṇād vyanakti pulako
vaidharmyam aṅga|śriyaḥ;
tasyā nūpura|padmarāga|mahasaḥ
pād'|âravinda|śriyo
bhedaṃ siñjitam eva vakti—kim ataḥ
śilpaṃ Vidher varṇyatām? [16]

1.37 *-darśanasmaraṇa-* J : *-darśanasparśaṇaśravaṇa-* Ś

---

[i] Árjuna and Karna are warriors in the "Maha·bhárata;" Govínda is Krishna.

Wonder is a mental transformation, not fully matured, produced by a marvelous sight or memory. For example:

> What god was not lost in wonder watching Árjuna
> fight?
> But Govínda had seen Karna's[i] bravery and wasn't
> much impressed.*

From the phrase "wasn't much impressed" we understand that the emotion is not fully matured.

When, in the case of the erotic or other rasa, the mental transformation that results from seeing something wondrous appears as a subordinate component, we have the erotic (or other) rasa. Where it appears as the dominant component, we have the amazing rasa. The following is an example where it is subordinate: 1.40

> The only thing that distinguishes her eyes
> from the lotuses
> at her ears is her tears of joy;
> the only thing that differentiates the beauty
> of her limbs
> from her golden jewelry is her goosebumps;
> and the only thing that separates the splendor
> of her lotus feet
> from the glow of her ruby anklet
> is its jingle—if God ever crafted anything
> finer than this
> it must beggar description.*

prādhānyena yathā:

vinā sāyaṃ ko 'yaṃ
samudayati saurabhya|subhagaḥ,
kirañ|jyotsnā|dhārām,
adhidharaṇi tārā|parivṛḍhaḥ,
dhanur dhatte smāraṃ,
tirayati vihāraṃ na tamasāṃ,
nirātaṅkaḥ* paṅke-
ruha|yugalam aṅke naṭayati. [17]

iti śrī|Bhānudatta|viracitāyāṃ Rasataraṅgiṇyāṃ
sthāyi|bhāva|nirūpaṇaṃ nāma prathamas taraṅgaḥ.

The following is an example where it is dominant:

What kind of moon is this, arising though it's
not yet night,
that's fragrant and spreads moonlight on the earth,
that does nothing to dispel the darkness, and carries
the bow of Love
and has no spot and sets a pair of lotuses to dancing
nearby?*

The end of the Description of the Stable Emotions,
the First Wave of Bhanu·datta's "River of Rasa."

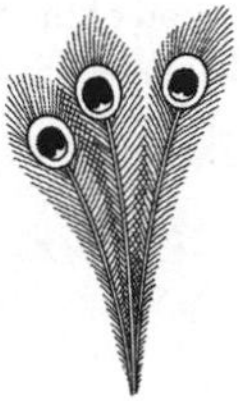

THE SECOND WAVE
DESCRIPTION OF THE FACTORS

2.1 ATHA VIBHĀVĀ NIRŪPYANTE. viśeṣeṇa bhāvayanty utpādayanti ye rasāṃs te vibhāvāḥ. te ca dvi | vidhā: ālambana | vibhāvā uddīpana | vibhāvāś c' êti. yam ālambya rasa utpadyate sa ālambana|vibhāvaḥ. yo rasam uddīpayati sa uddīpana|vibhāvaḥ. ālambana|vibhāvo yathā:

prāṇasya pratimūrtiḥ,
  praty|ātmā puṇya|latikāyāḥ,
adhidaivatam nayanayor
  sā mama yā kā 'pi, sā s" âiva. [1]

śṛṅgārasy' ôddīpana|vibhāvāḥ. tatra Bharataḥ:

ṛtu|māly'|âlaṅkāraiḥ
  priyajana|gāndharva|kāvya|sevābhiḥ
upavana|gamana|vihāraiḥ
  śṛṅgāra|rasaḥ samudbhavati.

2.5 candra | candan' | ādaya ūhanīyāḥ. uddīpana | vibhāvasy' ôdāharaṇaṃ yathā:

sandhyā|śoṇ'|âmbara|javanikā
    kāminoḥ prema nāṭyaṃ
  nāndī bhrāmyad|bhramara|virutaṃ
    māriṣaḥ ko 'pi kālaḥ
tārā|puṣp'|âñjalim iva kiran
    sūcayan puṣpa|ketor
  nṛty'|ārambhaṃ praviśati sudhā|
    dīdhitiḥ sūtra|dhāraḥ. [2]

THE FACTORS WILL now be described. The factors are called *vi·bhava* in Sanskrit because to a high degree (*vi*) they cause (*bhávayanti*) or engender the rasas. They are of two sorts, underlying factors and stimulant factors. An underlying factor is the thing or person that underlies the coming into being of rasa. A stimulant factor stimulates a rasa. An example of an underlying factor is the following: 2.1

> Exact copy of my life breath, the very image
> of the flowering vine of my merit from past births,
> the supreme deity for my eyes to worship—
> whatever she may be, she is mine and she alone.

The stimulant factors of the erotic have been discussed by Bhárata:

> "The time of year, garlands and ornaments, the presence of close friends, listening to music or poetry, outings to parks—these co-produce the erotic rasa."

One can extrapolate from this to such things as the full moon, sandalwood cream, etc. An example of a stimulant factor is the following: 2.5

> The passion of two lovers is a play:
> the red garment of twilight is the curtain,
> the buzz of flitting bees the invocation,
> the right hour the supporting actor,
> and entering, scattering stars—handfuls
> of flowers—to signal the start of the dance
> of the flower-bannered God of love
> comes the moon, director of it all.

atha hāsya|rasasya vibhāvāḥ. tatra Bharataḥ:

«viparīt'|âlaṅkārair,
vikṛt'|ācār'|âbhidhāna|veṣaiś ca,
vikṛtair artha|viśeṣair
hasat' îti rasaḥ smṛto hāsyaḥ.»

aṅga|vaikṛty'|ādaya ūhanīyā. yathā:

2.10 keyūraṃ ghargharayan,
bhramayan mauliṃ, vivartayan bāhum,
netr'|âñcalaṃ capalayan
naṭayati māyā|śiśuś chāyām. [3]

atha karuṇa|rasasya vibhāvāḥ. tatra Bharataḥ:

«iṣṭa|janasya vināśāc,
chāpāt, kleśāc ca, bandhanād, vyasanāt—
etair artha|viśeṣaiḥ
karuṇ'|ākhya|rasaḥ samudbhavati.»

bandhu|vaiklavy'|ādaya ūhanīyāḥ. yathā:

tvāṃ paśyato bhujaga|pāśa|nibaddha|deham
ady' âpi me yad asavo na bahiḥ prayānti—
netre nimīlayasi, paśyasi n' âiva tāvad
āsyaṃ madīyam iti, Lakṣmaṇa, yuktam eva. [4]

---

[i] Baby Krishna [ii] Rama speaks.

The factors* of the comic rasa have been discussed by Bhárata:

> "Ornaments askew, grotesque behavior or speech or costume: such grotesque things* provoke laughter—this is the comic rasa."

One can extrapolate from this to such things as grotesque movements of the body, etc. An example:

> Making his bracelet sound and shaking his head and waving his arms 2.10
> and rolling his eyes about, the magic child[i] made his shadow dance.

The stimulant factors of the sorrowful rasa have been discussed by Bhárata:

> "The loss of one's beloved, a curse, hardship, jail, misfortune are the specific things that co-produce the sorrowful rasa."

One can extrapolate from this to such things as the discomfiture of one's kin, etc. An example:[ii]

> To see you caught in the coils of this snake*
> and not to have the breath of life yet leave me—
> it's good your eyes are closed, Lákshmana,
> so you cannot see my mouth.

2.15 atha raudrasya vibhāvāḥ. tatra Bharataḥ:

«āyudha|khaḍg'|âbhibhavād,
vaikṛta|bhedād vidāraṇāc c' âiva,
ṣaṅgrāma|sambhav'|ârthād—
ebhyaḥ sañjāyate raudraḥ.»

vairi|darśana|nirbhartsan'|ādaya ūhanīyāḥ. yathā:

tanvantī timira|dyutiṃ, kṛtavatī
pratyarthi|cakra|vyathām,
eṣā, Bhārgava, tāvakī vijayate
nistriṃśa|dhārā niśā
yuddha|kruddha|vipakṣa|pakṣa|vidalan|
matt'|êbha|kumbha|sthalī|
bhraśyan|mauktika|kaitavena paritas
tār"|āvaliṃ varṣati. [5]

atha vīra|rasasya vibhāvāḥ. tatra Bharataḥ:

2.20 «utsāh'|âdhyavasāyād,
a|viṣāditvād, a|vismay|āmohāt,†
vividhād artha|viśeṣād
vīra|raso nāma sambhavati.»

2.20 *avismayāmohāt* NŚ : *avismayān mohāt* J

---

[i] Párashu·rama

The factors of the furious rasa have been discussed by Bhárata: 2.15

"From attack by arms, swords, and the like; from hideous injuries or wounds; from any untoward event of war—from such arises the furious rasa."

One can extrapolate from this to such things as the sight of an enemy, his insults, etc. An example:

It spreads a gleaming darkness,* and fills
with dread those *chakra* birds,* your foes,
and, in the guise of pearls scattered
about from the splitting forehead lobes*
of rutting elephants in the ranks
of enemies furious in battle,
the night that is your victorious sword blade,
O Bhárgava,[i] rains down a crowd of stars.

The factors of the heroic rasa have been discussed by Bhárata:

"From intentness on unleashing one's energy without despondency, pride, or confusion—from various events of this sort arises the heroic rasa."* 2.20

vinaya|bal'|ādaya ūhanīyāḥ. yuddha|vīra|vibhāvo† yathā:

«Laṅk"|âdhipaḥ saṃyati śaṅkanīyo
Jambh'|âri|dambh'|âpaha|bāhu|vīryaḥ.»
ity ālapantaṃ Hanumantam eṣa
Rāmaḥ smitair uttarayāṃ cakāra. [6]

dāna|vīrasya vibhāvo yathā:

vapuṣā vinayaṃ vahanti ke cid,
vacasā ke 'pi caranti cāru|caryām,
atithau samupāgate saparyāṃ
pulakaiḥ pallavayanti ke 'pi santaḥ. [7]

2.25 dayā|vīrasya vibhāvo yathā:

katham avirala|jāgrad|
bhakti|bhājo niśāyāṃ
tamasi dur|avagāhe
prāṇino vīkṣaṇīyāḥ—
iti kimu samudañcad|
dīpa|lekh"|âbhirāma|
dyutim urasi Murāriḥ
Kaustubhaṃ sambabhāra. [8]

2.21 *yuddhavīravibhāvo* Ś : om J

---

[i] Rávana [ii] Indra (literally "foe of [the demon] Jambha") is king of the gods [iii] Vishnu

One can extrapolate from this to such things as restraint, strength, etc. An example of the factor of the heroic in war:

"Lanka's lord[i] is formidable in battle,
strong enough to dispel Indra's[ii] pretensions."
As Hánuman gave his anxious report,
the only reply Rama gave was a smile.

An example of the factor of the heroic in munificence:

Some good men humbly bend their bodies,
others give welcome with words,
still others show hospitality by shivers
of delight when a guest arrives.

An example of the factor of the heroic in compassion: 2.25

Wondering how he might behold
his worshippers—whose devotion to him
was ever wakeful—during the nighttime
when the darkness is so dense,
Murári[iii] placed upon his chest
the Káustubha jewel that glowed
like a row of luminous lamps.

nanu sva | niṣṭha utsāhaḥ, katham uddīpana | vibhāvo bhavat' îti cet—satyam. uddīpana|vibhāvo jñāyamāna eva gamakaḥ. sa ca sva|niṣṭhaḥ para|niṣṭho v" êti na viśeṣaḥ. anubhāvas tu sva|niṣṭha eva gamakaḥ. tasy' ânumāpakatvena pakṣa|vṛttitv'|ādi|niyamād iti.

nanu dayā|vīraḥ kathaṃ karuṇa eva n' ântarbhavati? nirupādhi|para|duḥkha|prahāṇ'|êcchā dayā, sā ca karuṇayā vinā na sambhavat' îti cen—na, karuṇasya sthāyi|bhāvaḥ śoko, dayā|vīrasya sthāyi|bhāva utsāha, iti sthāyi|bhāva|bhedena bhedāt. nanu dayā|vīre karuṇa|rasatva|pratīteḥ kā gatir iti cet—satyam, karuṇayā vinā dayā|vīrasy' ân|anubhavād, iti tatra karuṇāyā anubhāvakatvād iti.

atha bhayānakasya vibhāvāḥ. tatra Bharataḥ:

2.30 «vikṛta|rava|sattva|darśana|
saṅgrām'|âraṇya|śūnya|gṛha|gamanāt,
guru|nṛpayor aparādhāt
kṛtakaś ca bhayānako jñeyaḥ.»

One might legitimately ask how, when the stable feeling of energy is located in Vishnu, the jewel that he himself wears can be a stimulant factor. The answer is that a stimulant factor is communicative merely upon becoming known; whether it is located in one person or another is immaterial. A physical reaction, on the other hand, is communicative only if it is located in oneself: since it prompts an inference, it must of necessity exist in the locus where the object of inference (the stable emotion) itself is located.

Another question: Why is the heroic in compassion rasa not included in the sorrowful rasa? For compassion is the desire to unconditionally alleviate the pain of others, and without a sense of sorrow such a desire cannot even exist. The answer is that the stable emotion of the sorrowful rasa is grief, whereas that of the heroic in compassion is energy, and since the two stable emotions are different, their associated rasas must be different. It would, however, be legitimate to rejoin that this is no solution, since we actually perceive in the heroic in compassion the fact of its being the sorrowful rasa. And accordingly, since we do not experience the heroic in compassion without the sorrowful rasa, that rasa can be said to enable our experience of it.

The factors of the fearful rasa have been discussed by Bhárata:

> "From a ferocious roar or seeing ferocious creatures 2.30
> or going to a battlefield, a jungle, or an empty house
> arises the fearful rasa; a transgression against a guru
> or a king produces fear of a secondary sort."*

ghāṭika | bandhu | bandhana | śravaṇa | śmaśāna | darśan' | ādaya ūhanīyāḥ. yathā:

udyat|kānti|kaṭhora|kesara|dalat|
pāthodhara|praskhalad|
vidyud|dīdhiti|kāñcanīkṛta|jagan|
niḥśeṣa|bhūmīdharaḥ,
sphūrjat|kaṇṭha|nināda|bhinna|vasudhā|
mārga|praviṣṭa|dvija|
prauḍh'|āśīr|vacana|praharṣita|Balir
vyāloki māyā|hariḥ. [9]

atha bībhatsasya vibhāvāḥ. tatra Bharataḥ:

«an|abhimata|darśanena ca,
gandha|rasa|sparśa|śabda|doṣaiś ca,
udvejanaiś ca bahubhir
bībhatsa|rasaḥ samudbhavati.»

2.35 a | hṛdya | vastūnāṃ śravaṇa | smaraṇ' | ādaya ūhanīyāḥ. yathā:

---

[i] The underworld [ii] The Man-Lion avatar of Vishnu

One can extrapolate from this to such things as the report of the arrest of a relative by a night watchman,* the sight of cremation grounds, etc. An example:

> Gilding all the mountains of the world
> with streaks of lightning falling from the clouds
> rent by the coruscating and rough
> strands of hair of his lion's mane
> and making Bali's realm[i] shudder
> at the fervent prayers uttered by the brahmins
> entering by the paths of the earth that split
> at his deafening roar, there appeared
> the magic Lion.*[ii]

The factors of the disgusting rasa have been discussed by Bhárata:

> "The sight of something displeasing, foul smells or tastes, touches or sounds—the many sources of revulsion such as these co-produce the disgusting rasa."

One can extrapolate from this to such things as hearing about or remembering unpleasant things. An example: 2.35

yodhānām adharair aśoka|kusumair,
netraiḥ sitair ambujair,
dantaiḥ kunda|dalaiḥ, karaiḥ sarasijaiḥ
sampādya puṣpa|śriyam,
jhillīṃ karṇa|yuge vidhāya, kariṇāṃ
rakt'|âvasikt'|âṅgakaiḥ
pretānāṃ baṭubhiḥ puraḥ Purabhido
nṛtyaṃ samārabhyate. [10]

ath' âdbhuta|rasasya vibhāvāḥ. tatra Bharataḥ:

«yat tv atiśay'|ârtha|yuktaṃ
vākyaṃ śilpaṃ ca karma|rūpaṃ ca,
tat|sambaddhair arthai
raso 'dbhuto nāma sambhavati.»

māy"|êndra|jāl'|ādaya† ūhanīyāḥ. yathā:

2.40 uddām'|ôddāma|mādyat|
pratibhaṭa|dalan'|ôdagra|jāgrat|prabhāvaḥ
so 'yaṃ devo mude vo
bhavatu Naraharis tārit'|â|śeṣa|viśvaḥ,
yasya prauḍha|pratāp'|ôd-
bhaṭa|vikaṭa|saṭā|koṭibhiḥ pāṭitānām
antrāṇy ambho|dharāṇāṃ
bahir iva niragur vidyutāṃ kaitavena. [11]

2.39 *jālādaya* G : *jālārthalābhādaya* J Ś

---

[i] Dances begin with an offering of flowers.

In front of Indra the dance of the dead begins
as the corpses of young soldiers strew lovely flowers[i]—
the red *ashókas* are their bleeding lips,
the lotuses the whites of their rolled-back eyes,
the jasmine petals their teeth, the crimson lilies
their bloody hands, while crickets on their ears
are their sounding earrings, and the gore
of slain elephants the lacquer on their feet.*

The factors of the amazing rasa have been discussed by Bhárata:

> "Hyperbolic speech or special effects or an extraordinary act*—events associated with such things produce the amazing rasa."

One can extrapolate from this to such things as magic, legerdemain, etc. An example:

May the god bring you joy, the Man-Lion 2.40
who rescued all the world, whose supreme
power was fully awakened when tearing to pieces
his wildly raving enemies
and whose terrible sharp-tipped mane, awesome
in its mighty power, rent the clouds
so much that their innards spilled across
the sky in the guise of lightning.

indra|jālo yathā:

vyomni prāṅgaṇa|sīmni sāndhya|kiraṇaṃ
vistārya cel'|âñcalaṃ,
dhvāntaiḥ kārmaṇa|pāṃśubhis tri|jagatāṃ
netrāṇi sammohayan,
tārā|śauktika|mauktikāni vihaga|
śreṇī|rava|cchadmanā
jiñjīkṛtya bahiḥ karoti vadanāt
Pañcāśugo māyikaḥ. [12]

iti śrī|Bhānudatta|viracitāyāṃ Rasataraṅgiṇyāṃ
vibhāva|nirūpaṇaṃ nāma dvitīyas taraṅgaḥ.

An example of legerdemain:

In the courtyard that is the sky
the magician that is Love
spread out his cape, the twilight glow,
and bedazzled the eyes of all the world
with his magic dust, the darkness,
and in the guise of birdcalls he cried
"Abracadabra!" and from his mouth produced
the oyster pearls that are the stars.

The end of the Description of the Factors,
the Second Wave of Bhanu·datta's "River of Rasa."

THE THIRD WAVE
DESCRIPTION OF THE PHYSICAL REACTIONS

3.1 ATH' ÂNUBHĀVĀ nirūpyante. ye rasān anubhāvayanty—anubhava | gocaratāṃ nayanti—te 'nubhāvāḥ kaṭ' | âkṣ' | ādayaḥ. karaṇatven' ânubhāvakatā. karaṇatvaṃ ca phal'|âyoga|vyavacchedena†* sambandhitvam.

nanu rase katham anubhāvak' | âpekṣ" êti cet—satyaṃ, sthāyī bhāvaḥ pūrṇo rasas, tasya c' ântaratvāj jñāpakena vinā kathaṃ jñānam, ity anubhāvakasy' âpekṣaṇīyatvāt.

nanu kaṭ'|âkṣ'|ādayaḥ katham uddīpana|vibhāvā na bhavanti? dṛṣṭe kaṭ' | âkṣ' | ādau kāminor* mano | vikāraḥ paripūrṇo bhavati. anubhava | siddhatven' âpahnotum a | śakyatvāt. kiṃ ca prācīna|sammatir api.

īṣad|vakrita|pakṣma|paṅktibhir, an|ā-
  kūta|smitair vīkṣitair*
etair eva tav' âdya, sundari, kara|
  kroḍe jagad vartate.
antaḥ|pāṃsula|hema|ketaka|dala|
  droṇī|durāpa|śriyo
dor|mūlasya vibhāvanād iha† punaḥ,
  krūre, kim ākāṅkṣasi?* [1]

3.1 *phalāyogavyavacchedena* Ś : *phalayogāvyavacchedena* J 3.4 *vibhāvanād iha* V J : *vibhāvanādiṣu* Ś

NEXT, THE PHYSICAL reactions will be described. Things that show a rasa being "reacted to"—in other words, that make a rasa an object of reaction—are called "reactions." These include sidelong glances, etc. Their being reactions derives from the fact that they are instruments, an instrument being something directly connected with an effect. 3.1

One might well ask why there should be any need for something that shows a rasa being reacted to. True enough, a rasa has been defined as a fully matured stable emotion, but since it is an internal phenomenon we cannot have knowledge of it without something else to make it known, hence the necessity of a physical reaction.

But one might also ask why sidelong glances and the like are not reckoned as stimulant factors, since when a sidelong glance is seen, a mental transformation in the two lovers becomes fully matured—this is proven by experience and so cannot be denied. Moreover, there is a consensus of the ancients on this point, as poems like the following show:

Your eyes with half-closed lashes, your aimless
smiles and idle glances
are enough to bring the whole world
into the palm of your hand.
So what can you be seeking here,
cruel lady, by revealing
a sight rarer than *kétaka*'s golden
stamen—your underarm?*

3.5 ity|ādaya iti cet—satyam. kaṭ'|âkṣ'|ādīnāṃ karaṇatven' ânubhāvakatvaṃ, viṣayatven' ôddīpana|vibhāvatvam. tathā c' ātmani† ras'|ânubhāvakatvena nāyakaṃ† prati kaṭ'|âkṣ'|ādayo 'nubhāvāḥ. te ca dṛṣṭi|gocarī|bhūtāḥ kāminor mano|vikāraṃ kārayanto viṣayatven' ôddīpana|vibhāvā iti.

te c' ânubhāvāḥ† kāyika|mānas'|āhārya|sāttvika|bhedāc caturdhā. kāyikā bhuj'|ākṣep'|ādayaḥ. mānasāḥ pramod'|ādayaḥ. nāṭye† Caturbhujatva|jñān'|ādaya āhāryāḥ. sāttvikā rom'|âñc'|ādayaḥ.

atha śṛṅgārasy' ânubhāvāḥ. tatra Bharataḥ:

«ayana|vadana|prasādaiḥ,
smita|madhura|vacaḥ|pramodaiś ca,
vividhair aṅga|vikārais
tasy' âbhinayaḥ prayoktavyaḥ.»*

kaṭ'|âkṣa|bhuj'|ākṣep'|ādaya ūhanīyāḥ. yathā:

3.5 *ātmani* Ś : *nāyakātmani* J 3.5 *nāyakaṃ* V : *nāyikāṃ* J Ś 3.6 *te cānubhāvāḥ* Ś : *sa cānubhāvaḥ* J 3.6 *nāṭye* J N : *nāṭya-* Ś

This is all true, but insofar as sidelong glances and the like are factors they can be classified as things that show rasa being reacted to; insofar as they are objects of perception they can be classified as stimulants. Accordingly, sidelong glances directed toward the *náyaka* are reactions insofar as they are a cause for showing the rasa being reacted to in herself.* When these glances themselves come under observation they bring about a mental transformation in the two lovers and hence, being objects, act as stimulant factors. 3.5

Physical reactions are of four kinds: voluntary, mental, costume-related, and involuntary. "Voluntary" refers to shaking the arms and so on; "mental" to joyfulness and so on; "costume-related" occurs in drama and consists in the representation of the Four-armed Vishnu and the like; "involuntary" refers to goose bumps, etc.

With regard to the physical reactions of the erotic rasa, Bhárata says:

> "It is to be represented by displaying clear eyes and a bright face, smiles, gentle words, joyfulness, and various movements of the limbs."

One can extrapolate from this to such things as sidelong glances, shaking the arms, etc. An example:

3.10 muktā|hāraḥ stana|kalaśayoḥ,
karṇayoḥ karṇikāraṃ,
maulau mālā paribhava|bhayād
eva dūre nyavāri.
dṛṣṭe 'bhīṣṭe samajani punaḥ
su|bhruvo bhūṣaṇāya
prātar|vāt'|ôttarala|kamala|
droha|dakṣaḥ kaṭ'|âkṣaḥ. [2]

atha hāsyasy' ânubhāvāḥ. tatra Bharataḥ:

«vikṛt'|ākārair vākyair
aṅga|vikāraiś ca vikṛta|veṣaiś ca†
hāsyaṃ janayed yasmāt
tasmāj jñeyo raso hāsyaḥ.»

asy' âdhara|vicaraṇa†|daśana|darśana|nāsā|kapola|spanda| dṛṣṭi|vyākośa|kuñcan'†|ādaya ūhanīyāḥ. yathā:

pātrī|kṛtya kapola|maṇḍalam idaṃ,
pīyūṣa|bhānoḥ kalāṃ
vartī|kṛtya, phaṇā|maṇiṃ phaṇi|pateḥ
sampādya tasyāṃ śikhām,
sāyaṃ dīpa|vidhiṃ vitanvati śiśau
mandaṃ hasantyā tayā
kiṃ cit kiṃ cid apāṅga|bhaṅga|kuṭilā
dṛṣṭiḥ samāropitā. [3]

3.12 *ca vikṛtaveṣaiś ca* NŚ : *vikṛtaviśeṣaiś* J : *vikṛtaveṣaiś ca* Ś

3.13 *-vicaraṇa-* V : *-vivaraṇa-* J Ś   3.13 *-vyākośakuñcana-* J : *-vyākuñcana-* Ś

A pearl necklace upon jug-like breasts, 3.10
a flower behind the ear,
a wreath in the hair—all were avoided
since all would pale in comparison.*
But at the sight of her lover something new
appeared on its own to adorn her:
a sidelong glance that could shame a lotus petal
trembling in the morning breeze.

With regard to the physical reactions of the comic rasa, Bhárata says:

> "Since by means of distorted speech, disfigured limbs, or disordered clothes one can provoke humor, the rasa is known as the comic."

One can extrapolate from this to such things as making the lips quiver, baring the teeth when laughing, flaring the nostrils or puffing out the cheeks, bugging out or squinting the eyes, etc. An example:

Turning the skull into an bowl,
the crescent moon into a wick,
and the jewel upon the hood
of the serpent into a flame,
her child tried to make a lamp
in the evening, and his mother
gently laughed and cast a glance
at him, just wrinkled at the edge.*

3.15 atha karuṇ'|ânubhāvāḥ. tatra Bharataḥ:

«niḥśvasitena ca ruditair†
moh'|āgamana|paridevanaiś c' âiva†
abhineyaḥ karuṇa|raso
deh'|āghāt'|ādibhiś c' âiva.»

mukha|śoṣaṇa†|pralāpa|vaivarṇy'|ādaya ūhanīyāḥ. yathā:

tāte nirgacchati* Gaṇapatau
nākam, ady' âpi tasyā
vācāṃ devyās tyajati śithilaṃ
kaṅkaṇaṃ n' âiva doṣṇoḥ,
ady' âpy ārdrī|bhavati kucayor
n' âiva† pāṭīra|paṅko,
netre niryat|payasi na punaḥ
kajjalaṃ sthairyam eti. [4]

atha raudrasy' ânubhāvāḥ. tatra Bharataḥ:

3.20 «nānā|praharaṇa|saṃkula|
śirasaḥ kampaiḥ, kar'|âgra|niṣpeṣaiḥ,*
ghorair artha|viśeṣais
tasy' âbhinayaḥ prayoktavyaḥ.»

bhru|kuṭī|dant'|âuṣṭha|pīḍan'|ādaya ūhanīyāḥ. yathā:

3.16 *ni[ḥ]śvasitena ca ruditair* J V N B : *niḥśvasitaśvasanaruditair* Ś
3.16 *mohāgamanaparidevanaiś caiva* Ś : *mohaiḥ pralāpaparidevanapralāpaiḥ* J 3.17 *-śoṣaṇa-* J : *-śoṣa-* Ś 3.18 *naiva* J : *nāpi* Ś

With regard to the physical reactions of the pitiful rasa, Bhárata says: 3.15

> "The pitiful rasa is to be represented by means of sighs, weeping, fainting, lamentation, beating the breast, etc."

One can extrapolate from this to such things as a sad face, raving, pallor, etc. An example:

> From the day my father, Gana·pati,
> went to heaven the bangles
> on the wrists of the goddess of language
> have been slipping off,
> the saffron cream on her breasts has not
> stayed moist,*
> and the dark rich lampblack
> on her eyes—with the tears streaming out—
> has not ceased to run.

With regard to the physical reactions of the furious rasa, Bhárata says:

> "By shaking the head ringing from multiple blows, 3.20
> by pounding the fist*—by dreadful things such as these should one represent the furious rasa."

One can extrapolate from this to such things as knitting the brow, gnashing the teeth, biting the lips, etc. An example:

ye ye Bhīmena baddha|
bhru|kuṭi|ghana|ravaṃ danta|niṣpīḍit'|ōṣṭhaṃ
vikṣiptā vyomni Vindhy'|â-
cala|caṭula|camatkāra|bhājaḥ kar'|îndrāḥ,
teṣām eṣā kapolād†
iva* bhaya|vidhutāt† kā cid uḍḍīya lagnā
bimbe pīyūṣa|bhānor
madhukara|paṭalī lāñchanasya cchalena. [5]

atha vīra|ras'|ânubhāvāḥ. tatra Bharataḥ:

«śauryair, vīryair, dhairyair,
utsāha|parākrama|prabhāvaiś ca,
vākyair ākṣepa|kṛtair
vīra|rasaḥ samyag abhineyaḥ.»

3.25 vijaya | bal' | ādaya ūhanīyāḥ. nanv atīndriyasya rasasya jñāpakāḥ śarīra|dharmā bhavitum arhanti. ta eva ca† sarvatr' ôktāḥ. tathā ca dhairy' | ôtsāhau na śarīra | dharmāv iti cet—satyam. dhairya|padena cāñcaly'|â|bhāva, utsāha|padena c' âśru|pulak'|ādayo vivakṣitāḥ. yad v" ânubhāvaś catur|vidhaḥ. tatra mānaso 'py anubhāva uktaḥ. tasya ca jñānam ev' ânubhāvakaṃ.† tac ca mānasam aindriyakaṃ c' êti na viśeṣaḥ.

3.22 *kapolād* Ś : *kapālād* J 3.22 *-vidhutāt* V B : *-vidhutā* J Ś *ca* J : om Ś 3.25 *ca* J : om Ś 3.25 *tasya ca jñānam evānubhāvakaṃ* J V : *sa ca jñāyamāna eva gamakaḥ* Ś

---

[i] One of the heroes of the epic "Maha·bhárata"

Knitting his brow and roaring an awful
roar and biting his lip, Bhima[i] hurled
the war elephants into the sky
like so many Vindhya peaks,
and from their cheeks as if shaking in fear
a swarm of bees flew into the sky
and attached themselves to the disk
of the moon in the guise of its jet-black streak.

With regard to the physical reactions of the heroic rasa, Bhárata says:

> "By boldness, heroism, steadfastness, energy, audacity, and magnificence, and by statements laden with double meanings,* is the heroic rasa properly represented."

One can extrapolate from this to such things as triumphalism, force,* etc. One might well object that the reactions have to be physical properties—and they have been so described elsewhere—if they are to give us some sense of rasa, which is itself imperceptible, but steadfastness and energy are not such properties. True enough, but by the word "steadfast" was meant the absence of physical movement, and by "energy," things like tears and horripilation. Or we could reply that the physical reactions are of four sorts, and mental reactions have been included among them. Awareness of that mental reaction is what makes clear the particular rasa being reacted to. It makes no difference whether that awareness is mental or perceptible.* 3.25

yuddha|vīrasy' ânubhāvo yathā:

«agre Vāsavajit samagra|samara|
vyāpāra|dīkṣā|guruḥ.
pārśve tasya vipakṣa|pakṣa|damana|
krīḍā|dhano Rāvaṇaḥ.»
itthaṃ jalpati sarvataḥ parijane
sandhyā|smṛtiṃ kurvataḥ
śrī|Rāmasya na kumbhakasya pavane
kṣuṇṇaḥ sa ko 'pi kramaḥ. [6]

dayā|vīrasy' ânubhāvo yathā:

dhvānta|stoma|dhare, jagad|vyayakare
pātho|dhare varṣati,
krodha|vyākula|vatsa|go|kula|dayā|
dīn'|ēkṣaṇaḥ Keśavaḥ
hasta|nyasta|mahīdhara|cyuti|bhiyā
n' âiv' âṅgulī|pallavair
veṇuṃ srastam urīkaroti, na tanoḥ
srastaṃ haraty aṃśukam. [7]

---

[i] Megha·nada, the son of Rávana [ii] Késhava (Krishna) protected the calves by holding over them a mountain like an umbrella.

An example of the physical reactions of the heroic in war:

"Before him stands Vásavajit,[i] high priest
in all the rituals of war.
At his side Rávana, master sportsman
in defeating the enemy ranks."
With his companions fretting at this thought
glorious Rama continued
with twilight worship and did not miss a step
in his yoga breathing.

An example of the physical reactions of the heroic in compassion:

As stormclouds, casting pitch darkness, terrifying
the world, began to burst,
Késhava looked with compassion at the herds
of cows and calves scared in his embrace,
and from fear of dropping the mountain he held
    in his hands[ii]
he would not pick up the flute
that he had let slip, nor pull up the garment
slipping off his body.

3.30 dāna|vīrasy' ânubhāvo yathā:

audāsyaṃ na vidhehi, gaccha na gṛhāt
saṃvīkṣya mṛd|bhājanaṃ.
yāce kin tu bhavantam etad a|khilaṃ,
Kautsa, kṣaṇaṃ kṣamyatām.
dāsaś ced aham, asmi ced, vasumatī
sarv" âiva saṃgṛhyatāṃ.
svarṇaṃ ced guru|dakṣiṇā, Dhanapater
ānīya sampādyate. [8]

atha bhayānakasy' ânubhāvāḥ. tatra Bharataḥ:

«kara|caraṇa|netra|mastaka|
sarv'|âṅgānāṃ prakampanaiś c' âiva,
śuṣk'|āuṣṭha|tālu|kaṇṭhair
bhayānako nityam abhineyaḥ.»

rom'|âñca|vadana|vaivarṇya|svara|bhed'|ādaya ūhanīyāḥ. yathā:

3.35 nyasta|srasta|tṛṇ'|âvalīḍha|vadana|
vyākīrṇa|phen'|ôccayaṃ,
kāku|vyākula|ghora|gharghara|ravaṃ,
sphārībhaval|locanam,
kampa|praskhalad|aṅghri, vāmana|tanu,†
śvās'|ōrmi|nunn'|âdharaṃ,
vistīrṇe bhujagasya vaktra|kuhare
Kṛṣṇasya gāvaḥ sthitāḥ. [9]

3.35 *vāmanatanu* Ś : *vāmanatanuḥ* J

[i] King Raghu speaks to his priest at the conclusion of a sacrifice where he gave away all his wealth. [ii] The god Kubéra [iii] Krishna and his cowherds entered the mouth of the demon Agha, mistaking it for a cave.

An example of the physical reactions of the heroic in munificence:[i] 3.30

Please do not, seeing this earthen bowl of mine,
leave my house in despair.
All that I would ask of you, Kautsa,
is to pause a moment.
If I am your slave, and still alive,
take the whole world for your own.
If gold is your teacher's gift, I'll get it
from the Lord of Wealth[ii] himself.

With regard to the physical reactions of the fearful rasa, Bhárata says:

"By the quivering of the hands, feet, eyes, head, and all the limbs, by parched lips, palate, and throat is the fearful rasa always to be represented."

One can extrapolate from this to such things as horripilation, pallor, a breaking voice, etc. An example:

Mouths smeared with foam and mouthfuls of grass 3.35
falling in a heap;
with an awful bellowing pierced with a screech,
and eyes bulging wide,
and bodies shrinking, quivering on tripping feet,
lips pounded by waves of sighs,
they stood in the vast gaping cave of the
serpent's maw,
those cows belonging to Krishna.[iii]

atha bībhats'|ânubhāvāḥ. tatra Bharataḥ:

«ānana|netra|vighūrṇana|locana|nāsā|pidhānaiś ca,
avyakta|pāda|patanair bībhatsaḥ samyag abhineyaḥ.»

sarv'|âṅga|saṃhāra|niṣṭhīvan'|ādaya ūhanīyāḥ. yathā:

kapaṭa|Harer* mukha|kuhare
vikṛte saṃvīkṣya dinakaraṃ Lakṣmīḥ
hata|daitya|palala|kavala|
bhrāntyā mukham aṃśukaiḥ pidadhe. [10]

3.40 ath' âdbhuta|ras'|ânubhāvāḥ. tatra Bharataḥ:

«sparśa†|grahaṇ'|ôllāsair,*
hā|hā|kāraiś ca, sādhu|vādaiś ca,
vepathu|gadgada|vacanaiḥ,
svara|bhedair abhinayas tasya.»

nirnimeṣa|prekṣaṇa|rom'|âñc'|ādaya ūhanīyāḥ. yathā:

Pāṇḍavaṃ vīkṣya dor|daṇḍa|
khaṇḍit'|ārāti|maṇḍalam,
ady' âpi nākināṃ netre
nimeṣā n' âiva jāgrati. [11]

iti śrī|Bhānudatta|viracitāyāṃ Rasataraṅgiṇyām
anubhāva|nirūpaṇaṃ nāma tṛtīyas taraṅgaḥ.

3.41 *sparśa-* Ś : *karasparśa-* J

---

[i] Hari (Vishnu) in the form of the Man-Lion devoured the demon Hiránya·káshipu [ii] Árjuna

With regard to the physical reactions of the disgusting rasa, Bhárata says:

> "By eyes rolling in one's head, by covering the eyes or nose, and by indistinct footfalls* is the disgusting rasa properly represented."

One can extrapolate from this to such things as physically recoiling, spitting, etc. An example:

> Lakshmi thought she saw the sun in the mouth,
> the gruesome mouth, of Hari in disguise,
> confusing it with gobs of the dead demon's flesh,
> and had to cover her face with her garment.[i]

With regard to the physical reactions of the amazing rasa, Bhárata says: 3.40

> "By an eager touching or grasping, with cries of 'Oh my!' or 'Bravo!' by quivering or stammering or a breaking voice is it to be represented."

One can extrapolate from this to such things as unblinking staring, horripilation, etc. An example:

> Once having seen the Pándava[ii] destroy
> the enemy ranks with his punishing arm,
> the eyes of those who live in heaven
> stay even today unblinkingly awake.*

The end of the Description of the Physical Reactions,
the Third Wave of Bhanu·datta's "River of Rasa."

THE FOURTH WAVE
DESCRIPTION OF THE INVOLUNTARY PHYSICAL REACTIONS

4.1 ATHA SĀTTVIKA|BHĀVĀ nirūpyante. tatra Bharataḥ:

«stambhaḥ, svedo, 'tha rom'|âñcaḥ,
svara|bhedo, 'tha vepathuḥ,
vaivarṇyam, aśru, pralaya
ity aṣṭau sāttvikā matāḥ.»

nanv asya sāttvikatvaṃ kathaṃ, vyabhicāritvaṃ na kutaḥ, sakala|rasa|sādhāraṇyād iti cet. atra ke cit: sattvaṃ nāma para|gata|duḥkha|bhāvanāyām atyant'|ânukūlatvam. tena sattvena dhṛtāḥ sāttvikā iti vyabhicāritvam an|ādṛtya sāttvika|vyapadeśa iti. tan na, nirveda|smṛti|dhṛtīnām api sāttvikatva|vyapadeś'|āpatteḥ. na ca para|gata|duḥkha|bhāvanāyām aṣṭāv eva† samutpadyanta ity anukūla|śabd'|ârthaḥ. ata eva sāttvikatvam apy eṣām iti vācyam. nirved'|āder api para|duḥkha|bhāvanāyām utpatter iti. atr' êdaṃ pratibhāti sattva|śabdasya prāṇi|vācakatvāt. atra sattvaṃ jīvac|charīraṃ, tasya dharmāḥ sāttvikāḥ. tathā ca śārīrā bhāvāḥ stambh'|ādayaḥ sāttvikā bhāvā ity abhidhīyante. sthāyino vyabhicāriṇaś ca bhāvā āntaratayā te śarīra|dharmā iti.

4.3 *eva* V : *ete* J Ś

NEXT, THE INVOLUNTARY physical reactions will be described. With reference to them, Bhárata says: 4.1

> "Paralysis, sweating, horripilation, a breaking voice,
> trembling, pallor, weeping, and absorption are held
> to be the eight involuntary reactions."

It could be asked why these are reckoned as involuntary reactions (*sáttvika*) rather than transitory feelings, given that they are likewise common to all the rasas. Some have answered that the word *sattva* refers to a feeling of deep sympathy for the experience of sorrow on the part of others, and this produces the involuntary physical reactions; that is why the designation *sáttvika* is used for them without regard to their transitory character. But that answer cannot be correct, since the designation *sáttvika* would then have to be applied to such transitory feelings as despair, remembrance, and fortitude.* Nor does the meaning of the word "sympathy" refer to the fact that only the eight reactions arise in response to the experience of sorrow on the part of others, since despair and so on also arise in response to another's sorrow. What seems to be at issue here is this: The word *sattva* refers to a living being, *sattva* in this context being the enlivened body. The properties of a *sattva*, or being, are called *sáttvika*, and accordingly bodily reactions are called *sáttvika* reactions. Because the stable emotions and the transitory feelings are internal they are not properties of the body.

śarīra|dharmatve sati gati|nirodhaḥ stambhaḥ. na ca nidr"|âpasmār'|ādāv ativyāptiḥ, śarīra|dharma|padena teṣāṃ vyāvartanāt. pralaya|bhāve tu ceṣṭā|nirodho na tu gati|nirodhaḥ. tasya vibhāvā harṣa|rāga|bhaya|duḥkha|viṣāda|vismaya|krodhāḥ. yathā:

4.5 «śroṇī pīnatarā, tanuḥ kṛśatarā,
bhūmī|dharāt pīvarā
vakṣojasya taṭī. kathaṃ nija|kuṭī,
mātar, mayā gamyate?»
ity udbhāvya, kadamba|kuñja|nikaṭe
nirviśya manda|smitaṃ
Govindaṃ samudīkṣya pakṣmala|dṛśā
stambhas tiro|dhīyate. [1]

vapuṣi salil'|ôdgamaḥ svedaḥ. asya vibhāvā manas|tāpa|harṣa|lajjā|krodha|bhaya|śrama|pīḍā|ghāta|mūrch"|ādayaḥ. yathā:

kānte, tava kuca|prānte rājante sveda|bindavaḥ
hṛṣyatā Madanen' êva kṛtāḥ kusuma|vṛṣṭayaḥ. [2]

---

[i] A term of affection here, addressed to her girlfriend [ii] Krishna

Paralysis, being a property of the body, is the obstruction of ambulatory movement. This definition is not so wide as to include transitory feelings such as sleep or possession, since those are excluded by the words "property of the body."* Paralysis is distinguished from absorption, where all motion is obstructed. Its factors are joy, passion, fear, sorrow, depression, wonder, and anger. An example:

"My hips are so wide, and my waist so thin, 4.5
and heavier than a mountain
are my breasts. How then, dear mother,[i]
    am I supposed
to go back to my own hut?"
So the lovely woman confessed, but when Govínda[ii]
entered the *kadámba* grove
slyly smiling, she looked up and saw him—
and at once her paralysis vanished.

Sweating is the arising of perspiration on the body. Its factors are remorse, joy, shame, anger, fear, fatigue, pain, distress, fainting, etc. An example:

My beloved, drops of sweat
are glistening on your breasts
like a rain of flowers showered down
by the joyful God of love.

vikāra | samuttha | rom' | ôtthānaṃ rom' | âñcaḥ. asya vibhāvāḥ śīt'|āliṅgana|harṣa|bhaya|krodhāḥ. yathā:

bakula|mukula|kośa|roṣa|niryan|
madhukara|kūjita|bhāji kuñja|bhūmau
pulakayati kapola|pāli|māli
smita|subhagaḥ katham adya Nanda|sūnuḥ? [3]

4.10 gadgadatva | prayojakībhūta | svara | bhāva | vailakṣaṇyaṃ svara | bhaṅgaḥ. asya vibhāvāḥ krodha | bhaya | harṣa | madāḥ. yathā:

«vyaktiḥ syāt svara|bhedasya
kopād, uktiḥ kriyeta cet.»
iti patyuḥ puro Rādhā
maunam ādhāya tiṣṭhati. [4]

bhāvatve sati śarīra|nispando vepathuḥ. bhāvatve sat' îti viśeṣaṇ'|ôpādānāt sūcaka|spand'|ādau n' âtivyāptiḥ. śarīra| padaṃ ceṣṭ"|āśraya|mātra|paraṃ, tena śarīr'|âvayava|kampe n' â | vyāptiḥ. asya vibhāvā āliṅgana | harṣa | bhīty | ādayaḥ. yathā:

kathaya, katham uroja|dāma|hetor
Yadu|patir eṣa cinoti campakāni,
bhavati kara|tale yad asya kampaḥ?
priya|sakhi, mat|smṛtir eva mat|sapatnī. [5]

---

[i] Krishna [ii] Krishna's principal mistress, angry here at his unfaithfulness [iii] One of Krishna's mistresses speaks. [iv] Krishna; the Yadus are his clan.

Horripilation is the bristling of hair in consequence of some transformation. Its factors are cold,* an embrace, joy, fear, and anger. An example:

In the grove filled with the buzz of bees
darting in anger from the *bákula* buds
why is Nanda's son[i] smiling today, and why
is the fuzz stiffening on his cheek?*

A breaking voice is a deformation in the nature of the voice that occasions stammering. Its factors are anger, fear, joy, and intoxication. An example: 4.10

"If I spoke, my voice
would clearly break in anger."
So Radha[ii] simply stood
in silence before her husband.

Trembling, in the discourse on aesthetic feeling, is a quivering of the body. The qualification "aesthetic feeling" is used to exclude gesturing toward something or twitching. The word "body" refers merely to the locus of the action, and thus the definition is not so narrow as to exclude the shaking of a body part. Its factors are an embrace, joy, fear, etc. An example:[iii]

Tell me, how can the Yadu lord[iv]
gather *chámpaka*s for my garland
when his hand is shaking so? Dear friend,
his thinking of me is my undoing!

vikāra | prabhava | prakṛta | varṇ' | ânyathā | bhāvo vaivarṇyam. asya vibhāvā moha | bhaya | krodha | śīta | tāpa | śramāḥ. yathā:

4.15 kukkuṭe kurvati kvāṇam ānanaṃ śliṣṭayos tayoḥ
divākara|kar'|ākrānta|śaśi|kāntim iv' ādadhau. [6]

vikāra | janitam akṣi | salilam aśru. asya vibhāvā harṣ' | â | marṣa | dhūma | bhaya | śoka | jṛmbhā | śīta | nirnimeṣa | prekṣaṇāni. yathā:

«visṛja, visṛja, citta, duḥkha|dhārām,
ayam upakaṇṭham upāgato Murāriḥ.»
iti kathayitum aśru|bindur akṣṇor
nipatati vakṣasi pakṣmal'|āyat'|âkṣyāḥ. [7]

śārīratve sati ceṣṭā | nirodhaḥ pralayaḥ. śārīratve sat' îti viśeṣaṇān nidr" | ādau n' âtivyāptiḥ. stambh' | ādayaḥ śarīra | dharmās teṣāṃ sāhacarya | kathanena pralayo 'pi śarīra | dharma eva. ten' âtra ceṣṭā | padena śarīra | ceṣṭ" âiv' âbhimatā. manasas tu karma bhavati na tu ceṣṭā. ata eva ceṣṭ" | āśrayaḥ śarīram iti śāstrīyaṃ lakṣaṇam. asya vibhāvā rāg' | āutkaṇṭhy'|ādayaḥ. yathā:

---

[i] Krishna

Pallor is a change in one's natural coloring as a result of some transformation. Its factors are confusion, fear, anger, cold, heat, and exhaustion. An example:

As the cock began to crow 4.15
their faces, lying cheek by cheek,
took on the pale glow of the moon
flooded by the rays of the sun.

Tears are water in the eyes produced by some transformation. Its factors are joy, vindictiveness, smoke, fear, grief, yawning, cold, and unblinking staring. An example:

"Give up, poor heart, give up this sorrow,
here is Murári[i] headed this way,"
the stream of tears proclaimed as it fell
upon the large-eyed woman's breast.

Absorption, being a bodily property, is the obstruction of all motion. By the qualification "being a bodily property" the definition is not so wide as to include transitory feelings such as sleep. Paralysis and the rest are properties of the body, and by being mentioned along with them, absorption too must be considered a property of the body. And thereby the word "motion" here must be taken as referring solely to the motion of the body. The mind has actions but not motions—thus the scientific definition of "body," namely, that it is the locus of motion. The factors of absorption are passion, longing, etc. An example:

no vaktraṃ namitaṃ, dhutaṃ na ca śiro,
vyāvartitaṃ no vapur,
vāso na ślatham āhṛtaṃ, nigaditaṃ
no vā niṣedh'|âkṣaram,
śoṇaṃ n' âpi vilocanaṃ viracitaṃ.
krīḍā|kalā|kātaraṃ
cetaḥ kevalam ānane Mura|ripor
vyāpāritaṃ Rādhayā. [8]

4.20 jṛmbhā ca navamaḥ sāttviko bhāva iti pratibhāti. yathā:

ujjṛmbh'|ānanam,† ullasat|kuca|yugaṃ,
svidyat|kapola|sthalaṃ,
kuñcat|pakṣma, galad|dukūlam, udayan|
nābhi, bhramad|bhrū|latam
bāl" âgr'|âṅguli|baddha|bāhu|paridhi,
nyañcad|vivṛtta|trikaṃ,
truṭyat|kañcuka|sandhi|darśita|lasad|
dor|mūlam ujjṛmbhate. [9]

ity | ādau Śṛṅgāra | tilak' | ādau ca sāttvika | bhāva | sāmānādhikaraṇya | darśanāt. na ca† sā† bhāv' | ânubhāva iti viparītam eva kiṃ na syād iti vācyaṃ. saty anubhāvatve bhāvatv' | â | virodhāt pulak' | ādīnāṃ tathā dṛṣṭatvāt. na c' âṅg' | ākṛṣṭi | netra | mardan' | ādīnām api bhāvatv' | āpattiḥ. teṣāṃ bhāva | lakṣaṇ' | â | bhāvāt. ras' | ânukūlo vikāra iti

4.21 *ujjṛmbhānanam* V : *ūrjann ānanam* J O 4.22 *na ca* V J : *nanu* Ś
4.22 *sā* V Ś : *sāttvika-* J

[i] Her eyes are red with passion.

She did not lower her face, shake her head,
turn her body aside,
catch her garment slipping down, or utter
a single simple "No,"
nor even turn toward him a reddened eye.[i]
All Radha did was focus
her mind, so bashful in the arts of love,
upon Murári's face.

Yawning would appear to be a ninth involuntary physical reaction. An example: 4.20

With mouth gaping, a pair of breasts heaving,
cheeks beaded with sweat,
drooping lashes, slipping dress, and navel
showing, eyebrows playing,
arms in a circle clasped by her small fingers,
hips turned and inclined,
with bodice bursting and armpits peeking through
the young girl stands there yawning.

In such poems as the above, and in the "Forehead Ornament of the Erotic"* and similar works, we find that yawning is referred to in parallel with other involuntary physical reactions. As for the argument that this should be reversed—that this yawning is an effect of an involuntary physical reaction—there is no force to it. So long as it is an effect there is nothing contradictory about its being a reaction, given that this is precisely what we see in such things as horripilation. Nor does this mean that things such

tasya lakṣaṇam. Kādambaryāṃ Mahāśvet'|ādīnāṃ sāttvika|
bhāva|varṇane tad|anulekhāc ca.† aṅg'|ākṛṣṭy|ādayo hi na
vikārāḥ kin tu śarīra|ceṣṭāḥ. pratyakṣa|siddham etad aṅg'|
ākṛṣṭir akṣi|mardanam ca puruṣair iṣṭatayā vidhīyate par-
ityajyate ca. jṛmbhā ca vikārād eva bhavati tan|nivṛttau ni-
vartate c' êti. yathā:

> ādhāya mānaṃ rahasi sthitāyāḥ
>   sambhāvya jṛmbhām Acal'|ātmajāyāḥ
> cuṭat†|kṛtiṃ smera|mukho Maheśaḥ
>   kar'|âṅgulībhiḥ kalayāṃ cakāra. [10]

iti śrī|Bhānudatta|viracitāyāṃ Rasataraṅgiṇyāṃ
sāttvika|bhāva|nirūpaṇaṃ nāma carturthas taraṅgaḥ.

4.22 *kādambaryāṃ mahāśvetādīnāṃ sāttvikabhāvavarṇane tadanulekhāc
ca.* add J   4.23 *cuṭat-* J : *caṭut-* Ś N

---

[i] In RT 1.5   [ii] A Sanskrit prose poem   [iii] Shiva and Párvati have
quarreled.

as stretching or batting the eyes would thereby also become involuntary physical reactions, for the simple reason that they do not share the definition of a reaction (which has been defined as a "transformation conducive to rasa"[i]), and because we find references to that effect in the description of the involuntary physical reactions of Mahá·shveta and others in the "Kadámbari."[ii] Things like stretching are not transformations but motions of the body. And it is furthermore empirically known that stretching or batting the eyes is something people do or do not do at will, whereas yawning arises from some transformation and ends when that ends.* An example:

As the daughter of the Mountain
nursed her love-anger in private
the Great Lord saw her yawn,* and smiling
started snapping his fingers.[iii]

The end of the Description of the Involuntary Physical Reactions,
the Fourth Wave of Bhanu·datta's "River of Rasa."

THE FIFTH WAVE
DESCRIPTION OF THE TRANSITORY FEELINGS

5.1 ATHA VYABHICĀRI|BHĀVĀO nirūpyante. tatra Bharataḥ:

«nirveda|glāni|śaṅk"|ākhyās,
tath" âsūyā|mada|śramāḥ,
ālasyaṃ c' âiva, dainyaṃ ca,
cintā, mohaḥ, smṛtir, dhṛtiḥ,
vrīḍā, capalatā, harṣa,
āvego, jaḍatā tathā,
garvo, viṣāda, autsukyaṃ,
nidr", âpasmara eva ca,
suptir, vibodho, '|marṣaś c' âpy,
avahittham, ath' ôgratā,
matir, vyādhis, tath" ônmādas,
tathā maraṇam eva ca,
5.5 trāsaś c' âiva, vitarkaś ca vijñeyā vyabhicāriṇaḥ.
trayas|triṃśat samākhyātā nāmnā tu vyabhicāriṇaḥ.»

itas tato raseṣu sañcāritvam aneka|rasa|niṣṭhatvam aneka|rasa|vyāpyatvaṃ vā vyabhicāritvam. na ca rom'|âñc'|ādāv ativyāptis, teṣām api saṃgrāhyatvāt. te ca bhāvāḥ śārīrā vyabhicāriṇaḥ. ete c' ântarā vyabhicāriṇaḥ, iyān viśeṣaḥ. nanu nirved'|ādeḥ sthāyitvaṃ vyabhicāritvaṃ ca katham iti cen—na. rasa|paryanta|sthāyitvam itas|tato|gāmitvaṃ c' êty upādhi|bhedam ādāy' ôbhaya|sambhavāt.

[i] That is, for the tranquil rasa

NEXT, THE TRANSITORY feelings will be described. With 5.1
reference to them, Bhárata says:

> "Despair, fatigue, worry, resentment, intoxication,
> exhaustion, torpor, despondency, pensiveness, con-
> fusion, remembrance, fortitude, shame, reckless
> ness, joy, shock, being dumbfounded, pride, de-
> pression, longing, sleep, possession, dreaming, wak-
> ing, vindictiveness, dissimulation, ferocity, wisdom,
> sickness, madness, dying, fright, and speculation 5.5
> are known as the transitory feelings, and they are
> thirty-three in number."

Their being transitory comes from the fact that they move to and fro transiently through the rasas, or because they relate to multiple rasas, or because they pervade them. It should not be objected that this definition is so wide as to include horripilation and so on, because the latter are in fact meant to be included: they are bodily transient feelings, whereas these are internal transient feelings—they differ only in this degree. The objection as to how despair, for example, can be both a stable emotion[i] and a transitory feeling is groundless. It can be both, given that it is subject to different conditions: in the first case it remains stable throughout the rasa; in the second, it moves to and fro through the rasas.

sv'|âvamānaṃ nirvedaḥ, saṃsāre heyatva|buddhir vā nirvedaḥ. tatra vibhāvās tattva|jñān'|â|parijihīrṣ"|ādayaḥ. anubhāvāḥ sveda|prakāśa|cint"|âśru|pāt'|ādayaḥ. yathā:

kṣoṇī|paryaṭanaṃ śramāya vihitaṃ,
vādāya vidy" ârjitā.
māna|dhvaṃsana|hetave paricitās
te te dhar"|âdhīśvarāḥ.
viśleṣāya saroja|sundara|dṛśām
āsye kṛtā dṛṣṭayaḥ.
ku|jñānena mayā Prayāga|nagare
n' ārādhi Nārāyaṇaḥ. [1]

glānir nirbalatā niḥsahatā vā. tatra vibhāvā raty|āyāsa|tṛṭ|kṣudh"|ādayaḥ. anubhāvā vaivarṇya|śaithilya|dṛg|bhramaṇ'|ādayaḥ. yathā:

5.10 vyāhartuṃ punar īkṣaṇāya na giraḥ
kaṇṭhād bahir niḥsṛtāḥ.
śeṣ'|āśleṣa|vidhiṃ vidhātum api vā
n' âiv' ônnatā dor|latā.
prātas talpam apāsya gacchati Harau
caṇḍ'|âṃśu|caṇḍ'|ātapa|
śliṣṭa|kliṣṭa†|kuraṅga|bhaṅgura|rucas
tasyāḥ sthitā dṛṣṭayaḥ. [2]

5.10 *śliṣṭakliṣṭa-* V N : *kliṣṭaśliṣṭa-* J Ś

[i] Vishnu [ii] The confluence of the Ganga and Yámuna rivers, also known as Allahabad [iii] Krishna; Radha watches him depart at dawn.

Despair is either self-reproach or the notion that life is not worth living. Its factors are cleaving to the truth about reality, etc. Its physical reactions are the appearance of perspiration, pensiveness, the shedding of tears, etc. An example:

I roamed the earth—and exhausted myself thereby.
I acquired knowledge—for mere debate.
I gained familiarity with many kings—
to the loss of my self-esteem.
I gazed on the face of lotus-eyed women—
only to lose them in the end.
What I didn't do, fool that I am,
is worship Naráyana[i] at Prayága.[ii]

Fatigue is either the absence of strength or the inability to bear something.* Its factors are the exertion of lovemaking, thirst, hunger, etc. The reactions are pallor, lassitude, rolling of the eyes, etc.* An example:

The words couldn't leave her throat to tell him 5.10
"Look at me one more time."
Nor could her arms be raised to give him
one remaining hug.
When early in the morning Hari[iii] left
the bed, she simply stared,
the light dying in her eyes like a doe's
struck by the blazing sunlight.

utkaṭa|koṭik'|âniṣṭa|pratisandhānam iṣṭa|hāni|vicāro vā śaṅkā. tatra durnaya|para|kraury'|ādayo vibhāvāḥ. kampa|kriyā|pracchādan'|ādayo 'nubhāvāḥ. yathā:

«ete citta|vilocanā guru|janā,
jihv"|âgra|doṣāḥ khalāḥ,
paurāḥ krūra|vacaḥ|prapañca|paṭavaḥ,
śvaśrūś ca cakṣuḥ|śravāḥ.
kiṃ syād ittham?» an|artha|bījam a|sakṛt
sañcintya vakṣo|ruhi
sphurjat|kiṃśuka|dāma vāma|nayanā
niḥśvasya vinyasyati. [3]

par'|ôtkarṣ'|â|sahiṣṇutā par'|ân|iṣṭa|cikīrṣā v" âsūyā. tatra vibhāvā manyu|daurjany'|ādayaḥ. anubhāvāḥ kopa|ceṣṭā|doṣ'|ôdbhāvan"|ādayaḥ. yathā:

«Hara|śirasi may" âpy a|labdha|vāse
nivasati k" âpi kalā tuṣāra|bhānoḥ!»
iti likhati Vidhuntudasya mūrtiṃ
pratibhavanaṃ pratibhūdharaṃ Bhavānī. [4]

5.15 harṣ'|ôtkarṣo madaḥ. duḥkh'|â|sambhinna|sukh'|ânubhava utkarṣaḥ.

---

[i] To hide the red nailmarks left by her lover [ii] Shiva [iii] Párvati

Worry is the expectation of something extremely bad or anxiety about the loss of something good. Its factors are poor advice, the cruelty of others, etc. The reactions are shaking, hiding one's actions, etc. An example:

> "My elders can see into my mind, and these villains
> have slurs on the tips of their tongues.
> The townsfolk are real experts in spreading slander,
> and my mother-in-law is a snake.*
> What will happen?" She sighed as she thought over
> the seeds of her misfortune,
> and then she laid upon her breast a garland
> of flame-red *kínshuka* flowers.[i]

Resentment is the inability to tolerate someone else's success or the desire to do something bad to someone else. Its factors are anger, wickedness, etc. The reactions are angry behavior, fault-finding, etc. An example:

> "On the head of Hara,[ii] where even I
> can't find a place,
> some little crescent of the cool-rayed moon
> has got her dwelling!"
> Thus thinking, Bhaváni[iii] sets about the task
> of drawing the face
> of the demon Eclipse on every house
> and every mountain.*

Intoxication is a superabundance of joy. "Superabundance" indicates the experience of happiness unalloyed with unhappiness. 5.15

tatra vibhāvaḥ pānam. anubhāva uttamānāṃ nidrā, madhyamānāṃ hasitam, adhamānāṃ rodanam. indriya|sammohana|rūp" âtra nidrā. tasmād indriya|sammohe nayana|ghūrṇana|sāmyena nidr" êva nidrā. na ca harṣa|vyabhicāri|bhāve 'tivyāptiḥ. tatra harṣa|mātrasya sattvāt. na tu tatra harṣ'|ôtkarṣa|niṣṭho jāti|viśeṣaḥ. kiṃ ca tatra mano|moho 'tra ca manaḥ|prasāda iti sva|rūpa|bhedāt. tatra nidrā|rodan'|ādayo 'tra ca pulak'|ādayo 'nubhāvā ity anubhāva|bhedāc ca. nanu «tiṣṭha tiṣṭha kṣaṇaṃ, mūḍha, madhu yāvat pibāmy aham,» ity|ādau vīra|rase 'pi mado dṛṣṭo 'sti. tatra nidrā rodanaṃ vā katham anubhāvo? na hi yodhaḥ saṃyati roditi nidrāti v" êti cet—satyam. rasa|bheden' ânubhāva|bhedaḥ, śṛṅgāre tu te 'nubhāvakāḥ. vīre nayan'|āruṇya|camatkār'|ādayaḥ. sāmānyena ca made nayana|ghūrṇana|vacana|skhalan'|ādayaś c' êti. yathā:

«rasanā rasayaty asau madhu;
   svayam asmākam an|arthakaṃ januḥ.»
iti tatra samastam indriyaṃ
   pratibimbasya miṣeṇa majjati. [5]

āyāsa|prabhavaḥ parābhavaḥ śramaḥ. tatra vibhāvā raty|adhva|gaty|ādayaḥ. anubhāvāḥ sveda|niḥsahat"|ādayaḥ. yathā:

---

[i] On the surface of the wine

The factor of intoxication is drinking. The reactions are, for the high characters, sleep; for the average, laughter; for the low, weeping.* Here "sleep" refers to sensory distortion; it is sleep-like, since when such distortion is present, one's eyes similarly roll back. Its definition is not so wide as to include the transitory feeling called joy, because there only joy itself is present, not the particular state pertaining to the superabundance of joy. Moreover, they differ both in form (since in the one case there is mental confusion, in the other, mental clarity), as well as in reactions (since in the one case there is sleep, weeping, and so on, in the other, horripilation, etc.). One may object that we find intoxication also in the heroic rasa, as in the verse "Wait, just wait a moment, you fool, while I drink my wine,"* and how could the reaction here be either sleep or weeping, given that a warrior neither weeps nor sleeps in battle. This is true enough, but reactions vary in accordance with the rasa. Those are the reactions in the case of the erotic rasa; in the heroic, the reactions are redness of the eyes, delectation, etc. Generally speaking, the reactions of intoxication are the rolling back of the eyes, slurred speech, etc. An example:

> "The tongue all by itself can taste the wine;
> as for us, existence has no point at all."
> As if with this in mind, all his senses,
> in the guise of his reflection,[i] seem to ebb.

Exhaustion is tiredness arising from exertion. Its factors are lovemaking, journeying, etc. The reactions are sweating, enervation, etc. An example:

sa Rāmacandraḥ saha nirgatāyāḥ
 sved'|âmbu|saṃsikta|payodharāyāḥ
apāṅga|pātair Mithil'|ātmajāyāḥ
 śramān aśeṣāṃ chithilī|cakāra. [6]

5.20 utthān'|ādy|a|kṣamatvam ālasyam. tatra vibhāvā garbh'|ādayaḥ. anubhāvāḥ kriyā|kātary'|ādayaḥ. yathā:

Haraṃ harantaṃ stana|hāra|yaṣṭiṃ
 kareṇa roddhuṃ na śaśāka tāvat
gireḥ sutā garbhavatī vihasya
 dṛg|añcalaṃ kātarayāṃ cakāra. [7]

duravasthā duḥkh'|âtireko vā dainyam. an|aujjvalyam iti ke cit. tan na. tasya bahir|viṣayatvena tad|anubhāvakatvāt. vibhāvā viraha|dāridry'|ādayaḥ. anubhāvāḥ kāya|kleśa|kṣut|pīḍ"†|ādayaḥ. yathā tāta|caraṇānām:

aṃse kuntala|mālikā, stana|taṭe
 netr'|âmbhasāṃ nimna|gā,
mādyan|Manmatha|kuñjar'|êndra|daśana|
 prānte vilagnaṃ manaḥ.
kiṃ c' ânyad|virah'|ânalena sa|rasaṃ
 sandahyamānaṃ vapur
gaṇḍe pāṇḍima|kaitavena su|tanoḥ
 phen'|ôccayaṃ muñcati. [8]

5.22 *-pīḍā-* V : *-pipāsā-* J : *-pīḍana-* Ś

---

[i] Sita

The daughter[i] of the king of Míthila
departed with Rama, the sweat coating
her breasts, but with his sidelong glances
he soothed her exhaustion, every bit.

Torpor is the inability to rise to one's feet, etc. Its factors are pregnancy, etc. The reactions are a reluctance to engage in action, etc. An example: 5.20

As Hara snatched her necklace away
Párvati in her pregnancy
hadn't strength enough to raise a hand,
only to laugh and flutter her eyes.

Despondency is a state of wretchedness, or extreme sorrow. Some define it as somberness, but that is incorrect because somberness, as an external object of perception, constitutes a reaction to sadness. Its factors are separation from a loved one, poverty, etc. The reactions are bodily pain, the pinch of hunger, etc. An example, from my honored father:

Her hair falls over her shoulders, a stream
of tears washes over her breasts,
her mind is caught on the tip of the tusk
of the raging bull elephant, Love.
And while the woman's fresh young body
burns with the fire of parting
it releases a white smoke on her cheek
under the guise of pallor.

cintā dhyānam. dhyai cintāyām ity anuśāsanāt. dhyānaṃ ca na smaraṇ'|ātmakaṃ smṛti|bhāvasy' âgre pṛthaktvena kathanāt, kin tu citt'|āikāgryam. tatr' êṣṭ'|ân|avāpti|prabhṛtayo vibhāvāḥ. anubhāvās tāpa|vaivarṇya|bāṣpa|śvās'|ādayaḥ. yathā:

5.25 Śambhuṃ dhyāyasi, Śaila|rāja|tanaye—
kiṃ nāma* jānīmahe?
tasy' âiv' âkṣi|tanūnapād iva tanau
tāpaḥ samunmīlati;
akṣṇor aśru|miṣeṇa gacchati bahir
Gaṅgā|taraṅg'|āvaliḥ;
pāṇḍimnaḥ kapaṭena candra|kalikā|
kāntiḥ samujjṛmbhate. [9]

moho vaicittyam. muha vaicittya iti dhātoḥ. mohanaṃ moha iti bhāva|vyutpanno moha|śabdaḥ. vaicittyaṃ kāry'|â|kāry'|â|paricchedaḥ. tatra vibhāvā bhīty|āveg'|ânucintan'†|ādayaḥ. anubhāvāḥ stambha|pāta|ghūrṇan'|ādarśana|vimaraṇ'|ādayaḥ. yathā:

antaḥ|smera|suvarṇa|ketaka|dala|
droṇī|dyuti|drohiṇīṃ
Lakṣmīṃ vīkṣya samudyad|indu|vadanāṃ
kṣīr'|âmbudher utthitām,
Śambhuḥ stambha|śat'|ākulaḥ, Śatamakhaḥ
kartavya|mūḍh'|êndriyaḥ,

5.26 *-anucintana-* Ś : *-anaucitya-* J

[i] Shiva holds the Ganga in his headdress.

Pensiveness is brooding, given the grammatical definition of the verbal root "to worry" as "brooding." Brooding is not memory, since the transitory feeling of remembrance is something separate that will be described below. Rather, it is singlemindedness. Its factors are failing to acquire what is desired, etc. The reactions are distress, paleness, weeping, sighing, etc. An example:

You are brooding on Shambhu, Párvati— 5.25
how do we know, you ask?
The fire in his own third eye has become
burning distress in your body;
in the guise of your tears the Ganga river[i]
is pouring out in waves;
and the glow of his crescent moon is spreading
in the form of your pallor.

Confusion is bewilderment, given that the root "to be confused" is defined as "bewilderment." The word is derived from the action word meaning "being confused." Bewilderment is the inability to decide what to do and what not to do. Its factors are fear, shock, worrying, etc. The reactions are paralysis, falling, staggering, inattentiveness, forgetfulness, etc. An example:

As Lakshmi emerged from the milk ocean,
lifting up her moon-like face,
putting to shame the radiance of the leaves
of a blooming golden *kétaka* tree,
Shambhu was utterly paralyzed, the god
of a hundred rites was confused what to do,

so 'py a|jñāna|bhujaṅga|pāśa|patito
jātas tri|lokī|patiḥ.* [10]

saṃskāra | janyaṃ jñānaṃ smṛtiḥ. saṃskāra | janyaṃ jñānaṃ pratyabhijñāna | rūpaṃ smaraṇa | rūpaṃ ca. saṃskāra | janyatven' ôbhaya | saṃgrahaḥ. anyathā pratyabhijñāyāḥ pṛthag | bhāvatv' | āpatteḥ. atra vibhāvāḥ saṃskār' | ôdbodhakāḥ sadṛś' | âdṛṣṭa | cint" | ādyāḥ.* anubhāvāḥ bhrū | samunnayan' | ādayaḥ. pratyabhijñā yathā:

Kālindī|sarasaḥ sametya nabhasaḥ
krode parikrīḍate
cakra|dvandvam idaṃ sudhā|kara|kalām
ākramya visphūrjati,
candro 'pi smara|cāpa|cāpala|camat|
kāraṃ samālambate.
tasmāt s" âiva kadamba|kuñja|kuhare
Rādhā paribhrāmyati. [11]

5.30 smṛtir yathā:

vadan'|âmbuja|lagna|dṛṅ|nipāte
mayi badhnaty avataṃsam aṃsa|mūle,
dara|kuñcita|dṛṣṭi Rādhikāyāḥ
smita|kirmīritam ānanaṃ smarāmi. [12]

dhṛtiḥ santoṣo, duḥkhe 'py a|duḥkha|buddhir vā. vibhāvā jñāna | śakty | ādayaḥ.* anubhāvā a | vyagra | bhog' | ādayaḥ. yathā:

---

i The three gods mentioned here are Shiva, Indra, and Brahma, respectively. ii Yámuna

and the lord of the triple world, even he, was caught
in the coils of the snake of ignorance.[i]

Remembrance is a form of knowledge produced by latent memories. The "form of knowledge produced by latent memories" can be in the form of either recognition or recollection, both being included in the category "produced by latent memories," since otherwise recognition would turn out to have some sort of separate existence. Its factors are the sight of something similar, concentration,* etc. The reactions are raising the eyebrows, etc. An example of recognition:

Reuniting from the pond
of the Kálindi river,[ii] this pair
of *chakras* plays in the sky's embrace,
rejoicing in their defeat of the moon,*
while the moon itself takes on
the look of instability
of the Love God's bow. Therefore
that must be Radha wandering
deep in the *kadámba* grove.*

An example of recollection: 5.30

I remember Radha's flashing
smile, with her eyes half closed,
as I placed an earring on her upper arm
and fixed my eyes on her lotus face.*

Fortitude is contentment even in the face of pain, or the notion that it is not in fact pain. Its factors are the power of knowledge, etc. The reactions are single-minded enjoyment, etc. An example:

bhūṣā bhasma|rajāṃsi, veśma vipinaṃ,
vṛddho vṛṣo vāhanaṃ,
celaṃ carma—tath" âpi Manmatha|ripor
bhogaḥ kimu bhraśyati,
īśatvaṃ kimu hīyate, kimu Mahā|
dev' êti no gīyate,
kiṃ vā tasya ca Deva|deva iti vā
saṃjñā janais tyajyate? [13]

svacchanda|kriyā|saṅkoco vrīḍā. na ca śaṅkāyāṃ trāse c' âtivyāptiḥ. tatra tatra kriyā|viraha eva na tu kriyā|saṅkocaḥ. atra vibhāvā durācār'|ādayo 'nubhāvāḥ śiro|namana|nayana|vadana|pracchādan'|ādayaḥ. yath" Âyodhyā|varṇanam:

5.35 bhittau bhittau pratiphala|gataṃ
bhāla|sindūra|binduṃ
dṛṣṭvā dṛṣṭvā kamala|nayanā
keli|dīpa|bhrameṇa
kānte cailaṃ harati haritaṃ
lolam ālokayantī
gātraṃ pracchād-
ayati sahasā pāṇi|paṅkeruheṇa. [14]

itar'|êtara|kriyā|karaṇaṃ* kriyāyāḥ śīghratā vā capalatā. mātsarya|dveṣa|rāg'|ādayo vibhāvāḥ. anubhāvā vaira†|darśana|vāk|pāruṣya|prahār'|ādayaḥ.* yathā:

5.36 *vaira-* V (pāṭha) : *vairi-* J Ś

---

i Shiva, in reference to his destruction of Kama

His ornaments are ash, his abode the woods,
his mount an aged bull,
his cloak a hide—and yet, does the foe of Love[i]
have any less enjoyment,
is his lordship diminished, is he not called
"the Great God" in hymns,
do people not use for him the epithet
"the very God of gods"?

Shame is a constraint on one's ability to act freely. This definition is not so wide as to include worry or fright, for in each of those cases there is a lack of, not a constraint on, action. Its factors are a wrongdoing, etc. The reactions are hanging the head, covering the eyes or face, etc. An example is this description of Ayódhya:

Her bright vermilion forehead dot 5.35
was reflected on each bedroom wall
and every time the woman looked
she thought it was the bedroom lamp.
So when she saw her lover begin
to gently remove her dark blue bodice,
she suddenly stretched out her lotus hand
to cover her body as best she could.

Recklessness is performing an act in a helter-skelter way or too hastily. Its factors are envy, hatred, passion, etc. The reactions are a display of hostility, verbal abuse, blows, etc. An example:

Laṅkā|cāriṇi, setu|kāriṇi, raṇa|
krīḍā|camatkāriṇi,
prauḍh'|ānanda|vacaḥ|prasāriṇi puro
Rāme dhanur dhunvati,
jātās tasya Daś'|ānanasya samara|
prārambha|dambha|sphurat|
keyūra|kvaṇit'|ânumeya|viśikha|
tyāgāḥ kara|śreṇayaḥ. [15]

cetaḥ|prasādo harṣaḥ. priya|darśana|putra|janm'|ādayo vibhāvāḥ. anubhāvāḥ pulaka|sved'|âśru|svara|bhed'|ādayaḥ. yathā:

pulakita|kuca|kumbha|pāli Rādhā
vrajati Mukunda|mukh'|êndu|vīkṣaṇāya
viracayati na madhya|bhaṅga|bhītiṃ
gaṇayati n' âpi nitamba|gaura|vāṇi. [16]

5.40 ākasmik'|êṣṭ'|ân|iṣṭ'|ôpapāta|vivartaḥ† sambhramo v" āvegaḥ. vairi|darśana|priya|śravaṇ'|ôtpāt'|ādayo vibhāvāḥ. anubhāvās tvarā|śarīra|skhalana|viparyās'|ādayaḥ. yathā:

5.40 *-vivartaḥ* Ś : *-mukhyakāraṇaṃ yasyeti* J

---

[i] Krishna [ii] Being so thin, according to the conceit, her waist could easily break.

As Rama—having made his way to Lanka,
built the bridge, enjoyed himself in battle,
delighted men of refinement with his words—
stood before him brandishing his bow,
one could infer from the sound of his bracelets
shaking in his arrogance at the start of battle
that the arrows had all at once been shot
by the twenty hands of ten-faced Rávana.

Joy is mental radiance.* Its factors are the sight of one's beloved, the birth of a son, etc. The reactions are horripilation, perspiration, weeping, a breaking voice, etc. An example:

As Radha made her way to see Mukúnda's[i]
moon-face, the down stiffening on her breasts,
she lost all fear of the fragility* of her waist[ii]
and gave not a thought to the heaviness of her hips.

Shock is either an internal transformation* arising from a completely unforeseen accident—whether welcome or unwelcome—or agitation.* Its factors are the sight of an enemy, receiving some news about one's beloved, an omen, etc. The reactions are impetuosity, physical stumbling, mental misapprehension, etc. An example: 5.40

eko vāsasi viślathe, sahacarī|
skandhe dvitīyaḥ karaḥ;
paścād gacchati cakṣur ekam, itarad
bhartur mukhe bhrāmyati;
ekaṃ kaṇṭaka|viddham asti caraṇaṃ,
nirgantum utkaṇṭhate
c' ânyad vairi|mṛgī|dṛśāṃ Raghu|pater
ālokya senā|carān. [17]

sakala|vyavahār'|â|kṣama|jñānavattā jaḍatā. na ca mūrch"|âpasmāra|nidrā|svapneṣv ativyāptiḥ. tatra jñāna|virahāt. na c' ālasya|bhīti|trāseṣv ativyāptiḥ. tatra tatra katipaya|vyavahārasya sattvāt. iṣṭ'|ân|iṣṭa|darśan'|ādayo vibhāvāḥ. anubhāvā an|avabhāṣaṇa|nirnimeṣa|prekṣaṇ'|êṣṭ'|ân|iṣṭ'|â|paricched'†|ādayaḥ. yathā:

duṣpāra|vāri|nidhi|pāram udāra|vīryam
āgacchato Hanumato hasitaṃ vitenuḥ;
udvīkṣya nīra|nidhi|nīram adhīra|vīciṃ
citr'|ârpitā iva punaḥ kapayo babhūvuḥ. [18]

ātmani sarv'|âdhikatva|buddhiḥ sarvasminn adhamatva|buddhir vā garvaḥ. bal'|āiśvary'|âbhijana|lāvaṇy'|ādayo vibhāvāḥ. anubhāvā avajñā|bhrū|dṛṣṭi|ceṣṭita|hasita|pauruṣa|prakāś'|ādayaḥ. yathā Paraśurāma|vākyam:

5.42 *-aparicchedа-* Ś : *-paricchedа-* J

One hand on the slipping garment,
the other on the handmaid's shoulder,
one eye glancing warily behind,
the other flitting on the husband's face,
one foot pierced by a thorn, the other
longing to get away—this is how
the wives of the enemy reacted
when they caught sight of Rama's soldiers.

Being dumbfounded is the awareness that one is incapable of communicating in any way. This definition is not so wide as to include fainting, possession, sleep, or dreaming, since there is no awareness in those states; nor torpor, fear, or fright, since some communication remains possible in those states. Its factors are the sight of something welcome or unwelcome. The reactions are non-responsiveness in speech, unblinking staring, inability to distinguish between what is welcome and what is unwelcome, etc. An example:

When the monkeys saw Hánuman bravely
approaching
the shore of the vast ocean, they chortled with joy,
but when they saw the ocean's crashing waves,
they stood as if painted in a picture.*

Pride is the sense of one's own superiority to everyone else, or of everyone's inferiority to oneself. Its factors are one's strength, lordliness, noble birth, beauty, etc. The reactions are scornfulness, particular movements of the brows or eyes, laughter, and a display of harshness. An example is this declaration of Párashu·rama:

5.45 niṣpīte kalaś'|ôdbhavena jaladhau
Gaurī|pater Gaṅgayā
hotuṃ hanta vapur lalāṭa|dahane
yāvat kṛtaḥ prakramaḥ,
tāvat tatra mayā vipakṣa|nagarī|
nārī|dṛg|ambhoruha|
dvandva|praskhalad|aśru|vāri|paṭalaiḥ
sṛṣṭāḥ payo|rāśayaḥ. [19]

iṣṭa|saṃśayo 'n|iṣṭa|jijñāsā vā viṣādaḥ. iṣṭa|padena jīvana|dhana|yaśaḥ|śarīra|putra|kalatr'|ādaya uktāḥ. aparādha|dhana|gaman'|ādayo vibhāvāḥ. anubhāvā uttamānāṃ sahāy'|ânveṣaṇ'|ôpāya|cintan'|ādayaḥ, madhyamānāṃ vimanaskatā, adhamānām iṣṭa|dhyāna|dhāvana|mukha|śoṣaṇa|nidrā|niḥśvās'|ādayaḥ. yathā:

pratyāvṛtya yadi vrajāmi bhavanaṃ,
vācāṃ bhavet pracyavo.
nirgacchāmi nikuñjam eva yadi vā,
ko veda kiṃ syād itaḥ?
tiṣṭhāmy eva yadi kva cid vana|taṭe,
kiṃ jātam etāvatā?
madhye|vartma kalā|nidheḥ samudayo,
mātaḥ,† kim ātanyatām? [20]

5.47 *mātaḥ* V N : *jātaḥ* J : *jātāḥ* Ś

---

[i] Radha has sneaked out at night to see Krishna and fears being revealed by the bright light of the moon.

When the sage born in an urn 5.45
had drunk up the ocean
and Ganga prepared to consign her body
to Shiva's forehead fire,
I created oceans with the floods
of tears that flowed gushing
from the lotus eyes of the women
in the cities of my foes.*

Depression is uncertainty about the arrival of something welcome, or preoccupation with the arrival of what is unwelcome. By the word "welcome" what is meant are life, wealth, great renown, a son, a wife, etc. The factors of depression are a transgression, the loss of wealth, etc. The reactions are, among the high character types, searching for help, pondering over remedies, and so on; among the average types, disheartenment; among the low, obsession with what is welcome, flight, parching of the mouth, falling asleep, sighing, etc. An example:

If I turn and go back home,
I'll be breaking my word,
but if I go on to the grove,
who knows what will come of it,
and what's the point of waiting somewhere
on the edge of the forest?
What to do, mother! with the moon rising
midway on my path?[i]

autsukyaṃ kāl'|â|sahiṣṇutā sakal'|êndriyāṇām ekad" âiva kriy"|ārambho vā. priya|saṃsmaraṇ'|ādayo vibhāvāḥ. anubhāvās tandrā|gātra|gaurav'|ādayaḥ. yathā:

ādyaḥ kair api keli|kautuka|mano|
 rājyair, dvitīyaḥ punar
mallī|kesara|cāru|campaka|nav'|âm-
 bhoja|srajāṃ gumphanaiḥ,
kāñcī|kuṇḍala|hāra|hema|valaya|
 nyāsais tṛtīyas tato
nītaḥ, sundari, vāsarasya. caramo
 yāmaḥ kathaṃ yāsyati? [21]

5.50 itarad indriyam apahāya manas tvaci yadā vartate tadā nidrā. suptasya kāraṇatvāt suptāt prāṅ nidrā Bharaten' ôktā. svapna|vaha|nāḍikāyāṃ mano yadā vartate tadā svapn'|ādi| sambhavaḥ. tatra vibhāvāḥ sva|bhāva|cint"|ālasya|klam'| ādayaḥ. anubhāvāḥ pārśva|karaṇa|nayana|bhrū|calana|vibhrama|vacana|svapna|darśan'|ādayaḥ. yathā:

gacchan kacchaṃ† tapana|duhituḥ
 piccha|gucch'|âvataṃsaḥ,
paśyann asmad|vadanam a|sakṛc
 cakṣuṣā kuñcitena,
snigdh'|âpāṅgaḥ, śithila|caraṇaḥ,
 stoka|vispaṣṭa|hāsaḥ
svapne dṛṣṭaḥ kamala|kalikā|
 maṇḍano megha|khaṇḍaḥ. [22]

5.51 *gacchan kacchaṃ* Ś : *gacchaṃs tīraṃ* J

---

[i] A longing *náyika* is addressing her girlfriend (or the reverse). [ii] Radha is describing Krishna.

Longing is impatience or the simultaneous engagement of all the senses. Its factors are recollecting the beloved, etc. The reactions are lassitude, heaviness of the limbs, etc. An example:

> The first watch of the day we passed
> in games and jokes and wishing;*
> the second, in stringing jasmine, *késara*,
> *chámpaka*, and fresh lotuses;
> the third, in putting on golden bracelets,
> necklaces, earrings, and belts.
> But how, my lovely, are we going
> to pass the fourth, the night?[i]

Sleep is when the mind, dissociating itself from the other senses, abides in the tactile sense alone. Because it is the factor of dreaming, sleep is treated by Bhárata prior to dreaming. Dreams and the like come about when the mind abides in the canal that conveys dreams. Its factors are one's particular nature, pensiveness, torpor, fatigue, etc. The reactions are rolling on the side, fluttering the eyes and brows, incoherent speech, seeing dreams, etc. An example: 5.50

> Going to the shore of the Yámuna river,
> a peacock's feather at his ear,
> looking repeatedly at my face
> from a half-closed eye,
> with luscious sidelong glances, weak-kneed,
> and a faintly visible smile—
> this I saw in my dream,* a lotus-bedecked
> mass of darkening cloud.[ii]

bhūta|sañcār'|ādi|sambhūta āveśo† 'pasmāraḥ. tatra vibhāvā apāvitrya|śūnya|gṛha|sthiti|dhātu|vaiṣamy'|ôtkaṭa|duḥkha|bhay'|ādayaḥ. anubhāvāḥ kampa|phena|niḥśvāsa|bhū|patana|viparyāsa|jihvā|lolan'|ādayaḥ. yathā:

udvelan|nava|pallav'|âdhara|rucaḥ,
paryasta|śākhā|bhujaḥ,
sphūrjat|koraka|phena|bindu|paṭala|
vyākīrṇa|deha|śriyaḥ,
bhrāmyad|bhṛṅga|kalāpa|kuntala|juṣaḥ,
śvās'|ânil'|ôtkampitāḥ
śailaṃ prekṣya kaper nipātitam apa-
smāraṃ dadhur bhūruhāḥ. [23]

mūrchā c' âtr' âiv' ântar|bhavati.

5.55 tvacam api vihāya manaḥ purītati† yadā vartate tadā suptam. nidrā vibhāvaḥ. anubhāvā netra|nimīlana|pralaya|śvās'|ôcchvās'|ādayaḥ. yathā:

śvās'|ôcchvāsa|pracalad|adhar'|ô-
pāntam, āmīlit'|âkṣaṃ
krīḍā|kuñje tapana|duhituḥ
supyataḥ śrī|Mur'|âreḥ
antaḥ|smeraṃ, nibhṛta|nibhṛtaṃ
k" âpi karṇ'|âvataṃsaṃ
kā cid bāhvoḥ kanaka|valayaṃ,
dāma muṣṇāti kā cit. [24]

5.52 *bhūtasañcārādisambhūta āveśo* conj. : *bhūtasañcārādisambhūto veśo* J : *grāhyādyāveśo* Ś 5.55 *purītati* Ś : *purītatīṃ* J

---

[i] Krishna

Possession is the state of being controlled by such things as a haunting ghost. Its factors are a state of impurity, residence in an empty house, disturbance of the bodily humors, extreme pain or fear, etc. The reactions are shaking, foaming at the mouth, sighing, falling to the ground, thrashing about, lolling the tongue. An example:

The *pállava* buds their swelling lower lips,
the tangled branches their arms,
the sprouting blossoms the flecks of foam
that dimmed their bodies' beauty,
the masses of flitting bees their wild hair,
the winds the sighs that shook them—
the mountains seemed possessed to behold
the peak dropped by the monkey.*

Fainting is included in possession.

"Dream" is when the mind withdraws from the tactile 5.55
body and abides in the canal of the heart. Its factor is sleep. The reactions are fluttering of the eyes, insentience, steady breathing, etc. An example:

As Murári[i] slept in the pleasure grove
of the Yámuna river,
the edge of his lips quivering with his breathing,
his eyes almost closed,
smiling secretly, ever so cautiously
one girl stole the flower
at his ear, one, the golden bracelets from his arms,
and a third, his garland.

indriyāṇāṃ prathama | prakāśo vibodhaḥ. nidrā | cchedo vibhāvaḥ. anubhāvā aṅg'|ākṛṣṭi|jṛmbh''|âkṣi|mardan'|âṅguli| moṭan'|ādayaḥ. yathā:

Rādhāyāḥ sahasā dṛśā kuvalaya|
droṇī|daridraṃ* nabhaḥ
kurvantyā kalakaṇṭha|kaṇṭha|ninadaiḥ
sāṅketikair jāgrataḥ
aṅg'|ākṛṣṭi|vivartamāna|vapuṣo
devasya Kaṃsa|dviṣo
lol'|âpāṅga|taraṅga|bhaṅga|caturaṃ
netr'|âmbujaṃ pātu vaḥ. [25]

par' | âhaṅkāra | praśaman' | ôtkaṭa | samīh'' âmarṣaḥ. vibhāvā avamān' | âdhikṣepaṇ' | ādayaḥ. anubhāvāḥ sveda | śiraḥ | kampa|nayan'|āruṇy'|ādayaḥ. yathā:

5.60 ady' ājñā n' âiva bhartuḥ.†
sarasija|nayanā|sūnu|senā|sametaṃ
baddhvā lāṅgūla|mūle
Daśa|mukham abhito bhū|tale bhrāmayāmaḥ?
śaśvan mārg'|âvaloka|
pracala|nayanayā Sītayā sākam enāṃ
Laṅkām utpāṭya kiṃ vā
Raghupati|caraṇ'|âmbhojayor yojayāmaḥ? [26]

5.60 *adyājñā naiva bhartuḥ* V N J : *ājñā ced adya bhartruḥ* Ś

---

[i] Krishna, who killed his uncle Kansa [ii] Soldiers in Rama's monkey army speak. [iii] Megha·nada, the son of Rávana and Mandódari

Waking is the first light of the senses. Its factor is being roused from sleep. The reactions are stretching the limbs, yawning, rubbing the eyes, cracking the fingers, etc. An example:

As Radha, beggaring all of space
of its dark lotus petals by her own eyes,
suddenly let out a cuckoo's cry
telling of their rendezvous, the god
Kansa's foe,[i] awoke and began
to twist his body as he stretched his limbs—
and may the graceful sidelong glances
cast from his lotus eyes be your salvation.

Vindictiveness is the powerful desire to destroy a rival's arrogance. Its factors are being scorned, insulted, etc. The reactions are perspiring, shaking the head, redness of the eyes, etc. An example:[ii]

We have as yet no order from our commander. 5.60
Should we tie up with our tails
Ten-faces and the whole army of his fair wife's
offspring,[iii] and twirl them about on the ground?
Or should we rip up Lanka by the roots
and place it at Rama's lotus feet,
along with Sita, her eyes ever darting
to watch the road for his approach?

ākāra|vyavahāra|saṅgopanam avahittham. vibhāvā vrīḍā|dhārṣṭya|kauṭilya|gaurav'|ādayaḥ. anubhāvā anyathā|karaṇ'|ânyathā|prekṣaṇ'|ânyathā|kathan'|ādayaḥ. yathā:

«tyaktvā veśma Vibhīṣaṇaḥ sa gatavān,
baddhaḥ sa pātho|nidhiḥ,
kiṃ cit krudhyati so 'pi Sāraṇir; ataḥ
Sītā parityajyatām.»
ity ākarṇya suhṛd|gaṇasya vacanaṃ
smer'|ānano Rāvaṇo
muktā|dāma kareṇa kaṇṭha|savidhe
Kīrasya vinyasyati. [27]

ugratā nirdayatā. vibhāvā aparādha|doṣa|kīrtana|caury'|ādayaḥ. anubhāvās tarjana|tāḍan'|ādayaḥ. yathā Rāmaṃ prati Paraśurāma|vākyam:

kodaṇḍaṃ raṇa|bhinna|bhū|pati|bhujā|
daṇḍaiḥ pracaṇḍaiḥ kṛtaṃ.
tatra jyā pratipakṣa|rāja|ramaṇī|
veṇī|guṇair gumphitā.
krūr'|ākāra|kuṭhāra|tāra|patana|
prabhraṣṭa|duṣṭa|dvipa|
truṭyad|danta|dalaiḥ kṛto 'sti viśikhas,
tal lakṣyam udvīkṣyate. [28]

---

[i] Sárani (usually Sárana) and Kira (usually Shuka; both names mean "parrot") were counselors sent by Rávana to assess Rama's might.

Dissimulation is hiding one's expression or actions. Its factors are shame, impudence, slyness, vanity, etc. The reactions are doing something different, looking elsewhere, or speaking of something else, etc. An example:

"Vibhíshana quit his house and left,
the ocean has been spanned,
even Sárani[i] is in a rage.
Let Sita be released."
Rávana listened to the words
of his friends and smiled,
and took a string of pearls and placed it
on the throat of Kira.*

Ferocity is pitilessness. Its factors are a transgression, the recitation of one's shortcomings, theft, etc. The reactions are threats, blows, etc. An example is the statement of Párashu·rama to Rama:

My bow is made of the strong arm bones
of kings slain in battle.
Its string is woven of strands of hair
of the wives of enemy princes.
And my arrow is made of the broken tusks
of wild elephants killed
by the sharp blows of my cruel axe—
and it's been seeking a target.*

5.65 yath"|ârtha|jñānaṃ matiḥ. atra vibhāvāḥ śāṣtra|cintan'|ādayaḥ. anubhāvāḥ śiṣy'|ôpadeśa|bhrū|kṣepa|kara|cālana|cātury'|ādayaḥ. yathā:

Lāṭī|netra|puṭī|payodhara|ghaṭī|
krīḍā|kuṭī|dos|taṭī|
pāṭīra|druma|varṇanena kavibhir
mūḍhair dinaṃ nīyate.
Govind' êti, Janārdan' êti, jagatāṃ
nāth' êti, Kṛṣṇ' êti ca
vyāhāraiḥ samayas tad|eka|manasāṃ
puṃsāṃ parikrāmati. [29]

naya|vinay'|ânunay'|ôpadeś'|ôpālambhā* atr' âiv' ântarbhavanti. upadeśo yathā:

vasu pradeyaṃ, khalato 'vadheyaṃ,
mano nidheyaṃ caraṇe Harasya.
nijaṃ vidheyaṃ kṛtibhir vidheyaṃ,
vidher vidheyaṃ vidhir eva vetti. [30]

upālambho 'pi dvi|vidhaḥ, praṇay'|ātmā kop'|ātmā c' êti. praṇay'|ātmā yathā:

5.70 pāṣāṇe yadi mārdavaṃ, yadi payo-
dhārā hutāś"|ôdare,
vyālīnāṃ vadane sudhā yadi, raver
garbhe himānī yadi,
sthemā kiṃ ca samīraṇe yadi, tadā
svapne bhavet satyatā—
kiṃ nāma, Smara|bhūmi|pāla bhagavan,
krodhān mudhā dhāvasi? [31]

Wisdom is correct knowledge. Its factors are reflection on the holy texts, etc. The reactions are raising one's eyebrows when teaching students,* or gesturing with one's hands, or displaying skill, etc. An example: 5.65

Stupid poets spend their days describing
Lata women's eyes and breasts and arms,*
pleasure domes and sandalwood trees.
Men singlemindedly devoted to god
will pass their time uttering his names: Govínda,
Janárdana, Lord of the world, and Krishna.

Included in wisdom are the teaching of good judgment, comportment, and obedience, or reproof thereof. An example of teaching:

Give away wealth, watch out for rogues,
direct your thoughts to the feet of Hara.
Wise men should do the duties they must,
what fate will do fate alone can know.

Reproof can be either affectionate or angry. An example of affectionate reproof:

If there were softness in stones, and streams 5.70
of water in the belly of fire,
if there were nectar in serpents' mouths
and ice in the womb of the sun,
if there were fixity in the wind,
there might be truth in dreams—
so why, O Love God, blessed king,
do you rage about in vain?

kop'|ātm'|âmarṣa ev' ântarbhavati. yathā:

janayasi jagad eva, deva|dev'|ā-
bharaṇa, sudhā|rasa|śītalaṃ, sudh"|âṃśo;
urasi vahasi me tath" âpi tāpaṃ—
Yadu|pati|vaktra|sakh" âsi. kiṃ bravīmi? [32]

jvar'|ādi|vikāro vyādhiḥ. kupita|dhātu|bhaya|kāma|kleś'|ādayo vibhāvāḥ. anubhāvā deha|kārśy'|ādayaḥ.†* yathā:

dātuṃ svīyam an|arghya|dīdhiti|padaṃ
tasyāḥ kuraṅgī|dṛśaḥ
keyūraṃ kanak'|âṅgulīyakam iv' ā-
netuṃ bahir gacchati.
anyat, Kṛṣṇa, nivedayāmi. kim ito
veṇī|miṣāt Kāliyo
dṛṣṭvā locana|vāri Kāliya|saro|
bhrāntyā paribhrāmyati. [33]

5.75 vinā vicāram ācāra unmādaḥ. na c' â|gamyā|gamane 'tivyāptiḥ. vinā vicāram iti padena tad|vyāvartanāt. tatra sukham uddeśyaṃ, tad|aṃśe vicāra eva kriyā. na samīcīn" êty anyad etat. a|prekṣya|kārit" ônmāda iti yasya mataṃ, tatr' êdaṃ dūṣaṇam. tatra vibhāvāḥ priya|viyoga|vibhava|bhraṃś'|ādayaḥ. anubhāvā vṛthā|vilapita|vṛthā|hasita|vṛthā|rodan'|ādayaḥ. yathā:

5.73 *dehakārśyādayaḥ* conj. V : *daśopadravāḥ* J

---

[i] Radha speaks. [ii] A girlfriend of Radha's speaks to Krishna. [iii] A serpent that lived in a black pond near the Yámuna river

Angry reproof is included in vindictiveness. An example:[i]

Ambrosial moon, jewel of the god of gods,
you cool the whole world with your liquid nectar,*
and yet to me you bring burning heartache—
what can I say? You are the peer of Krishna's face.

Sickness is a physical change such as fever. Its factors are an imbalance in the humors, fear, desire, pain, etc. The reactions are the wasting away of the body, etc. An example:[ii]

The bracelet of the doe-eyed girl
has quit its splendid place
and gone away, it seems, to get
a golden ring instead.*
What more to say, Krishna? Káliya,[iii]
in the guise of her braid,
sees her tears and wanders there,
mistaking it for his pond.

Madness is acting without thinking. The definition is not 5.75
so wide as to include having sexual relations with inappropriate women, since that is excluded by the use of the phrase "without thinking." In such sexual relations pleasure is one's objective, and in that respect at least there is thinking; the fact that the act is wrong is another matter altogether. The same criticism applies to the view that madness is acting without foreseeing the consequences. The factors of madness are separation from the beloved, loss of wealth, etc. The reactions are irrational lamenting, laughing, weeping, etc. An example:

«n' âiṣā k" âpi cakāsti kāñcana|latā,
s" āiv' âsti me Rādhikā.
pṛṣṭā cen na kuto 'pi jalpati, tadā
sammūrchitā vartate.»
ittham, hanta, vicintya siñcati muhur
nīrair a|dhīrair dṛśor,
vātaṃ vyātanute kareṇa, bhujayor
ādhāya sambhāṣate. [34]

prāṇa|niṣkramaṇaṃ nidhanam. vibhāv'|ânubhāvau spaṣṭau. yathā:

paryast'|âṅghri, vikīrṇa|bāhu patataḥ
saṅgrāma|bhūmau bhiyā
Laṅk"|ēśasya na keśa|pāśam anilaḥ
sprastuṃ samākāṅkṣati.
uṣṇaṃ n' ôṣṇa|karaḥ karaṃ kirati vā
vaktr'|âravinde, na vā
sve sve dhāmni mithaḥ kathām api surāḥ
pravyaktam ātanvate. [35]

mano | vikṣobhas trāsaḥ. tathā ca vicār' | ôttho manaḥ | kṣobho bhītiḥ. ākasmika | manaḥ | kṣobhas trāsa iti vikṣobheṇ' âiva dvayor apy ekatven' ôpasaṃgrahaḥ. tatra vibhāvā ghora | svana | śravaṇa | ghora | sattva | darśan' | ādayaḥ. anubhāvāḥ stambha|sveda|rom'|âñca|srasta|gātrat"|ādayaḥ. yathā:

---

[i] A girlfriend of Radha's describes Krishna's behavior.

"That's no golden vine coming into view,
it's my beloved Radha.
But why is she not responding when asked?
It must be because she's fainted."*
Lost in these thoughts, alas, he sprinkled it
with his tumbling tears,
fanning with his hand, folding in his embrace,
soothing with his words.[i]

Death is the departure of one's life breaths. Its factors and reactions are obvious. An example:

As Lanka's king fell on the battlefield,
limbs splayed, arms outstretched,
the wind would not dare to touch his hair,
paralyzed with fear,
the hot-rayed sun would not shine a hot ray
upon his lotus face,
and even the gods, in their private abodes,
would not discuss it freely.

Fright is mental shock. That is to say, fear is mental shock that arises upon reflection, whereas fright is sudden mental shock. The two may be categorized as one only by reason of this shock. Its factors are hearing a dreadful sound, seeing a dreadful creature, etc. The reactions are paralysis, sweating, horripilation, going weak in the knees, etc. An example:

5.80 śṛṇvāno Hari|nāma Rāma|vadanād,
Indrasya śaṅkāṃ vahan,
kurvan kātaram āntaraṃ sa bhagavān
Maināka|bhūmidharaḥ
kuñcat|pakṣati, bhugnita|śruti, kṛta|
pratyaṅga|cel'†|āvṛti,
tyakta†|vyāhṛti sindhu|paṅka|kuhare
nirmaṅktum ākāṅkṣati. [36]

vicāro vitarkaḥ. vibhāvāḥ vipratipatti|saṃśaya|sādhaka|bādhaka|māna|samudbhavan'|ādayaḥ. anubhāvāḥ śiraḥ|kampa|bhrū|cālan'|ādayaḥ. vitarkaś catur|vidho, vicār'|ātmā saṃśay'|ātm" ân|adhyavasāy'|ātmā vipratipatty|ātmā c' êti. an|adhyavasāya utkaṭa|koṭikaḥ saṃśayaḥ. pratyekam udāharaṇāni:

Kālindī|viluṭhat|kaṭhora|kamaṭha|
krūraṃ dhanuḥ Śāmbhavaṃ;
Rāmo bāla|mṛṇāla|komala|vapur;
vaṃśo 'vataṃso bhuvaḥ;
vyāhāra|prakharāḥ khalāḥ; kṣiti|bhṛtāṃ
goṣṭhī gariṣṭhā yatas,
tasmāt kevalam eṣa tiṣṭhati mama
śreyas|karo bhāskaraḥ. [37]

5.80 *-cela-* V N : *-cola-* J Ś   5.80 *tyakta-* Ś : *vyakta-* J

Hearing the name of Hari from Rama's mouth, 5.80
blessed Mount Mainàka
was racked with worry that Indra might be near
and took faint within.
With his wings folded and his ears pinned back,
wrapped up tight in a cloak,
in total silence he sought a place to hide
in the ocean's muddy cave.*

Speculation is reflection. The factors are disagreement, doubt, the co-presentation of positive and negative evidence, etc. The reactions are shaking the head, raising the brows, etc. Speculation is of four types, depending on whether it consists of reflection, doubt, indecision, or disagreement. Indecision is a doubt based on a irresolvable dilemma. An example of each:

The bow of Shambhu is hard as the shell
of a tortoise
adrift in the Kálindi,
while Rama's body is softer than a lotus;
my clan adorns the world,
but villains say cruel things, and yet the assembly
of kings is very weighty.
So the only source of succor for me
is the lordly sun above.*

saundaryasya Manobhavena gaṇanā|
lekhā kim eṣā kṛtā?
lāvaṇyasya vilokituṃ trijagatīm
eṣā kim udgrīvikā?
ānanda|druma|mañjarī nayanayoḥ
kiṃ vā samujjṛmbhate?
Rādhāyāḥ kimu vā sva|bhāva|subhagā
rom'|ālir unmīlati? [38]

kathaya, kathaya, k" êyaṃ khañjanaṃ khelayantī
viharati Yamunāyāḥ pāthasi svarṇa|valliḥ?
ayam udayati ko vā śāradaḥ śīta|bhānus
tad|upari timirāṇām eṣa ko vā vivartaḥ. [39]

5.85 iyaṃ na vilasat|sudhā|
kara|kal"|âdhikā Rādhikā:
karaṃ kiraṇa|mālinaḥ
kimu saheta v" âsyā† vapuḥ?
na vā kanaka|mañjarī,
vahati khañjarīṭaṃ yatas.
tataḥ Smara|mad'|ālasā,
kathaya, k" êyam unmīlati? [40]

5.85 *vāsyā* J : *tasyā* Ś

[i] The images refer respectively to the woman's eyes, body, face, and hair.

Is this a tally mark made by Love
counting up his beauties?
Or Charm itself craning its neck
to behold the world?*
Or a sprig of the tree of Bliss
appearing before the eyes?
Or is it the hair at Radha's navel
in all its natural beauty?

Tell me, is that a golden vine
that makes the wagtail dance
and bobs about so playfully
on the Yámuna stream?*
And is that the autumn moon
rising in the sky?
And there above the moon, is that
a thick mass of darkness?[i]

'That's not my beloved Radha, a woman lovelier 5.85
than the crescent moon,
for how could her body bear the touch
of the rays of the beaming sun?
Nor is it a golden sprig, since sprigs don't flutter
like two wagtail birds.
So tell me, what is that coming into view,
languorous with Love's passion?

nanu daś'|âvasthāsv abhilāṣa|guṇa|kathā|pralāpā vyabhicāri|bhāv'|âbhyantare na gaṇitās, tat kiṃ sva|tantrā eva te sant' îti cen—na. autsukye 'bhilāṣasya varṇan'|ātmaka|smṛtau guṇa|kathāyā unmāde pralāpasy' ântarbhāvāt.

atra pratibhāti cchalam adhiko vyabhicāri|bhāva iti.

ekatr'|āsana|saṃsthitiḥ parihṛtā
pratyudgamād dūratas;
tāmbūl'|āharaṇa|cchalena rabhasā
śleṣo 'pi saṃvighnitaḥ;
ālāpo 'pi na miśritaḥ parijanaṃ
vyāpārayantyā tayā.
kāntaṃ praty upacārataś caturayā
kopaḥ kṛt'|ârthī|kṛtaḥ. [41]

iti śṛṅgāre darśanāt. raudre c' êndra|jāl'|ādi|darśanāt. hāsye ca vyapadeś'|âny'|âpadeśayor darśanād, vīthī|bheda|gaṇanāc ca.

5.90 saṅgupta|kriyā|sampādanaṃ chalam. vibhāvā avamānana|pratipakṣa|ku|ceṣṭ"|ādayaḥ. anubhāvā vakr'|ôkti|nibhṛta|smita|nibhṛta|vīkṣaṇa|prakṛti|pracchādan'|ādayaḥ. śṛṅgāre yathā:

---

[i] See RM 265.

Three items listed among the "ten conditions,"[i] namely yearning, recounting the beloved's good qualities, and raving, have not been numbered among the transitory feelings. Does this mean they are entirely independent? No, insofar as yearning is included in longing, the recounting of good qualities in remembrance of the sort that consists of description, and raving in madness.

On this topic it would appear that trickery is an additional transitory feeling.* This is so because in a poem like the following,

> She avoided sitting on the same seat with him
> by rising when at a distance;
> by the trick of rushing to bring him paan
> she stopped him from embracing her;
> she didn't exchange words with him by engaging
> her servants in conversation.
> By politesse toward her lover she quickly
> satisfied her anger.*

we see trickery in the case of the erotic rasa; similarly, we see the use of magic in the case of the furious rasa, and being deceived and deceiving others in the case of the comic rasa. Moreover, trickery is counted as an additional transitory feeling according to different schools of thought.

Trickery is engaging in surreptitious activity. Its factors 5.90
are being scorned, ill-treatment on the part of an enemy, etc. The reactions are indirection in speech, secret smiling, secret glances, hiding one's true feelings, etc. An example in the case of the erotic rasa:

saṅketī|kṛta|kānanaṃ praviśator
anyonya|kautūhalād,
anyatva|pratibhānam āracayator
anyonyam uttrasyatoḥ,
kuñcat|kāyam itas tataḥ kisalayair
ātmānam āvṛṇvato
Rādhā|Mādhavayor nikuñja|kuharād
udgrīvikā pātu naḥ. [42]

saṅgrāme yathā:

sapt' âpi kḷptān kapaṭ'|âmbu|rāśīn
pur'|ôpakaṇṭhe punar īkṣamāṇaḥ
dṛśau kap'|îndrasya mukhe sa|khedam
āyojayām āsa sa Rāmacandraḥ. [43]

sarvāṇi vyabhicāri|sthalāni vistara|bhayān n' ôdāhṛtāni.

5.95 ālasy'|āugrya|jugupsāḥ sambhoge varjyāḥ. vipralambhe c' ālasya|glāni|nirveda|śrama|śaṅkā|nidr"|āutsuky'|âpasmāra|supta|vibodh'|ônmāda|jāḍy'|âsūyā vyabhicāriṇaḥ. hāsye 'vahitth'|ālasya|nidrā|supta|prabodh'|âsūyā vyabhicāriṇaḥ. karuṇe moha|nirveda|dainya|jāḍya|viṣāda|śram'†|âpasmār'|

5.95 *-śrama-* Ś : *-bhrama-* J

[i] Krishna [ii] Rávana had seven moats magically built around Lanka.
[iii] Hánuman

As they entered the rendezvous thicket
equally desirous,
and trying to disguise the way they looked
equally timorous,
and, bending their limbs this way and that, covered
their bodies with fronds, Radha
and Mádhava[i] craned their necks to peer from
the bower—
and may that look protect you.

And in the case of battle:

As he looked again at the seven magical lakes[ii]
constructed around the city,
Rama·chandra painfully fixed his eyes*
on the face of the lordly monkey.[iii]

Lest this book become overly long, not all instances of transitory feelings have been cited.

In the erotic enjoyed subtype, torpor, ferocity, and revulsion are to be avoided; in the erotic frustrated, the transitory feelings torpor, fatigue, despair, exhaustion, worry, sleep, longing, possession, dreaming, waking, madness, being dumbfounded, and resentment; in the comic rasa, the transitory feelings dissimulation, torpor, sleep, dreaming, waking, resentment; in the pitiful rasa, transitory confusion, despair, despondency, being dumbfounded, depression, exhaustion, possession, madness, sickness, torpor, remembrance, trembling, paralysis, a breaking voice, tears; in the furious rasa, the transitory feelings energy, remembrance, sweating, shock, vindictiveness, horripilation, 5.95

ônmāda | vyādhy | ālasya | smṛti | vepathu | stambha | svarabhed' | âśrūṇi vyabhicārīṇi. raudra utsāha|smṛti|sved'|āveg'|âmarṣa| rom' | âñca | cañcalat" | ôgratā | svarabheda | kampā vyabhicāriṇaḥ. vīre utsāha | dhṛti | mati | garv' | āveg' | âmarṣ' | āugrya | romāñcā vyabhicāriṇaḥ. bhayānake stambha | sveda | gadgadatā | romāñca | vaivarṇya | śaṅkā | moh' | āvega | dainya | cāpala | trās' | âpasmāra | pralaya | mūrchā vyabhicāriṇaḥ. bībhatse 'pasmāra | moh' | āvega | vaivarṇyāni vyabhicārīṇi. adbhute stambha | sveda | gadgadat" | âśru | romāñca | vibhrama | smayā vyabhicāriṇaḥ. anye ca vyabhicāri | bhāvā ras' | ânukūlāḥ svayam ūhyāḥ.

sthāyino 'pi vyabhicaranti. hāsaḥ śṛṅgāre. ratiḥ śānta | karuṇa | hāsyeṣu. bhaya | śokau karuṇa | śṛṅgārayoḥ. krodho vīre. jugupsā bhayānake. utsāha|vismayau sarva|raseṣu.

iti śrī|Bhānudatta|viracitāyāṃ Rasataraṅgiṇyāṃ
vyabhicāri|bhāva|nirūpaṇaṃ nāma pañcamas taraṅgaḥ.

recklessness, ferocity, a breaking voice, shaking; in the heroic rasa, energy, fortitude, wisdom, pride, shock, resentment, ferocity, horripilation; in the fearful rasa, the transitory feelings paralysis, sweating, stammering, horripilation, pallor, worry, confusion, shock, despondency, recklessness, fright, possession, absorption, fainting; in the disgusting rasa, the transitory feelings possession, confusion, shock, pallor; in the amazing rasa, paralysis, sweating, stammering, tears, horripilation, confusion, surprise. One may extrapolate on one's own from these to other transitory feelings that are appropriate to a given rasa.

Stable emotions can become transitory: the humorous in the case of the erotic rasa; desire in the case of the tranquil, pitiful, and comic rasas; fear and grief in the case of the pitiful and erotic rasas; anger in the case of the heroic rasa; revulsion in the case of the fearful rasa; energy and wonder in all the rasas.

The end of the Description of the Transitory Feelings,
the Fifth Wave of Bhanu·datta's "River of Rasa."

THE SIXTH WAVE
DESCRIPTION OF RASAS

6.1 ATHA RASĀ NIRŪPYANTE. vibhāv' | ânubhāva | sāttvika | bhāva|vyabhicāri|bhāvair upanīyamānaḥ* paripūrṇaḥ sthāyī bhāvo rasyamāno rasaḥ. bhāva|vibhāv'|ânubhāva | vyabhicāri | bhāvair mano | viśramo yatra kriyate sa vā rasaḥ. prabuddha|sthāyi|bhāva|vāsanā vā rasaḥ. prabodhakā vibhāv' | ânubhāva|vyabhicāri|bhāvāḥ. na ca yūnoḥ pratham' | ânurāge ' | vyāptiḥ pūrv' | ânubhav' | â | bhāvād iti vācyam. tatr' âpi janm'|ântarīy'|ânubhava|sattvād iti.

sa ca raso dvi | vidho, laukiko ' | laukikaś c' êti. laukika | sannikarṣa|janmā raso laukiko, '|laukika|sannikarṣa|janmā raso ' | laukikaḥ. laukikaḥ sannikarṣaḥ ṣoḍhā viṣaya | gataḥ. a | laukikaḥ sannikarṣo jñānam. teṣu c' ânubhūteṣu sākṣād etaj|janm'|ân|anubhūteṣv api teṣu prāktana|saṃskāra|dvārā jñānam eva pratyāsattiḥ. a | laukiko rasas tridhā: svāpniko, mānorathika, aupanayikaś c' êti. aupanayikaś ca kāvya | pada | pad' | ârtha | camatkāre nāṭye ca. parantu dvayor apy ānanda | rūpatā. nanu mānorathiko raso na prasiddha iti cet—satyam.

THE RASAS WILL now be described. When a stable emotion is represented by the factors, the voluntary and involuntary physical reactions, and the transitory feelings and thereby becomes fully matured, it is "tasted" and thus becomes a rasa. Another definition: rasa is that upon which the mind is brought to focus by the emotions, the factors, the physical reactions, and the transitory emotions. Yet another definition: a rasa is the trace memory of a stable emotion when this trace has been awakened, and what awakens it are the factors, the physical reactions, and the transitory emotions. This last definition is not so narrow as to exclude the love at first sight of two young people, on the grounds that they have no previous experience (and hence no memory). For even in their case there exists an earlier experience—namely, in a former birth. 6.1

Rasa is of two sorts, ordinary and extraordinary.* The former is produced by ordinary contact, the latter by extraordinary contact. Ordinary contact is of six types* and depends on a physical object; extraordinary contact is mental. That is, the mental state itself supplies the contiguity, either directly, when the causes and so on have actually been experienced, or by way of latent memories, when these factors have been experienced but not in the present birth. Extraordinary rasa is of three sorts, occurring in a dream, in the imagination, or in a representation. The last is found in the beauty of drama as well as in the beauty of the words and themes of poetry; both these forms consist of bliss that is pure and unmixed.* It might be fair to object that the rasa occurring in the imagination has no traditional standing. But in a poem such as the following,

dhanyānāṃ giri|kandare nivasatāṃ,
jyotiḥ paraṃ dhyāyatām,
ānand'|âśru payaḥ pibanti śakunā
niḥśaṅkam aṅke|śayāḥ.
asmākaṃ tu mano|rath'|ôparacita|
prāsāda|vāpī|taṭa|
krīḍā|kānana|keli|kautuka|juṣām
āyuḥ parikṣīyate. [1]

ity | ādau mānorathika | śṛṅgāra | śravaṇāt śāstre sukhasya traividhya|gaṇanāc ca rasena vinā ca sukh'|ân|utpatter iti.

6.5 tatra viśeṣāḥ. yath" āha Bharataḥ:

«śṛṅgāra|hāsya|karuṇā|
raudra|vīra|bhayānakāḥ
bībhats'|âdbhuta|saṃjñau ca
nāṭye c' âṣṭau rasāḥ smṛtāḥ.»

sakal' | âdhidaivataṃ Viṣṇuḥ. sa ca śṛṅgārasy' âpi daivatam. tena sakal' | ākāṅkṣā | viṣayatven' ārādhyatayā ca prathamaṃ śṛṅgār' | ôpanyāsaḥ. nanu vātsalyaṃ, laulyaṃ, bhaktiḥ, kārpaṇyaṃ vā kathaṃ na rasaḥ? ārdrat"|âbhilāṣa|

Fortunate are those who dwell in mountain caves
and contemplate the highest light
as birds alight in their laps without fear
and drink their flowing tears of joy.
As for my life, it wastes away in endless
pursuit of diversions in pleasure groves
or on the ledges of pools or palaces
imagined only in my dreams.*

we are actually reading about an erotic fantasy; moreover, bliss is reckoned in authoritative texts to be threefold,* and bliss cannot come into being without rasa.

Now to the particularities. According to Bhárata: 6.5

"The names of the eight rasas in drama are: the erotic, the comic, the sorrowful, the furious, the heroic, the fearful, the disgusting, and the amazing."

The presiding deity over all these rasas is Vishnu. He is also the deity of the erotic. Accordingly, since he is the object of all desires and worship, the erotic will be treated first. One might ask why affection for a child, covetousness, devotion to a god, and even avarice are not rasas, given the presence there of the stable feelings of tenderness, craving, faith, and greed respectively. The answer is that these (affection for a child and so on) are not stable feelings but instead transitory emotions, all aspects of desire. One might then well ask what rasas they are supposed to be transitory emotions of. The answer is that in the case of affection for a child, the rasa is the sorrowful; in the case of covetousness, the comic; in the case of devotion to a god, the tranquil;*

śraddhā|spṛhāṇāṃ sthāyi|bhāvānāṃ tatra sattvād iti cen—na, teṣāṃ vyabhicāri|raty|ātmakatvāt.* nanu kasya rasasya te vyabhicāri|bhāvā bhaveyur iti cet—satyam, vātsalye karuṇa eva raso, laulye hāsyo, bhaktau śāntaḥ, kārpaṇye 'pi hāsya eva. nanv evaṃ paratra* kḷptatvād atra vyabhicāritven' āvaśyakatvād, dharmi|kalpanāto* dharma|kalpanāyāṃ laghutvāc ca vyabhicāriṇī ratir ev' âstu; kiṃ karuṇen' êti cen—na, rateḥ śoka iti śoka|kāraṇatāyāṃ rater upakṣayāt.*

kiṃ ca rateḥ kasya rasasya vyabhicāritvam? na śṛṅgāra|hāsya|raudra|vīrāṇāṃ yuva|mithuna|paraspara|prīti|hāsa|krodh'|otsahānāṃ tatr' â|bhāvāt. na vā bībhatsasya, jugupsāyās tatr' â|bhāvāt. n' âpy adbhutasya vismayasy' âpi tatr' â|sthiratvāt. tasmāc chokasya sthāyitayā śoka|sthāyi|bhāvakaḥ karuṇ'|ākhyo 'tirikto rasa iti.

in the case of avarice, likewise the comic. But why then (in the case of love for a child) shouldn't desire as a transitory emotion alone be in operation? What is the need for bringing in the sorrowful rasa? For in the former case the phenomenon is actually in existence, whereas in the latter it has to be postulated through there being an emotion that is transitory for it, and it is more parsimonious to postulate a property (in this case, desire) than an entity (in this case, the sorrowful rasa). The reason is that the desire expends itself in producing grief, since grief comes from desire.

Moreover, for what other rasa could this kind of desire (found in affection for a child) be a transitory emotion? Not for the erotic, the comic, the furious, or the heroic, since the corresponding stable emotions of these rasas, i.e., a couple's lovemaking or mutual affection (that constitutes the desire of the erotic), laughter, anger, or energy are not found in it. Nor for the disgusting, since the corresponding stable emotion, revulsion, is not found in it. Nor for the amazing, since wonder isn't stably connected with that kind of desire. Accordingly, since what is stable in this (affection for a child) is grief, the only possible rasa is the remaining one, the sorrowful, whose stable emotion is grief.

nanu ratir ev' âstu, kiṃ hāsyen' êti cet. kasy' âsau vyabhicāriṇī, karuṇa | raudra | vīra | bhayānaka | bībhatsānāṃ na tatr' ân | avakāśāt. n' âpy adbhutasya, vismayasya tatr' â | sthiratvāt. na śṛṅgārasya, rateḥ sthāyitv' | â | patteḥ. parantu ratyā saha hāsasya sāṅkaryam. nanu rati | hāsayor a | saṅkīrṇa | sthal' | â | bhāvāt pṛthaktvaṃ kathaṃ syād iti cen—na. hetor a | sādhāraṇyād. a | sādhāraṇyam atra sthāyitvam. yathā rati | sāṅkarye 'pi sthāyi | śokād a | sādhāraṇāt kāraṇāt karuṇo bhidyate tathā tat|sāṅkarye 'pi sthāyi|hāsa| bhāvād a | sādhāraṇāt kāraṇādd hāsyo bhidyate. śānte 'py evam ūhyam. na ca vātsaly' | ādāv apy a | sādhāraṇā hetava ārdrat"|ādayaḥ sant', îti teṣām api rasatv'|āpattir iti vācyam, ārdrat"|ādīnām api ratitvāt. tasyāś ca tatra tatr' â|sādhāraṇye śṛṅgāra|rasatv'|āpattiḥ. nan' ûtsāha|krodhāv ubhayatra, tasmād vīra|raudrayor anyatara eva raso vartatām iti cen—na, sthāyi | bhedena bhedāt. utsāha | vāsanā vīre, na tu raudre. krodha|vāsanā raudre, na tu vīre.

Why again, one might ask, shouldn't desire alone be in operation in the case of covetousness? What is the need for bringing in the comic rasa? Yet as a transitory emotion the kind of desire found in covetousness has to pertain to some rasa, and what other rasa could it pertain to? Not the sorrowful, the furious, the heroic, the fearful, or the disgusting, since their stable emotions have no place in that kind of desire. Nor the amazing, since wonder isn't stably connected with that kind of desire. Nor the erotic, since then it would become a stable emotion and not a transitory one. There is, on the other hand, an essential commingling of laughter and the kind of desire or craving that is found in covetousness. One might ask how, if there are no places where desire and the comic are not commingled, they can be separate entities. The answer is because the cause of each is unique. Here, uniqueness signifies an emotion's stability. For example, even though there may be an admixture of desire in the sorrowful rasa, given that the stable emotion of the sorrowful, namely grief, is unique to it, the sorrowful is a distinct rasa. Similarly, though desire may be admixed in the comic, given that the stable emotion of the comic, namely, laughter, is unique to it, the comic is a distinct rasa. The same may be extended to the tranquil rasa. In the case of affection for a child and the others, however, one may not claim that since the factors, the feelings of tenderness and so on, are unique to them they must accordingly turn out to be rasas, for the simple reason that those feelings too are nothing more than desire, and if desire were to be unique to each of these, they would turn out to be the erotic. One might further object that since energy and anger are in both

yūnoḥ parasparaṃ paripūrṇaḥ pramodaḥ samyak|pari-
6.10 pūrṇa|rati|bhāvo vā śṛṅgāraḥ. yūnor ekasya pramoda|
ratyor ādhikye nyūnatāyāṃ vyatireke vā paripūrter a|bhā-
vād ras'|ābhāsa iti. sa ca dvi|vidhaḥ, saṃbhogo vipra-
lambhaś c' êti. tatra darśana|sparśana|saṃlāp'|ādibhir itar'|
êtaram anubhūyamānaṃ sukhaṃ paraspara|saṃyogen' ôt-
padyamāna ānando vā saṃbhogaḥ. saṃyogo bahir|indriya|
sambandhaḥ. asya daivataṃ Viṣṇur, varṇaḥ śyāmaḥ. yathā:

stobhena cāṭu|vacanāni parāhatāni,
pāṇiḥ payodhara|gato jaḍatāṃ jagāma.
Lakṣmyāḥ paran tu pṛthu|vepathur eva nīvīṃ
visraṃsayan suhṛd abhūn Madhusūdanasya. [2]

yathā vā:

nidrāṇ'|ēkṣaṇam unnamayya vadanaṃ
kānte kuc'|ântaḥ|spṛśi,
srasta|vyasta|dukūla|darśita|vali|
pravyakta|nābhi|śriyaḥ
Rādhāyā dara|ghūrṇad|utpala|dala|

[i] Madhu·súdana is Vishnu; Lakshmi (Shri) is his consort.

the heroic and the furious, only one of these should be a rasa. But they are different because their stable emotions differ. The trace memories of energy are found only in the heroic, not in the furious, whereas the trace memories of anger are found only in the furious and not in the heroic.

The fully matured mutual pleasure of a young couple, 6.10
or the properly matured feeling of desire, is the erotic. If one of the pair has greater pleasure or desire than the other, or a lesser feeling, or if there is any differential, we have the absence of full maturation and hence what is termed a semblance of rasa. The erotic is of two sorts, enjoyment and frustration. Enjoyment is the pleasure mutually experienced through seeing, touching, or conversing, or the bliss arising from union with one other. Enjoyment is external sensory contact. Its superintendent deity is Vishnu, and its color is dark blue. An example:*

> His sweet nothings were thwarted by stuttering,
> and his hand fell limp the moment it touched
> her breasts.
> But Madhu·súdana[i] had an ally, Lakshmi's intense
> trembling, which caused her skirt to slip right off.

Another:

> As her lover lifted Radha's face—eyes closed*
> in sleep—and touched her breasts
> her silk dress fell in a heap to reveal her lovely
> navel amidst her curves,
> but what made their passion so long-lived
> were the waves

droṇī|mada|drohibhir
dṛk|koṇasya taraṅgitair viracito
dīrgh'|āyur eva smaraḥ. [3]

deśānāṃ samayānāṃ nāyikānāṃ ca bhedena nāyakayor avasthā|bhedena ca bahavo bhedās. te ca Rasa|mañjaryāṃ viśeṣato darśitā, iha punar vistara|bhiyā na pradarśyanta iti.

6.15 atha hāvā nirūpyante. tatra Bharataḥ:

«līlā|vilāso, vicchittir, vibhramaḥ, kilakiñcitam,
moṭṭāyitaṃ, kuṭṭamitaṃ, bibboko, lalitaṃ tathā,
vihṛtaṃ c' êti vijñeyā daśa hāvās tu yoṣitām.»

nārīṇāṃ śṛṅgāra|ceṣṭā hāvaḥ. sa ca svabhāva|jo nārīṇām. nanu bibboka|vilāsa|vicchitti|vibhramāḥ puruṣāṇām api sambhavant' îti cet—satyaṃ, teṣāṃ tv aupādhikāḥ, svabhāva|jāḥ strīṇām eva. nanv evaṃ yadi, tāsāṃ sad" âiva te kathaṃ na bhavant' îti cet—satyam. uddīpak'|ânvaya|vyatirekābhyāṃ nāyikānāṃ hāv'|āvirbhāva|tirobhāvāv iti. līlā|vilāsa|vicchitti|vibhrama|lalitāni śārīrāṇi. moṭṭāyita|kuṭṭamita|bibboka|vihṛtāny āntarāṇi. kilakiñcitam ubhaya|saṅkīrṇam iti.

of glances from her eyes
that put to shame the pride of the petals
of bobbing dark lotuses.

There are many differentiations of the erotic according to differences of time, place, type of female character, and mental state of the male and female characters. These have been examined in detail in the "Bouquet of Rasa" and will not be examined further here lest this book grow too long.

Now the charms will be described. According to Bhárata: 6.15

"The ten charms of women are mimicry, coquetry, negligence, disarray, turmoil, coyness, saying no when meaning yes, giving the cold shoulder, adornment, and reticence."

A charm is an erotic action on the part of a woman, and it is something natural to women. It might be objected that giving the cold shoulder, coquetry, negligence, and disarray are found among men, too. But among men they are conditional, whereas they are natural to women. It might be further objected that if women are permanently in possession of these charms, then they could never not have them. The answer is that women show or hide these charms according to the presence or absence of their stimulant factors. Mimicry, coquetry, negligence, disarray, and adornment are physical; coyness, saying no when meaning yes, giving the cold shoulder, and reticence are internal; turmoil is an intermingling of the two.

priya | bhūṣaṇa | vacan' | ādy | anukṛtir līlā. tatra vibhāvāḥ sakhī|kautuka|kalāpaḥ. anubhāvāḥ priya|parihāsāḥ. yathā:

cand'|âṃśau caram'|âdri|cumbini, mano
 jijñāsituṃ subhruvāṃ
nyañcat|kautukayā tayā viracite
 vaṃśī|rave Rādhayā,
«eṣa sphūrjati kasya niḥsvana?» iti
 krodhād vrajan kānanaṃ,
Rādhāṃ vīkṣya latā|pratāna|pihitāṃ
 smero Hariḥ pātu vaḥ. [4]

6.20 gamana | nayana | vadana | bhrū | prabhṛtīnāṃ yaḥ kaś cid utpadyate viśeṣaḥ, sa vilāsaḥ. atra vibhāvāḥ priya | darśana | smaraṇ' | ādayaḥ. anubhāvā abhilāṣa | vaidagdhya | prakāśan' | ādayaḥ. yathā:

kūjat|kāñci, dara|sphurad|vali, naṭad|
 bhrū|valli, vellad|vapur,
valgat|kuṇḍala|kānti, sāci|valita|
 grīvaṃ vadantyā vacaḥ
prātar nartita|puṇḍarīka|pariṣat|
 pāṇḍitya|pāṭaccarī
dṛṣṭir yaṃ prati jāyate vara|tanor
 vakrā, sa Śakr'|âdhikaḥ. [5]

---

[i] Krishna's [ii] Indra

Imitating one's lover's ornamentation, language, and so on is called mimicry. Its factors* are amusements for the sake of girlfriends. The reactions* are gentle mockery of the lover. An example:

> Just as the sun kissed the western hills,
> the lovely Radha grew keen to amuse
> her lovely friends and learn Hari's[i] mind,
> and so she raised the sound of his flute.
> He rushed to the grove and in anger cried,
> "Who's making that sound?" and there saw Radha
> hidden in the lattice of the vines,
> and smiled—and may he thus protect you.

A special variation in the gait or in the play of the eyes or mouth or brows is called coquetry. Its factors are the sight or memory of the beloved. The reactions include a display of desire, sophistication, etc. An example: 6.20

> Jewel belt jingling, midriff on display,
> eyebrows dancing, earrings flashing
> as her body sways, head tilted as she speaks,
> the woman casts a sidelong glance—
> a glance that plagiarizes the learning
> of the assembled lotuses dancing at dawn—
> at a man who must be far more blessed
> than Shakra,[ii] king of all the gods.

katipaya|bhūṣaṇa|vinyāso vicchittiḥ. tatra vibhāvā saukumārya|priya|saubhāgya|saundarya|garva|krodha|kleś'|ādayaḥ. anubhāvāḥ garva|māna|kleśa|prakāśan'|ādayaḥ. yathā:

keyūraṃ na kare, pade na kaṭakaṃ,
maulau na mālā punaḥ;
kastūrī|tilakaṃ tath" âpi tanute
saṃsāra|sāraṃ śriyam.
sarv'|ādhikyam alekhi bhāla|phalake
yad Vedhasā subhruvo,
jānīmaḥ kimu tatra Manmatha|mahī|
pālena mudrā kṛtā. [6]

vāg|aṅga|bhūṣāṇāṃ sthāna|viparyāso vibhramaḥ. tatra vibhāvā dhana|mada|rāg'|āutkaṭy'|ādayaḥ. anubhāvāḥ priya|sakhy|ādy|upahās'|ādayaḥ. yathā:

6.25 tyakte keli|vidhau nij'|âṃśuka|dhiyā
Pītāmbarasy' âṃśukaṃ
Padmāyāḥ paridhāya padma|śayanāt
prātaḥ prayāntyā bahiḥ
ādātuṃ vasan'|âñcalaṃ capalayan,
kopaṃ dṛśā darśayaṃ,
vācā kautukam ācaran, smita|sudhā|
snigdho Hari pātu vaḥ. [7]

[i] Lakshmi [ii] Vishnu

Wearing only a few pieces of jewelry is called negligence. Its factors are the woman's delicacy, her sexual power over her lover, her pride in her beauty, the perturbation of anger, etc. The reactions are displaying pride or the perturbation of jealous anger, etc. An example:

She wore no bracelet on her wrist, no anklet
on her foot, no wreath on her head,
and yet she bore a forehead mark of musk,
the essence of worldly beauty.
The Creator inscribed her sovereignty,
I guess, upon her forehead,
and that must be the seal by which
Love, the king, confirmed it.

A disorderliness in the arrangement of body ornaments or words is called disarray. Its factors are pride of wealth,* wild passion, or the like. The reactions are the laughter of the beloved, the girlfriend, etc. An example:

When they had left off making love, 6.25
Padma[i] put on his yellow robe
thinking it was her own and began
to leave the lotus bed at dawn.
But Hari[ii] shook the garment's hem
to get it back, looked crossly, began
to tease, and broke out in a tender smile—
and may this god keep you from harm.

śram'|âbhilāṣa|garva|smita|harṣa|bhaya|krodhānāṃ saṅkaraḥ kilakiñcitam. tad āhuḥ:

«śram'|âbhilāṣa|garvāṇāṃ,
smita|harṣa|bhaya|krudhām
a|sakṛt saṅkaraḥ prājñair
vijñeyaṃ kilakiñcitam.»

iti. atra vibhāvā nava|yauvan'|ôdbheda|cāñcaly'|ādayaḥ. anubhāvāḥ kartavy'|â|nirdhāraṇ'|ādayaḥ. yathā:

kodaṇḍam ārohati caṇḍimānaṃ,
madhu|vrataḥ kāṅkṣati śoṇimānam,
padmaṃ sudhāṃ varṣati vepamānaṃ,
svarṇ'|âcalaḥ khidyati—kiṃ nidānam? [8]

6.30 yathā vā:

krodh'|āgāra|samutthitāḥ, samudayat|
saṃtrāsa|tail'|ârditā,*
vrīḍābhiḥ parimarditāḥ, smita|sudhā|
dhārābhir udvartitāḥ,
snātāḥ sneha|rasair, mano|bhava|kalā|
mālābhir ābhūṣitāḥ—
pāyāsur mayi Śaila|rāja|duhituḥ
sphītāḥ kaṭ'|âkṣa|cchaṭāḥ. [9]

---

[i] The references are to the girl's brows, eyes, face (and ambrosial words), and breasts. [ii] The goddess Párvati

A mixture of fatigue, desire, pride, smiling, joy, fear, and anger is called turmoil. Thus it is said:

> "The continuous mixing of fatigue, desire, pride, smiling, joy, fear, and anger is how the learned define turmoil."*

Its factors are the fickleness occasioned by the coming of puberty, etc. The reactions are uncertainty about what to do, etc. An example:*

> The bow is bending,* the black bees are reddening,
> the trembling lotus is showering nectar,
> and those golden mounds are making so much
> trouble[i]—what could be the cause?

Another: 6.30

> Leaving her room—her jealous anger—and salved
> with the oils of her mounting concern,
> massaged by modesty, lathered with streams
> of ambrosial smiles, bathed in affection's
> waters, and ornamented with a wreath
> of all the arts of the God of love—
> may those lustrous glances of the daughter
> of the Mountain king[ii] provide me refuge.*

vārtā|vaimukhye sati nibhṛta|bhūyo|darśana|spṛhā moṭṭāyitam. atra vibhāvāḥ sapatnī|trāsa|lajj"|ādayaḥ. anubhāvāḥ manaḥ|prema|kathana|saṅketa|nivedan'|ādayaḥ. yathā:

na snehasya kathā|rasaṃ katham api
śrotuṃ samutkaṇṭhate
Rādhā, kin tu vikīrṇa|ratna|kapaṭād
āgatya saudhād bahiḥ,
nṛtyan|netra|puṭi, sphurat|kuca|ghaṭi,
sved'|ôllasad|dos|taṭi,
vyāvalgad|bhru|kuṭi, skhalat|kaṭi* punaḥ
Kṛṣṇ'|ântike bhrāmyati. [10]

sukhe duḥkha|ceṣṭā kuṭṭamitam. atra vibhāvā rāg'|āutkaṇṭhya|daśana|karaja|kṣata|kuntal'|âdhara|grahaṇ'|ādayaḥ. anubhāvāḥ kapaṭa|kāya|saṅkoca|kapaṭa|sītkār'|ādayaḥ. yathā:

6.35 roddhuṃ pāṇiḥ pracalati cirād,
aṅgulir niścal" âsau,
bhrū|vikṣepo bhavati kuṭilo,
netram antaḥ|prasannam;
gāḍh'|āśleṣe bhavati sutanor
ardha|mātro na|kāraḥ;
kampo mūrdhnaḥ prasarati, mukhaṃ
sammukhaṃ ca prayāti. [11]

A keenness to secretly behold the lover repeatedly while seeming to be indifferent to any talk about him is called coyness. Its factors are fright or shame before the co-wives, etc. The reactions are revealing the love in her heart, hinting at the rendezvous place, etc. An example:

Radha has no desire at all
to hear sweet talk of love,
she simply leaves her house, pretending
to gather her scattered jewelry.
And with eyelids fluttering, breasts bobbing,
arms glistening with sweat,
eyebrows playing, and hips swaying
she finds her way to Krishna.

Acting as if in pain when actually feeling pleasure is saying no when meaning yes. Its factors are the lover's pulling her hair or the lower lip, scratching with his nails, or biting her in the grip of passion. The reactions are pretending to shy away, pretending to gasp, etc. An example:

Her hand goes out to stop him too late 6.35
and the fingers will not move,
she arches her brows in anger and yet
her eyes are soft within,
when he takes her in his arms she cries
"No" but it's only half-said,
and even while shaking her head
her face draws near his face.

garv'|âbhimāna|sambhūto vikāro 'n|ādar'|ātmā bibbokaḥ. atra vibhāvā yauvana|mada|dhana|mada|kula|mada|priy'|âparādh'|ādayaḥ. anubhāvā avahittha|durvacana|duḥpreksạṇ'|ādayaḥ. yathā:

kṛt'|âñjaliḥ, kātara|dṛṅ|nipātaḥ
prāṇ'|ēśvaraḥ pārśvam upājagāma.
sakhī|mukhe kuṇḍala|ratna|lekhām
eṣā punaḥ prekṣitum ācakāṅkṣa. [12]

sakal'|âṅga|samīcīna|bhūṣaṇa|vinyāso lalitam. atr' âiva smit'|ādayo 'ntar|bhavanti. tatra vibhāvā manaḥ|prasāda|priyatam'|ādar'|ânurāga|dhīratv'|ādayaḥ. anubhāvāḥ priya|vaśīkaraṇa|lok'|ânurāga|camatkār'|ādayaḥ. yathā:

kala|kvaṇita|mekhalaṃ,
capala|cāru|netr'|âñcalaṃ,
prasanna|mukha|maṇḍalaṃ,
śravaṇa|sañcarat|kuṇḍalam,
sphurat|pulaka|bandhuraṃ,
lapita|śobhamān'|âdharaṃ,
vihasya rati|mandiraṃ
vrajati kasya śāt'|ôdarī? [13]

A mental transformation arising from arrogance and egotism and consisting of scorn is called giving the cold shoulder. Its factors are pride in youthful beauty, wealth, or family; a transgression on the part of the lover, and so on. The reactions are dissimulation, insults, dirty looks, and so on. An example:

As her lover came beside her
with hands folded and a sheepish look,
she continued to study the earring
aglow upon her girlfriend's face.

The proper ornamentation of the whole body is adornment; smiling and the like are also included in it. Its factors are being well disposed toward the lover, respect for him, the continuity of passion, etc. The reactions are the enchantment of the lover, the admiration and attraction of other people, etc. An example:

With jeweled belt gently tinkling,
tender glances quivering,
with countenance serene, and earrings
gently swinging at the ear,
the soft down on the body stiffening,
the lower lip adorned with small talk—
whose bedroom has the slender girl
gone off to visit with a smile?

6.40 priya | sannidhāv abhilāp' | â | paripūrtir* vihṛtam. tatra vyāja|lajj"|ādayo vibhāvāḥ. anubhāvā anyathā|ceṣṭit'|ânyathā|vyavahār'|ādayaḥ. vyājād yathā:

abhilaṣati kapole candra|cūḍe vidhātuṃ
 tilakam, udayad|antaḥ|kopa|bhājā Bhavānyā
phaṇi|pati|bhaya|kūṭād aṅgam utkampayantyā
 pracala|vasana|vātair vighnitāḥ keli|dīpāḥ. [14]

lajjāto yathā:

«ānanda|bhājo Yadunandanasya
 kar'|âvarodhaṃ na kareṇa kuryāḥ.»
sakhīṃ lapantīm iti sañjaghāna
 cakora|netrā culuk'|ôdakena. [15]

yūnor anyonyaṃ muditānāṃ pañc' | êndriyāṇāṃ sambandh' | â | bhāvo 'bhīṣṭ' | â | prāptir vā vipralambhaḥ. na ca mān' | ātmake vipralambhe ' | vyāptir iti vācyam. mudita | pañc' | êndriya | sambandh' | â | bhāva | rūpasya viśiṣṭ' | â | bhāvasya tatr' âpi sattvāt. tadānīṃ yūnor indriyāṇāṃ muditatvāt.†* nanu yā priyam abhisarati sā priya|yuktā bhaved iti cet—satyaṃ, sā priya | yukt" âiva. a | cira | darśana | pratyāś" | ânuvṛtta|pramodena viraha|dharmasy' âśru|pāt'|āder a|sambhava iti.

6.44 *muditatvāt* B : *muditatvābhāvāt* J

---

[i] Shiva [ii] Párvati [iii] Belonging to Krishna

Breaking off talking in the presence of the lover is reticence. Its factors are pretense or shame. The reactions are acting or behaving in some distracting way. An example of pretense: 6.40

As the moon-crested god[i] sought to draw on
her cheek
an ornament, Bhaváni[ii] grew angry* and with limbs
trembling, pretending to recoil in fear
from the snake,
she snuffed the lamp with the breeze from her
rustling dress.

An example of shame:

As her girlfriend was saying "You shouldn't block
Yadu·nándana's[iii] hand with your hand
when he's overcome with bliss,"
the large-eyed woman silenced her
with the water held in her cupped hands.

The absence of any joyous mutual sensory connection between a young couple or the failure to attain their desire is called frustration. This definition is not so narrow as to exclude frustration in the case of love-anger. For in the case of love-anger, too, we find this particular type of absence, namely, the absence of a joyous sensory connection, since the couple's senses are at the time still joyous. There is some truth to the objection that while going on a secret rendezvous to her lover a woman can be said to be separated (from her lover, and thus be frustrated), but in fact she is really only separated. There is no weeping, and none of the

6.45 sa ca vipralambhaḥ pañcadhā, deś'|ântara|gamanād, guru|nideśād, abhilāṣād, īrṣyāyāḥ, śāpāc c' êti. samayād, daivād, viḍvarād† ity|ādayo 'py unneyāḥ.

deś'|ântara|gamanād yathā:

prasthānāya kṛt'|ôdyame priyatame
doḥ|kaṅkaṇena cyutaṃ,
dhairyeṇa skhalitaṃ, madena galitaṃ,
netr'|âmbhasā niḥsṛtam,
jīven' âpi yiyāsunā «Śiva, Śiva!»
prārambhi vāma|bhruvaḥ
kamp'|ândolita|kiṅkiṇī|kala|rava|
vyājena Vainya|smṛtiḥ. [16]

yathā vā tāta|caraṇānām:

vīṇām aṅke katham api sakhī|
prārthanābhir nidhāya
svairaṃ svairaṃ sarasija|dṛśā
gātum ārabdham eva.
tantrī|buddhyā kim api viraha|
kṣīṇa|dīn'|âṅga|vallīm
enām eva spṛśati bahuśo
mūrchanā—citram etat. [17]

6.45 *viḍvarād* B G : *dviḍvarād* J : *vidravād* Ś

---

[i] Prithu, son of Vena, one of the epic heroes sometimes invoked before a journey

other expressions of her missing him are present, because she is continuously joyful with the hope of seeing him again shortly.

Frustration has five varieties, depending on whether it results from the lover's going to another country, the orders of a parent, desire, jealousy, or a curse. Additional causes can be supposed, such as time, fate, or a calamity. 6.45

An example of frustration caused by the lover's going to another country:

When her lover started to go,
the woman's bracelet fell from her wrist,
her steadiness tripped, her passion dipped,
the tears poured from her eyes,
and in the guise of the sweet sound of bells
tinkling on her shaking arm
her life, about to leave, cried out
"Dear god!" and turned its thoughts to Vainya.[i]

Another example, from my honored father:

Her friends implored her, and finally
the lotus-eyed woman
took the lute upon her lap
and slowly began to sing.
But—how strange—her limbs were so sadly
wasted from separation
that Fainting* thought they were the strings
and touched them repeatedly.

6.50 guru|nideśād yathā:

bhāsvāmś cūta|tarur, *gurur* manasijaḥ,
ko 'py eṣa bhṛṅgas *tamo*,
mando gandha|vahaḥ, *sito* malayajo,
*doṣ'|ākaro** mādhavaḥ,
aṅgāro nava|pallavaḥ, para|bhṛto
vijño—guror ājñayā
niryāto 'si; vicāritāḥ katham amī
krūrās tvayā na grahāḥ? [18]

abhilāṣād yathā:

āgār'|âbhimukhaṃ mukhaṃ racayator,
vakrī|kṛta|grīvayor,
vyastaṃ colam ajānatoḥ, kva cid api
vyājāt punas tiṣṭhatoḥ,
mārgaṃ vismaratoḥ kva cit, kva cid api
tyakt'|âkṣaraṃ jalpatoḥ
sāci|prekṣitam āvayor yad abhavad,
bhūyas tad āśāsmahe. [19]

---

i A woman speaks to her secret lover before his departure.

An example of frustration caused by the orders of a parent: 6.50

The mango tree is *gleaming* ⁝ *the sun*;
the God of love is *a guru* ⁝ *Jupiter*; the black bee is
darkness ⁝ *Eclipse*;
the breeze is *gentle* ⁝ *Saturn*; the sandalwood is
pure white ⁝ *Venus*;
the spring is *a source of faults* ⁝ *the moon*;
the new sprout burns like *a firebrand* ⁝ *Mars*;
the cuckoo is *adept* ⁝ *Mercury*—
you left at the command of my father but why
did you not first take thought for these cruel planets?

An example of frustration caused by desire:[i]

Directing our heads toward the rendezvous house
and twisting our necks,
garments on inside out, standing around
idly on a pretext;
forgetting the way, leaving things half said—
may the two of us have,
time and again, the furtive glances we had
in all these different acts.

īrṣyāto yathā:

prāṇ'|ēśasya prabhavati!* manaḥ|
　　prema hema|prasūnaṃ,
cetaś cūtaṃ, dṛg api kamalaṃ,
　　jīvanaṃ bandhujīvam.
āśā|sūtre grathitam a|khilaṃ
　　vedhasā, yasya bhaṅge
syād eteṣām api nipatanaṃ—
　　caṇḍi, mānaṃ vimuñca. [20]

śāpād yathā:

anyatra yadi nirgantum icchā, nirgaccha dūrataḥ;
priyā|viraha|tāpena śāpa|dagdho bhaviṣyasi. [21]

samayād yathā:

viśleṣa|jīvana|vrīḍā|
　　pīḍā|vidhura|mānasā
tasthau prātaḥ priyaṃ vīkṣya
　　cakrī vakrī|kṛt'|ānanā. [22]

daivād yathā:

jīvane '|sati† viśleṣo,
　　viśleṣe '|sati† jīvanam.
dvayor apy anayor yūnām
　　aham eva nidarśanam. [23]

6.61 *'sati* V (?) : *sati* J　6.61 *'sati* V (?) : *sati* J

An example of frustration caused by jealousy:

The love in the heart of your husband 6.55
is a golden flower, the mind
a mango bud, the eye a lotus,
and life itself a *bandhu·jiva* bloom.
The creator has strung these all together
upon the string called hope, and if
you break that string the flowers are lost—
so no more anger, hot-headed girl.

An example of frustration caused by a curse:

If you really want to leave,
go far away or you'll be burned
by a curse from the burning pain
of separation from your beloved.*

An example of frustration caused by time:

Brokenhearted at the painful shame
of surviving even though parted,
the *chakra·vaki* bird gazed at dawn
on her mate and hung her head.*

An example of frustration caused by fate: 6.60

Some people are never separated while alive,
and some never live once separated.
But here am I, alone among youths,
an example of both.*

viḍvarād†* yathā:

kelī|gṛhe vā maṇi|mandire vā
  śaśāma Laṅkā|nagare hut'|âśaḥ.
itas tataḥ prasthitayor na yūnor
  viyoga|janmā virarāma vahniḥ. [24]

iti Śrī|Bhānudatta|viracitāyāṃ Rasataraṅgiṇyāṃ rasa|nirūpaṇaṃ nāma ṣaṣṭhas taraṅgaḥ.

6.62 *viḍvarād* B G : *dviḍvarād* J : *vidravād* Ś

An example of frustration caused by an calamity:

The flames in Lanka city burned themselves out
in jeweled palaces and pleasure rooms,
but the fire of young couples' separation was
unceasing
as they wandered thence from place to place.*

The end of the Description of Rasas, the Sixth Wave of Bhanu·datta's "River of Rasa."

THE SEVENTH WAVE
DESCRIPTION OF RASAS CONTINUED

7.1 HĀSASYA PARIPOṢO hāsyaḥ. varṇo 'sya śuklo† śuddho, daivataṃ pramathaḥ. sa ca dvi|vidhaḥ: sva|niṣṭhaḥ para|niṣṭhaś c' êti. tāv apy uttama|madhyam'|âdhama|bhedāt tridh" êti ṣaḍ|vidhaḥ. sva|niṣṭho 'pi ṣaḍ|vidhaḥ. para|niṣṭho 'pi ṣaḍ|vidha iti dvādaśa|vidho hāsyaḥ. tathā hi uttamānāṃ sva|niṣṭhe para|niṣṭhe ca smita|hasite. madhyamānāṃ sva|niṣṭhe para|niṣṭhe ca vihasit'|ôpahasite. adhamānāṃ sva|niṣṭhe para|niṣṭhe c' âpahasit'|âtihasite. uttamānām īṣad|vikasita|kapolam, a|vyakta|daśanam, apāṅga|suṣṭhu|vīkṣaṇaṃ smitam. utphulla|kapolaṃ, kiñcil|lakṣita|daśanaṃ hasitam. madhyamānāṃ samay'|ôcitam uttama|svanam, ākuñcita|mukham, āvirbhūta|vadana|rāgaṃ vihasitam. utphulla|nāsā|puṭaṃ, kuṭila|vīkṣitaṃ, kuñcita|grīvaṃ, sphuṭa|svanam upahasitam. adhamānām uddhatam, udyad|aśru, kampita|mauli, sphuṭatara|svanam apahasitam. atyuddhataṃ, bahal'|âśru, sphuṭatama|svanam, āśliṣṭa|pārśva|janam, ārabdha|kara|tālam atihasitam.

7.1 *śuklo* Ś : *śuddho* J

---

[i] Goblin-like companions of the god Shiva

THE FULL DEVELOPMENT of the humorous stable emotion is called the "comic" rasa. Its color is white, and its presiding deity is the troop of the *prámathas*.[i] The comic is of two types: self-directed and other-directed.* Each of these is divided into high, average, and low,* giving six varieties. The self-directed and other-directed comic together have twelve varieties. To be specific: In the case of high characters, the self-directed and other-directed comic consist of smiling and laughing; in the case of average characters, the self-directed and other-directed comic consist of chuckling and chortling; in the case of low characters, the self-directed and other-directed comic consist of guffawing and belly-laughing. In the case of high characters we have smiling, which consists of partially puckered cheeks with the teeth hidden and subtle sidelong glances, and laughing, which consists of cheeks fully blossomed and teeth partially visible; in the case of average characters, we have chuckling, which consists of modulating the pitch of one's voice as appropriate to the occasion, the head slightly inclined, the face blushing, and chortling, which consists of the nostrils flaring, sly looks, neck fully inclined, and a shrill pitch of the voice; in the case of low characters, we have guffawing, which consists of intense whooping with head shaking and tears starting, and belly-laughing, which consists of very intense shrieking, tears pouring out, hugging the people at one's side, and wildly clapping the hands. 7.1

sva|niṣṭhaṃ smitaṃ yathā:

lekhanīm ita ito vilokayan
  kutra kutra na jagāma Padmabhūḥ.
tāṃ punaḥ śravaṇa|sīmni lambhitāṃ
  prāpya, sannata|mukhaṃ smitaṃ dadhau. [1]

sva|niṣṭhaṃ hasitaṃ yathā:

7.5 vyom'|âṅkuraṃ vyoma|gataṃ rad'|âgram
  ugra|dyutiṃ svīyam udīkṣya Viṣṇoḥ
yad āsa hāsyaṃ kimu tat payodhāv
  ady' âpi phena|stabakāyamānam. [2]

para|niṣṭhaṃ smitaṃ hasitaṃ ca yathā:

Hara|vṛṣabha|mukhe sa|khelam āyo-*
  jayati suvarṇa|sa|varṇa|kānti|parṇam,
dṛśi Bhujaga|pateḥ śiśuḥ Ṣaḍāsyaḥ
  kalayati kajjalam antike Bhavānyāḥ. [3]

para|niṣṭhaṃ vihasitaṃ yathā:

niśāsu tailasya dhiyā gṛhītair
  masī|jalair lipta|mukh'|âravindam
gopaṃ prabhāte skhalad|aśru|nīram
  a|dhīra|nādaṃ jahasus taruṇyaḥ. [4]

---

[i] In his Boar incarnation [ii] Párvati watches her son Skanda playing with Shiva's bull and the cosmic snake Shesha.

An example of self-directed smiling:

Here and there and everywhere
Brahma went searching for his pen,
and when he found it fixed behind
his ear, he lowered his face and smiled.

An example of self-directed laughing:

When Vishnu saw his dreadful tusk[i] 7.5
flash in the sky like a root of the sky
he laughed—and even today that laugh
remains in the form of the foam of the sea.*

An example of other-directed smiling and laughing:*

Playfully, the Six-headed god, her little child,
put a golden leaf on Nandi's snout
and painted the eyes of the Lord of serpents
with lampblack, as Bhaváni was looking on.[ii]

An example of other-directed chuckling:

At night the cowherd took a pot of ink,
thinking it oil, and rubbed it on his face,
and at dawn the girls laughed at him,
the sound half-suppressed, tears welling
in their eyes.

7.10 para|niṣṭham upahasitaṃ yathā:

«yo nirodho may" ārabdha...»
iti padyaṃ paṭhan budhaḥ
śaśvad|utphulla|nāsena
taṭasthen' ôpahasyate.† [5]

para|niṣṭham apahasitaṃ yathā:

rat'|ôtsave vallabha|yajña|sūtraṃ
kaṇṭh'|âvalagnaṃ parimocayantīm
dvij'|âṅganāṃ dīrghataraṃ śvasantīṃ
tāra|svaraṃ vāra|vadhūr jahāsa. [6]

para|niṣṭham atihasitaṃ yathā:

7.15 coraḥ Kāma|ripor gṛhaṃ niśi gataḥ
śūlaṃ kapālaṃ haran,
bījaṃ dhūrta|phalasya taṇḍula|dhiyā
nītvā punar bhuktavān.
vyāvalgan, pracalan, skhalan, paripatan,
muhyan, vighūrṇan, hasann,
aṭṭ'|âṭṭa|dhvani mukta|mauli|kusumaṃ
svar|veśyayā hāsyate. [7]

7.11 *upahasyate* Ś : *upahāsyate* J

An example of other-directed chortling: 7.10

As the poet recited his verse
saying, "I cunt begin to tell … "*
the bystanders burst out laughing at him,
their nostrils flaring wide with glee.

An example of other-directed guffawing:

The courtesan began to roar with laughter
when she caught sight of the brahmin's wife
breathlessly trying to untangle the sacred thread*
around her husband's neck when making love.

An example of other-directed belly-laughing:

A thief at night went to the house of Shiva 7.15
and stole his trident and skull bowl,
and took and ate some datura* seeds,
thinking they were grains of rice.
And as he swayed and tottered and stumbled
        and fell,
swooned and spun and laughed out loud,
the whores of heaven were in stitches, teeth
        flashing white,
flowers spilling from their hair.

śokasya paripoṣaḥ karuṇaḥ. āśā|vicchede sati sarv'|êndriya|klamo vā. na ca vipralambhe 'tivyāptiḥ. tatr' êṣṭ'|āśāyāḥ sattvāt. tad|vicchede tu sa vipralambhaḥ karuṇa eva. śoko duḥkham. varṇo 'sya kapota|citrito, daivataṃ Varuṇaḥ. sa ca sva|niṣṭhaḥ para|niṣṭhaś ca. sva|śāpa|bandhana|kleś'|ân|iṣṭair vibhāvaiḥ sva|niṣṭhaḥ. par'|êṣṭa|nāśa|śāpa|bandhana|kleś'|ādīnāṃ darśana|smaraṇair vibhāvaiḥ para|niṣṭhaḥ.

sva|niṣṭho yathā:

tava, nātha, śaraḥ, śar'|āsanaṃ
  tava dehena sah' âiva bhasmasāt.
aham asmi, tataḥ pratīyate:
  tava n' âsm' îti—kim ucyatām itaḥ? [8]

para|niṣṭho yathā:

7.20 anuvanam anuyāntaṃ, bāṣpa|vāri tyajantaṃ,
  mṛdita|kamala|dāma|kṣāmam ālocya Rāmam,
dinam api ravi|rocis|tāpam antaḥ prasūte;
  rajanir api vidhatte tārakā|bāṣpa|bindūn. [9]

[i] Rati, the wife of the God of love, laments at his death by fire from Shiva's third eye.

The full development of the stable emotion grief is called the pitiful rasa. Or it may be thought of as a deadening of all the senses when all hope is lost. This definition is not so wide as to include the rasa called the erotic frustrated, because there hope of the beloved still exists; it is precisely when all such hope is lost that the erotic frustrated becomes the pitiful rasa. Grief is sorrow. Its color is speckled dove gray, and its presiding deity is Váruna. The pitiful rasa, too, is either self-directed or other-directed. The former comes about through such underlying factors as a curse upon oneself, one's imprisonment, or some catastrophe or other unwelcome occurrence. The latter comes about through such underlying factors as another's losing some cherished person, a curse upon him, his imprisonment or other troubles, whether actually seen or only remembered.

An example of the self-directed pitiful rasa:

Your bow and arrows, master, are truly yours,
since when your body burned they were burned,
too.
But I remain alive, and so I know—
what else to say?—I was not really yours.[i]

An example of the other-directed pitiful rasa:

Watching Rama shedding tears and wandering 7.20
from forest to forest, weak as a trampled lotus,
even the day felt pain—the blazing sun—
even the night shed tears in the shape of stars.

paripūrṇaḥ krodho raudraḥ, sarv'|êndriyāṇām auddhatyaṃ vā. varṇo 'sya rakto, daivataṃ Rudraḥ. yathā:

caṇḍ'|âṃśuḥ kiṃ na cakraṃ,
bhujaga|patir asau vartate vā na pāśaḥ?
kuntāḥ kiṃ danti|dantā,
na ca girir aśaniḥ? kiṃ na śastraiḥ kim anyaiḥ?
Bhīmo 'haṃ duṣṭa|Duryo-
dhana|nidhana|samud|
daṇḍa|bāhu|prakāṇḍaḥ*
pratyāvṛtta|prakopa|
pralaya|hutavaho—
n' âsmi kasy' âpi vaśyaḥ. [10]

yathā vā:

krīḍā|tuṅga|turaṅga|ṭāpa|paṭalī|
kharvī|kṛt'|ôrvīdhara|*
śreṇī|sphūrjita|dhūli|dhoraṇi|tamaḥ|
stom'|âvalīḍhaṃ jagat
baddha|spardha|kar'|îndra|vṛnda|caraṇa|
vyābhugna|bhog'|īśvara|
vyagr'|ôdagra|phaṇ'|âgra|ratna|rucibhir
vidyotayāmo vayam. [11]

7.25 paripūrṇa utsāhaḥ sarv'|êndriyāṇāṃ praharṣo vā vīraḥ. varṇo 'sya gauraḥ. daivataṃ Śakraḥ. sa ca tridhā: yuddha|vīra|dāna|vīra|dayā|vīra|bhedāt. iyāṃs tu viśeṣaḥ. sa c' ôtsāho yuddha|vīre pratāp'|âdhyavasāy'|ādi|prabhavaḥ. dāna|vīre dāna|sāmarthy'|ādi|prabhavaḥ. dayā|vīre ārdrat"|ādi|prabhavaḥ. yuddha|vīro yathā:

Fully matured anger—or a state of intensification of all the senses—is the furious rasa. Its color is red, and its presiding deity is Rudra. An example:

> Isn't the sun a discus, the cosmic serpent
> a rope? Aren't elephant tusks lances,
> and mountains crashing bolts? I have no need
> for any other armaments.
> I am Bhima, my tree-trunk arm upraised
> to kill the wicked Duryódhana,
> the doomsday fire of my anger reignited—
> and I answer to no one.*

Another example:

> The world's been swallowed in a mass of darkness
> from the blanket of dust thrown up
> by the string of mountains that were flattened
> by their galloping spirited warhorses,
> but with the rays from the gems on the upraised
> hood of Shesha, brought low by the feet
> of the herds of our competing elephants,
> we shall shed illumination.*

Fully matured energy—or an enlivenment of all the senses—is the heroic rasa. Its color is pale yellow, and its presiding deity is Indra. It is threefold: the heroic in war, in munificence, and in compassion. The difference here is only that in the first case, the energy arises from intentness on martial fervor, and so on; in the second, from the capacity for bestowing gifts, and so on; and in the last, from feelings of pity, and so on. An example of the heroic in war: 7.25

saṅgrām'|âṅgaṇam āgate Daśamukhe
Saumitriṇā vismitaṃ,
Sugrīveṇa vicintitaṃ, Hanumatā
vyālolam ālokitam.
śrī|Rāmeṇa paraṃ tu pīna|pulaka|
sphūrjat|kapola|śriyā
sāndr'|ānanda|ras'|ālasā nidadhire
bāṇ'|âsane dṛṣṭayaḥ. [12]

dāna|vīro yathā:

abhyāgacchati mandiraṃ dvija|kule,
«khaṇḍāya khaṇḍ'|âmbudhiṃ,
kṣār'|âbdhiṃ lavaṇāya, dugdha|jaladhiṃ
dugdhāya ced dāsyati,
durvāro viraho bhaved,» iti bhiyā
dīn" êva divy'|âpagā
yasy' âṅghriṃ na jahāti, vipra|vapuṣe
Rāmāya tasmai namaḥ. [13]

dayā|vīro yathā:

7.30 dayā|bījaṃ Harer netram,
aṅkuras tatra bhāskaraḥ,
tataḥ samutthitāv etau
pallavau Rāma|Lakṣmaṇau. [14]

---

[i] Párashu·rama [ii] The sun is Vishnu's right eye, as well as the progenitor of the clan to which Rama and Lákshmana belonged.

When Rávana reached the battlefield,
Lákshmana stood amazed,
Sugríva fretted, Hánuman
looked anxiously about.
But glorious Rama, the hair bristling
thickly on his cheeks,
set his eyes, heavy with rapturous
bliss, upon his bow.

An example of the heroic in munificence:

As the horde of brahmins assembled at the temple
the Ganga wondered: "If he gives
the salt sea to them for salt, the candy sea
for candy, the milk sea for milk,
I will inevitably be bereft,"
and so as if dejected the river
cleaves to his feet in fear*—all praise to him,
that Rama in the brahmin's form.[i]

An example of the heroic in compassion:*

Vishnu's eye was the seed of compassion, 7.30
the sprout from this seed was the sun,
and from it there arose those two
blossoms, Rama and Lákshmana.[ii]

bhayasya paripoṣaḥ sarv'|êndriyāṇām vikṣobho vā bhayānakaḥ. varṇo 'sya śyāmaḥ. daivatam Yamaḥ. sa ca sva|niṣṭhaḥ para|niṣṭhaś ca.

aparādhāt sva|niṣṭho yathā:

gopī|kṣīra|ghaṭī|viluṇṭhana|vidhi|
vyāpāra|vārtā|vidoḥ
pitros tāḍana|śaṅkayā śiśu|vapur
devaḥ prakāśya jvaram,
rom'|âñcaṃ racayan, dṛśau mukulayan,
pratyaṅgam utkampayan,
sīt|kurvaṃs tamasi prasarpati gṛhaṃ
sāyaṃ samāgacchati. [15]

para|niṣṭho yathā:

7.35 Gaṅgāyāḥ salile nimajjati, jaṭā|
jūṭe paribhrāmyati,
bhraśyaty akṣi|hut'|âśane, phaṇi|phaṇ'|ā-
bhoge kva cil līyate,
kubjī|bhūya Harasya karṇa|suṣiraṃ
nirgantum utkaṇṭhate—
Rāhor āsyam udīkṣya kiṃ na kurute
bālas tuṣāra|dyutiḥ? [16]

---

[i] Krishna [ii] Shiva's attributes include a crescent moon in his headdress, along with the Ganga and matted locks, a fiery third eye in the middle of his forehead, and a snake around his neck.

The full development of the stable emotion fear—or an agitation of all the senses—is called the fearful rasa. Its color is blue-black, and its presiding deity is Yama. It can be self-directed or other-directed.*

An example of the self-directed fearful rasa arising from a transgression:

His parents had heard talk of his behavior,
how he looted the milkmaids' pots,
and so the god in a child's body[i] was scared
they'd spank him. He pretended fever,
produced chills, and kept his eyes half shut,
trembling in every limb and groaning
as he made his way home in the evening
with darkness coming on apace.

An example of the other-directed fearful rasa:

It plunges into Ganga's waters, 7.35
wanders among the matted hair,
leaps into the third eye's fire,
disappears amid the snake's coils,
and even makes itself a midget
trying to escape through Shiva's ear—
when it sees the yawning mouth of Eclipse,
what won't the crescent moon attempt?[ii]

vikṛta|ninadāt para|niṣṭho yathā:

kurvāṇe daśabhir mukhair Daśa|mukhe
nādaṃ, suraiḥ kampitaṃ,
diṅ|nāgaiś cakitaṃ, Harer api hayair
utpuccham ādhāvitam.
Sugrīvas tu samucchalaj|jala|nidhi|
vyālola|vīci|bhrami|
bhraśyat|setu|viśaṅkayā Hanumato
vaktre dṛśau sandadhe. [17]

jugupsāyāḥ paripoṣo bībhatsaḥ, sarv'|êndriyāṇāṃ saṅkoco vā. varṇo 'sya nīlo, daivataṃ Mahākālaḥ. sa ca sva|niṣṭhaḥ para|niṣṭhaś c' êti.

sva|niṣṭho yathā:

7.40 Kālī|Kuṇḍalinī|kutūhala|mithaḥ|
prārabdha|thūthūt|kṛti|
nyañcad|vīci|calad|vihāyasi valaj|
jhillī|nipāta|spṛśi
baddha|spardha|vipakṣa|pakṣa|rudhira|
srotasvinī|srotasi
bhraśyaty, udbhramati, skhalaty atha raṇa|
krodh'|ākulo Bhārgavaḥ. [18]

---

[i] Rávana [ii] A form of Shiva [iii] Malevolent forms of the mother goddess

An example of the other-directed fearful rasa arising from a gruesome sound:

As Ten-heads[i] raised a battle cry in all
ten mouths at once the gods trembled,
the heavenly elephants quaked, even the Sun's
horses bolted, their tails in the air.
But Sugríva, fearing that the bridge
would break as the wild waves were cresting
over the heaving ocean, fixed his gaze
upon the face of Hánuman.

The full development of the stable emotion revulsion—or a recoiling of all the senses—is called the disgusting rasa. Its color is blue, and its presiding deity is Mahá·kala.[ii] It can be self-directed or other-directed.

An example of the self-directed disgusting rasa:

Kali and Kúndalini,[iii] with equal rclish, 7.40
started to gibber and squeal,
the sky itself moved under the crashing waves,
circling vultures swooped down,*
and in that swift current of the river of blood
of contending enemy ranks
Bhárgava, blind with battle rage, began
to slip and slide and fall.

para|niṣṭho yathā:

«chatraṃ kumbh'|îndra|karṇair
viracaya, vitataṃ† cāmaraṃ vāji†|pucchair,
mālāṃ muṇḍaiḥ pracaṇḍaiḥ
sṛja, gaja|jaghanair maṇḍapaṃ† yojayasva,
antrair nīrājanāyāḥ
kalaya vidhim.» iti preta|vṛddh'|âṅganānām
ālāpaḥ Kuṇḍalinyās
tanaya|pariṇay'|ārambha|janmā babhūva. [19]

vismayasya samyak samṛddhir adbhutaḥ, sarv'|êndriyāṇāṃ tāṭasthyaṃ vā. varṇo 'sya pīto, daivataṃ Brahmā. sa ca sva|niṣṭhaḥ para|niṣṭhaś ca.

sva|niṣṭho yathā:

7.45 līlā|nibaddha|pāthodhir,
helā|hata|Daś'|ānanaḥ
sa Rāmaḥ Sītay" āśliṣṭam
ātmānaṃ bahv amanyata. [20]

para|niṣṭho yathā:

tyaktā jīrṇa|dukūlavad vasumatī,
baddho 'mbudhir binduvad,
bāṇ'|âgreṇa jarat|kapotaka iva
vyāpādito Rāvaṇaḥ,
Laṅkā k" âpi Vibhīṣaṇāya sahasā
mudr" êva hast'|ârpitā—
śrutv" âivaṃ Raghu|nandanasya caritaṃ
ko vā na romāñcati? [21]

7.42 *vitatam* Ś : *tanu taṃ* J : *tanutāṃ* V B N 7.42 *vāji-* Ś : *vyāla-* J
7.42 *maṇḍapaṃ* Ś : *maṇḍalaṃ* J

An example of the other-directed disgusting rasa:

"Fashion a parasol from elephant ears,
a wide one, a fly whisk from horses' tails,
string a garland of gruesome hairless skulls,
build a marriage hall of elephant parts,
perform the holy lamp ceremony
with entrails." So the old women
among the ghosts gave orders to commence
the wedding of Kúndalini's son.

The proper expansion of the stable emotion wonder—or a neutralization of all the senses—is the amazing rasa. Its color is yellow, and its presiding deity is Brahma. It can be self-directed or other-directed.

An example of the self-directed amazing rasa:

Though he had bridged the ocean in sport 7.45
and slain ten-headed Rávana for fun,
Rama only took pride in himself
when Sita took him in her arms.

An example of the other-directed amazing rasa:

To give up the earth like a worn-out garment,
to bridge the sea like a droplet,
to put an end to Rávana with an arrow
like an age-worn pigeon,*
to hand Lanka straightway to Vibhíshana
like a signet ring—
who could listen to these acts of Rama's
and not succumb to shivering?

atyukti|bhram'|ôkti|citr'|ôkti|virodh'|ābhāsa|prabhṛtayo 'dbhutā eva.

atyuktir yathā:

7.50 bhūyād eṣa satāṃ hitāya bhagavān
kol'|âvatāro Hariḥ,
sindhoḥ kleśam apāsya yasya daśana|
prānte sthitāyā bhuvaḥ
tārā hārati, vāridas tilakati,
svar|vāhinī mālyati,
krīḍādarpaṇati kṣapā|patir, ahar|
devaś ca tāṭaṅkati. [22]

yathā vā:

divya|Harer mukha|kuhare
vistīrṇe parṇati vyoma,
cūrṇati candraḥ, kramukati
Kanaka|giriḥ, khadirasārati khar'|âṃśuḥ. [23]

bhram'|ôktir yathā:

tīvrais tigma|rucaḥ karaiḥ paricitāṃ
sektuṃ kapola|sthalīṃ
nīrāṇāṃ nikaraṃ kareṇa haratā
tucchī|kṛte vāridhau,
Maināka[i]ṃ samudīkṣya paṅka|patitaṃ,
śālūka|śaṅkā|juṣo
Herambasya punātu danta|śikhara|
vyāpāra|līlā|rasaḥ. [24]

[i] The mountain that took refuge in the ocean when Indra was cutting off the mountains' wings

Hyperbole, misinterpretation, fantasy, and apparent contradiction are all forms of the amazing rasa.*

An example of hyperbole:

May Vishnu bring welfare to the good 7.50
in his Boar incarnation
when Earth sat poised on the tip of his tusk,
set free from the ocean's chafing,
and the stars made her a necklace, the cloud
a forehead ornament,
the heavenly river a garland, the moon
a mirror, the sun an earring.

Another:

In the vast maw of the divine Lion*
the sky was a betel leaf,
the moon lime paste, the Golden Mountain
areca, the sun cutch juice.*

An example of misinterpretation:

When his cheek was burned by the hot rays
of the blazing sun
and he drew water in his trunk to bathe it
and thereby emptied the ocean,
Ganésha saw Mainákai fallen in the mud,
and thinking him a root,
he played with him with the tip of his tusk—
and may that play protect you.

7.55 yathā vā:

antaḥ|krodh'|âgni|jāgrat|
kapaṭa|Narahari|sphāra|niḥśvāsa|vāta|
vyādhūtā vāri|vāhāḥ
kula|dharaṇibhṛtaḥ sānuṣu praskhalantaḥ
diṅ|nāgair nāga|buddhyā,
vana|hariṇa|kulaiḥ śaṅkayā śādvalānāṃ,
chāyā|bhrāntyā kirātaiḥ,
śiti|vasana|dhiyā vīkṣitāḥ svar|vadhūbhiḥ. [25]

citr'|ôktir yathā:

girir vamati mauktik'|ā-
valim, ali|dvayaṃ sthāvaraṃ,
śarat|tuhina|dīdhitir
vyajana|mārutaṃ vāñchati,
dhanuḥ svapiti mānmathaṃ,
śithila|bandham andhaṃ tamo,
namo manasi|jāya te,
kim api kautukaṃ tanvate. [26]

lakṣaṇikam akhilaṃ citr'|ôktir eva.

7.60 virodh'|ābhāso yathā:

ko 'py asau tava, Mukunda, *nandako*
'|nandako bhavati Kaṃsa|sampadaḥ;
kuṇḍalī tvam asi, Kāliyaṃ kuto
dūrato nayasi—tan nivedaya. [27]

---

[i] The God of love [ii] Mukúnda, or Krishna, killed his uncle Kansa and the serpent Káliya.

Another: 7.55

The winds of the mighty sighs of that artifice,
the Man-Lion, awakened by the fire of his anger,
tossed the clouds about and they went scuttling
onto the slopes of the ancient mountain:
The guardian elephants of the quarters believed
them other elephants; the herds of forest deer,
mounds of grass; the country people, shadows;
and the women of heaven, elegant black gowns.

An example of fantasy:

A mountain that spits out pearls, a pair
of bees absolutely still,
an autumn moon that calls, yearning
for a breeze from a fan,
a bow of Love that lies asleep,
deep darkness that falls disheveled—
praise be to you who are born in the mind,[i]
and who so excite our fancy.*

Fantasies as such are based entirely on metaphorical or metonymical identification.

An example of apparent contradiction: 7.60

How remarkable, Mukúnda, is *your source of joy : your sword* named Nándaka,
for it was no source of joy to the fortunes of Kansa,
and you *are a coil-possessing snake : wear earrings*
and yet you drive Káliya away[ii]—tell me why.

nāṭye ca sarve rasā ānanada|rūpāḥ, adbhut'|ākhyāḥ, para|niṣṭhā eva.*

citta|vṛttir dvedhā, pravṛttir nivṛttiś ca. nivṛttau yathā śānta|rasas, tathā pravṛttau māyā|rasa iti pratibhāti. ekatra ras'|ôtpattir, aparatra n', êti vaktum a|śakyatvāt. na ca sa ratir eva. tarhi sa kasy' âstu vyabhicārī? na śṛṅgārasya, tad|vairiṇo bībhatsasy' âpi tatra sattvād; ata eva na bībhatsasy' âpi. na hāsyasya, tad|vairiṇaḥ karuṇasy' âpi tatra sattvād; ata eva na karuṇasy' âpi. na raudrasya, tad|vairiṇo 'dbhutasy' âpi tatra sattvād; ata eva n' âdbhutasy' âpi. na vīrasya, tad|vairiṇo bhayānakasy' âpi tatra sattvād; ata eva na bhayānakasy' âpi. n' âpi śāntasya tad|virodhitvāt.

na ca sāmānya eva rasas, tad|viśeṣā itare bhavanti. śānta|rasasya tarhi ras'|ābhāsatv'|āpatteḥ. kiṃ tu vidyuta iva rati|hāsa|śoka|krodh'|ôtsāha|bhaya|jugupsā|vismayās tatr' ôt-

In drama, all rasas are joyful, are fundamentally the amazing rasa, and are solely other-directed.

Now, there are two basic states of mind, engagement and disengagement. In the case of disengagement we have the tranquil rasa, and in the same way, in the case of engagement it would appear we have a rasa of phenomenal reality,* for we cannot argue that rasa arises in the former case but not in the latter. Nor can this phenomenal rasa be desire as such (counterposed to the absence of desire in the tranquil rasa), since were that so, phenomenal rasa would then have to be a transitory feeling of some other rasa—but which one? Not the erotic, because of the presence in the phenomenal rasa of the disgusting, which is inimical to the erotic—and so desire could not be a transitory feeling for the disgusting, either. Nor the comic, because of the presence in the phenomenal rasa of the pitiful, which is inimical to the comic—and so it could not be a transitory feeling for the pitiful, either. Nor the furious, because of the presence in the phenomenal rasa of the amazing, which is inimical to the furious—and so it could not be a transitory feeling for the amazing, either. Nor the heroic, because of the presence in the phenomenal rasa of the fearful, which is inimical to the heroic—and so it could not be a transitory feeling of the fearful, either. Nor the tranquil, because it is diametrically opposed to the phenomenal rasa.

Furthermore, this phenomenal rasa cannot be purely a genus, of which the other rasas are species, for then the tranquil would be excluded and thereby turn out to be a semblance of rasa. Instead, like flashes of lightning, desire

padyante vilīyante ca. tena tatra te vyabhicāri | bhāvā iti. lakṣaṇaṃ ca prabuddha | mithyā | jñāna | vāsanā māyā | rasaḥ. mithyā | jñānam asya sthāyi | bhāvaḥ. vibhāvāḥ sāṃsārika | bhog'|ârjaka | dharm'|â | dharmāḥ. anubhāvāḥ putra | kalatra | vijaya | sāmrājy'|ādayaḥ. yathā:

7.65 vāṭī lāṭī | dṛg | ambho |
ruha | rabhasa | karī, vāpikā k" âpi kāntā,
talpaṃ candr'|ânukalpaṃ,
prakaṭayati mithaḥ kāminī kāma | nītim,
rūpaṃ kām'|ânurūpaṃ,
maṇimaya | bhavanaṃ,
bandhuraṃ bandhu | rāgo—
loke, Lokeśa, kasya
tvam asi na bhavane sarvadā sarva | dātā? [28]

nāṭya | bhinne paraṃ nirveda | sthāyi | bhāvakaḥ śānto 'pi navamo raso bhavat' îti. nirvedasya paripoṣaḥ śānto raso, doṣa | praśamo vā. doṣāḥ kāma | krodh'|ādayaḥ. asya viṣaya | doṣa | vicāra | virakty | ādayo vibhāvāḥ. anubhāvā ānand'|âśru | pulaka | harṣa | gadgada | vacan'|ādayaḥ. yathā:

---

[i] Actions leading to good and bad karma respectively

together with humor, grief, anger, energy, fear, revulsion, and wonder arise and vanish in this phenomenal rasa, and hence for it, all these stable emotions function as transitory feelings. The definition of phenomenal rasa is this: it is a latent impression, consisting of false consciousness, that comes to be stimulated. This false consciousness is its stable emotion; its underlying and stimulant factors are dharma and adharma,[i] which underwrite experience in the world, whereas its reactions are such things as a child, a wife, success, pre-eminence. An example:

A garden that enchants with the lotus eyes 7.65
of Lata women, a lovely pond,
a bed like the moon, a beloved who reveals
her mastery of love in union,
a body suited for love, a jeweled mansion
so beautiful, affectionate kin—
O lord of the world, upon whose house in the world
don't you always bestow everything?*

Except in drama there is a ninth rasa, the tranquil, whose stable emotion is dispassion. The full development of dispassion—or an extinguishing of the vices—is called the tranquil rasa. The vices are desire, anger, etc. Its underlying factors and stimulant factors are reflection on the baseness of worldly objects, disenchantment, etc. Its reactions are tears of bliss, horripilation, stammering, etc. An example:

heyaṃ harmyam idaṃ, nikuñja|bhavanaṃ
śreyaṃ,†* pradeyaṃ dhanaṃ;
peyaṃ tīrtha|payo, Harer bhagavato
geyaṃ pad'|âmbhoruham;
neyaṃ janma cirāya darbha|śayane,
dharme nidheyaṃ manaḥ,
stheyaṃ tatra sit'|âsitasya savidhe,
dhyeyaṃ purāṇaṃ mahaḥ. [29]

yathā vā:

Vedasy' âdhyayanaṃ kṛtaṃ, paricitaṃ
śāstraṃ, Purāṇaṃ śrutaṃ—
sarvaṃ vyartham idaṃ, padaṃ na Kamalā|
kāntasya cet kīrtitam.
utkhātaṃ, sadṛśī|kṛtaṃ, viracitaḥ
seko 'mbhasā bhūyasā—
sarvaṃ niṣphalam, ālavāla|valaye
kṣiptaṃ na bījaṃ yadi. [30]

7.70 iti śrī|Bhānudatta|viracitāyāṃ Rasataraṅgiṇyāṃ
rasa|nirūpaṇaṃ nāma saptamas taraṅgaḥ.

7.67 *śreyam* G : *śreyaḥ* J Ś

---

[i] The confluence of the Ganga and Yámuna, that is, Prayága

Mansions should be abandoned, a forest hut
made home, and money given away;
water at sacred fords should be drunk, the feet
of blessed Vishnu intoned in song;
life should be lived* every night on *darbha* grass
and one's thoughts given to dharma,
one's time should be spent where white water
meets black,[i]
and the ancient light contemplated.

Another example:

You can study the Vedas, learn the shastras
and listen to the Puránas,
but this will all be for nought if you do not
extol the feet of Vishnu.
You can dig and level the ground and sprinkle
water night and day,
but it will all be fruitless unless you place
into the hole a seed.

The end of the Description of Rasas Continued, 7.70
the Seventh Wave of Bhanu·datta's "River of Rasa"

THE EIGHTH WAVE MISCELLANY

8.1 STHĀYI | BHĀVA | JĀ dṛṣṭir aṣṭadhā: snigdhā, hṛṣṭā, dīnā, kruddhā, dṛptā, bhītā, jugupsitā, vismitā c' êti. vyabhicāri | bhāva | jā dṛṣṭir viṃśatidhā: śūnyā, malinā, śrāntā, lajjitā, śaṅkitā, mukul", ârdha | mukulā, glānā, jihmā, kuñcitā, vitarkit", âbhitaptā, viṣaṇṇā, lalitā, kekarā, vikośā, vibhrāntā, vidyutā, trastā, madirā c' êti. rasa|bhedād aṣṭadhā rasa | dṛṣṭiḥ: kāntā, hāsyā, karuṇā, raudrā, vīrā, bhayānakā, bībhats", âdbhutā c' êti ṣaṭ|triṃśad|bhedā dṛṣṭayaḥ. kuṇitā, vikasit", ârdha|vikasitā, cakitā, suptā, ghūrṇit", âlasā, vivartit", ârdha | vivartitā, paryastā, śunyā, stimitā c 'êty | ādayo dṛṣṭi|bhedā ūhanīyāḥ. tatra lalitā yathā:

manasija|nṛpatir vā,
    maṇḍanaṃ vā mado vā,
  śaśi|mukhi, bhavanaṃ vā,
    yauvanaṃ vā, vayaṃ vā—
akhilam api kṛt'|ârthaṃ
    vīci|vikṣepa|khelat|
  kamala|vijaya|līlā|
    śālinā locanena. [1]

glānā yathā:

paryast'|âlaka|rociṣaḥ, śrama|juṣaḥ,
    praspanda|gaṇḍa|tviṣaḥ,
  Śambhau śīkara|śītalena śaśinā

FROM THE STABLE emotions are produced looks,* which are of eight types: the amorous, amused, sad, angry, energetic, afraid, disgusted, and wonder-struck. From the transitory emotions also are produced looks, which are of twenty types: the vacant, dark, exhausted, embarrassed, doubtful, closed, half-closed, fatigued, side-long, skewed, speculative, distressed, depressed, seductive, squinty, wide-eyed, wild-eyed, flashing, timorous, and drunken. And given the differentiation among rasas, there are also eight rasa-looks: the loving, funny, piteous, furious, heroic, fearful, disgusting, and amazing. There are thus in sum thirty-six looks. Other types of looks can be extrapolated from these, including the hurt, blossomed, half-blossomed, frightened, sleepy, rolling, languorous, open, half-open, crossed, vacant,* frozen, etc. An example of the seductive look: 8.1

His majesty the God of love,
your jewelry and passion,
the house where you live, O moon-faced girl,
your youth, and we ourselves
have all found their purpose in life
thanks to something lovely
as a lotus playfully bobbing
on a wave-swept pond—your eye.

An example of the fatigued look:

As she lay exhausted, her glorious hair disheveled,
her cheeks glistening with sweat,
and Shiva fanned her with his crescent moon*
cooled by droplets of nectar,

vātaṃ samātanvati,
jīyāstām Acal'|âdhirāja|duhitur
niḥspanda|nīl'|ôtpala|
cchāyā|nidrita|cañcarīka|mithuna|
spardhā|samṛddhe dṛśau. [2]

8.5 evam anyā apy udāharaṇīyāḥ.

atha rasānāṃ janya|janaka|bhāvaḥ. tatra Bharataḥ:

«śṛṅgārāt tu bhavedd hāsyo,
raudrāc ca karuṇo mataḥ;
vīrāt syād adbhut'|ôtpattir,
bībhatsāc ca bhayānakaḥ.»

ayam utsargaḥ, pareṣām api rasānāṃ kārya|kāraṇa|bhāva| darśanāt. pūrva|granthakāra|sammatir api:

«kathā|saṅgraha|yogāc ca, vivakṣā|vaśataḥ kaveḥ,
anyonyaṃ janya|janakā rasa|bhāvā bhavanty amī.»

8.10 yathā:

mātur dṛṣṭvā dṛg|ambho|
ruha|yugala|galad|bāṣpa|dhārām udārāṃ,
tātasya prekṣya vakṣaḥ|
sthala|rudhira|cayaṃ, krudhyatā Bhārgaveṇa
haste nyastaḥ Sahasr'|Âr-
juna|damana|samārambha|gambhīra|vīrya|
sphūrjad|dor|valli|hallī-
saka|sakala|kalā|sūtra|dhāraḥ kuṭhāraḥ. [3]

---

[i] Shiva's wife, Párvati, daughter of the Himálaya

the daughter of the Mountain King[i] looked
at him—
and all glory to those eyes
that vied in beauty with two bees asleep
in the shade of a motionless lotus.

In the same way illustrations for all the others could be adduced. 8.5

Rasas can have a generative relationship with other rasas. Thus Bhárata:

> "The comic can be produced by the erotic, the pitiful by the furious; the amazing can arise from the heroic, and the fearful from the disgusting."*

This is only a general formulation, since we find that other rasas, too, stand in causal relationship with yet other rasas. Earlier scholars likewise concur in this view:

> "Depending on the construction of the narrative or the intention of the poet, rasas and feelings can be mutually generative."*

An example: 8.10

Seeing the swollen stream of tears that gushed
from his mother's lotus eyes,
and the blood that streamed from his father's chest,
Bhárgava flew into a rage
and took in hand his axe, that dancing master
expert in all the ballet arts
of arms entwined in the heroic undertaking
of killing Thousand-armed Árjuna.*

atra vīraṃ prati karuṇa|bībhatsayoḥ kāraṇatā. yathā vā tāta|pādānām:

kuraṅg'|âkṣyā veṇīṃ,
subhaga, viparīte rati|vidhāv
adhi|skandhaṃ dṛṣṭvā
kim api nipatantīm ari|bhaṭaḥ,
adhi|grīvaṃ yuṣmat|
pracala|karavāla|vyatikaraṃ
smarann eva stabdho
viramati parīrambhaṇa|rasāt. [4]

atra bhayānakaṃ prati śṛṅgārasya kāraṇatā. yathā vā:

8.15 yudhi kupita|kṛt'|ânta|
syandana|spardhi|nādaṃ
diśi diśi Daśa|kaṇṭhas
tyaktavān vārid'|âstram.
taḍiti Janaka|putryāḥ
sāmyam ālokyamānas
tyajati na pavan'|âstraṃ
Rāghavaḥ svinna|pāṇiḥ. [5]

atra śṛṅgāraṃ prati vīrasya kāraṇatā.

---

[i] Sita [ii] The Wind Weapon counteracts the Cloud Weapon by dispersing it.

In the above poem, the rasas of pity and disgust function as causes with respect to the heroic rasa.* Another example, from my honored father:

As the doe-eyed girl was making love
on top, your enemy,
my lucky king, caught sight of her long braid
somehow falling upon his shoulder,
and remembering the action of your sword
as it once swept by his throat,
he went stiff as a board and lost his taste
for the pleasure of her embrace.

In the above poem, the erotic rasa functions as a cause with respect to the fearful. Another example:

As the battle raged Ten-necked 8.15
Rávana released far and wide
a Cloud Weapon that equaled the din
of the chariot of wrathful Death,
but seeing the likeness of Jánaki[i]
in the lightning of the clouds,
Rama began to sweat and his hands
couldn't wield the Wind Weapon.[ii]

In the above poem, the heroic rasa functions as a cause with respect to the erotic.

eteṣām aṅg'|âṅgi|bhāv'|āpannānāṃ rasa|saṅkara iti nāma lokā lapanti. rasānāṃ mitho virodho 'pi. tatra Bharataḥ:

«śṛṅgāra|bībhatsa|rasau,
tathā vīra|bhayānakau,
raudr'|âdbhutau, tathā hāsya|
karuṇau vairiṇau mithaḥ.»

vairi|rasa iva vairi|rasasya vibhāv'|ânubhāva|vyabhicāri| bhāvā api rasa|hāni|karā, iti tān api vārayet. tatra prācīna| sammatiḥ:

8.20 «na ca vairi|rasaṃ brūyād, vairiṇo na vibhāvakam,
n' ânubhāvaṃ, na sañcāri|bhāvaṃ c' âpi kadā cana.»

iti. kin tv aṅg'|âṅgi|bhāv'|ân|āpannayor eka|deśe sati vairam. deśa|bhede sati na vairam, vṛkṣe kapi|saṃyoga|tad| a|bhāvayor iva. samaya|bhede sat' îty api na vairam, bhū| tale ghaṭa|tad|a|bhāvayor iva. vairaṃ yathā:

priyeṇ' āliṅgyamānāyāḥ priyāyāḥ kuca|kumbhayoḥ
karaja|kṣata|nirmuktaṃ rudhiraṃ kuṅkumāyate. [6]

These rasas can enter into a relationship of dominant and subordinate, to which people give the name "commingling of rasas." Rasas can also be mutually contradictory, as Bhárata says:

> "The erotic and the disgusting rasas, the heroic and the fearful, the furious and the amazing, the comic and the pitiful stand in a relationship of mutual conflict."*

Just like a conflictual rasa itself, its underlying factors, stimulant factors, reactions, and transitory emotions can cause damage to the rasa and so should be avoided. The ancients are in consensus on this point:

> "One should not give voice to a conflictual rasa, 8.20
> nor to its factors, reactions, or transitory emotions, under any circumstances."*

However, with respect to two rasas that have not entered into a relationship of dominant and subordinate, there is conflict only if they are located in a single place; if they are in different places there is no conflict, as in the case of a monkey in one part of tree but not in another. There is also no conflict if they occur at different times, as in the case of a pot that at one time is on the ground but at another time is not. An example of conflict:

> As the lover embraced his beloved, the blood
> bloomed like vermilion on her breasts where he had
> scratched her.

deśa|bhede sati virodh'|âbhāvo yathā:

ekaḥ Sindhubhuvaḥ kare vilulitaś,
cakre dvitīyaḥ sthitaḥ,
Kāma|dhvaṃsini Kālakūṭa|kavala|
kliṣṭe tṛtīyo dhṛtaḥ,
bhūyaḥ kṣīra|nidher ghana|pramathane
saktaś caturthas tathā—
pāyāsuḥ Kamalā|pater bhagavato
nānā|rasāḥ pāṇayaḥ. [7]

8.25 atra śṛṅgāra|raudra|karuṇ'|âdbhutānāṃ rasānāṃ virodh'|â|bhāvaḥ. samaya|bhedena yathā:

bhagnaṃ Kāma|ripor dhanuḥ, parihṛtaṃ
rājyaṃ, sthitaṃ kānane,
nirbhinnas Triśirāḥ, Kharasya piśitaṃ
spṛṣṭaṃ, kapir lālitaḥ,
Laṅk''|ēśo dalitaś, cirāya ruditaṃ
Laṅkā|vadhūnāṃ śrutaṃ,
nītā sadma Videha|bhūs—tad|akhilaṃ
Rāmasya lok'|ôttaram. [8]

atr' âdbhuta|śānta|bhayānaka|raudra|bībhatsa|hāsya|vīra|karuṇa|śṛṅgārāṇāṃ virodh'|âbhāvaḥ.

---

[i] Tri·shiras and Khara are two *rákshasas* slain by Rama. [ii] Sita

If there is a difference of place, there is no contradiction. An example:

One trembles on the hand of Sea-born Lakshmi,
the second takes up the discus,
the third holds Shiva, slayer of Love, tormented
by swallowing the cosmic poison,
the fourth stands ready to continue churning
the primeval ocean of milk—
may blessed Vishnu's hands and their many rasas,
provide you with protection.*

In the above poem there is no contradiction among the rasas: the erotic, the furious, the pitiful, and the amazing, respectively. Nor if they occur at different times, as in the following example: 8.25

Breaking the bow of Shiva, renouncing kingship,
dwelling in the dreadful jungle,
slaying Tri·shiras, touching Khara's mangled flesh,[i]
coddling the monkey king,
killing the lord of Lanka, listening long
to the weeping Lanka women,
taking Vaidéhi[ii] home—all this is the work,
the supernatural work, of Rama.

In the above poem there is no contradiction among the rasas: the amazing, tranquil, fearful, furious, disgusting, comic, heroic, pitiful, and erotic, respectively.

aṅg'|âṅgi|bhāv'|ân|āpannānāṃ rasānāṃ niveśo yatra sa rasa|śabala iti veditavyam. tasy' âpy etad ev' ôdāharaṇam.

aṅgayor vaire 'pi na rasa|hānir, bhaṭayor vaire prabhor iva. yathā:

8.30 Sītāṃ saṃsmarya vīci|
pracala|kuvalaya|spardhi|cakṣuḥ kṣipantīṃ,
senāṃ saṃvīkṣya rakṣaḥ|
śara|dalita|vapuḥ|śoṇit'|āsāra|siktām,
Rāmeṇa krodha|dṛpyad|
Daśa|mukha|nipatan|muṇḍa|lābha|pramoda|
krīḍat|Kālī|karāla|
bhru|kuṭi|sahacarī sandadhe cāpa|yaṣṭiḥ. [9]

atra śṛṅgāra|bībhatsayor virodhe 'pi na rasa|hāniḥ. evam aṅg'|âṅgi|bhāv'|âpannayor virodhinor ekatra bhāve 'pi na rasa|hāniḥ. yathā:

bhaujaṅgamaṃ, girimayaṃ, jalad'|ātmakaṃ vā
śastraṃ yad eva mumuce Daśa|kandhareṇa,
sarvaṃ Videha|tanayā|virah'|ākulena
Rāmeṇa vahnimaya|śastram iva vyaloki. [10]

Where there is an arrangement of rasas that have not entered into a relationship of dominant and subordinate we have what is known as a mosaic of rasas. The preceding poem serves as an illustration of this as well.

While two subordinate rasas might be in conflict, there is no damage to the rasa, just as there is no damage to a king when two of his soldiers are in conflict. An example:

> Thinking of Sita, how she would cast her glances 8.30
> that vied with blue lotuses stirred by waves,
> and seeing his army splashed with streams of blood,
> their bodies torn by *rákshasa* arrows,
> Rama took his bow in hand, the very image
> of the frowning awful brows of Kali
> dancing for joy at each falling skull she took
> from the furious Ten-faced demon.

In the above poem there is no damage to the rasa even though there is a contradiction between the erotic and the disgusting. Similarly, even when two contradictory rasas in a relationship of dominant and subordinate are found in a single place, there is no damage to the rasa. An example:

> Whatever weapon Rávana launched—
> serpentine, aqueous, adamantine—
> seemed to Rama, in his longing
> for Sita, to become a weapon of fire.*

nanu bībhatsa | śṛṅgārayoḥ saha | jaṃ vairam kutaḥ? madhu nipīya niṣṭhīvatoḥ sambhoga | darśanād iti cet— satyam. bībhatsasya jugupsā sthāyi|bhāvaḥ. sā ca tad|darśanena taṭa|sthasya bhavati, na tu tayo, rāg' | āutkaṭyād iti. nanu tath" âpi bībhatse śṛṅgāro dṛśyate. tathā hi:

yad api hṛdi viśālā muṇḍa|mālā, na pāṇis
tyajati nara|kapālaṃ, rauravaṃ carma|cailam,
tad api Giri|sutāyāḥ pakṣa|pātaḥ Purārau
samudayati—vicitraḥ kāminoḥ prema|bandhaḥ.
[11]

8.35 ity|ādāv iti cet, satyam. nija|bhartur adhame 'pi bhūṣaṇe bhakty | atiśayena patnyās tatra jugups" âiva n' âvatarati. jugupsitatvena pratīyamānam eva hi jugups" | ôtpādakaṃ bhavati. kiṃ ca priya|sambandh'|ôpādhikam adhikaṃ tatra prem' âiv' ôtpadyate. tasmāt sthāyi|bhāv'|â|bhāvād bībhatsas tatra na jāyata iti.

nanu vīrasya yudhi gacchataḥ sarpa|sparśe cakitatā dṛśyate, raudre c' ākasmik' | ôtpāt' | âtipāte vismaya iti cet— satyaṃ; cakitatā vismayaś ca tatra tatra ras' | āveśān na

One might object that the disgusting and the erotic are not irreducibly conflictual, since we find such things as lovers taking pleasure in drinking and spraying each other with rum. That may be true, but revulsion is the stable emotion of the disgusting, and that arises in an outside observer of the act, not in the two who are in the throes of passion. Even so, one might object further, we find the erotic in the disgusting, in such poems as the following:

> Although he wears upon his chest
> a necklace of heads and his hand
> never releases the human skull
> or the antelope skin he wears,
> still the Mountain's daughter adores
> the Enemy of the City—
> how inscrutable the bond of affection
> that unites two lovers.*

While that may be true, there is not the slightest sense 8.35
of revulsion in the wife at her husband's lowly adornment because of the high degree of her devotion to him. For only something that is perceived as revolting can become a source of revulsion. On the contrary, what actually arises in this case is a more intense love conditioned by their bond of affection. Accordingly, given the absence of the requisite stable emotion, the disgusting rasa does not come into being in this poem.

One might further object that when a hero is heading into battle, we find that he might touch a snake and be frightened; or when a man is in a fury, that he might feel wonder at the sudden appearance of a portent. While that

bhavaty eva, sati vā viṣaya|bhedo. vīrasya na pratibhaṭād bhayaṃ, kin tu bhujaṅgāt. raudre ca na pratibaṭa|bal'|ādhikye vismayaḥ, kin t' ûtpāte.

rasa|vairasy' ôtpādakam akhilam avadheyam. tatra pūrv'|ācāryāḥ:

«anyac ca rasa|vairasy' ôtpādakaṃ vacanaṃ tathā
na vācyaṃ rasa|bhāva|jñair nāṭya|śāstra|viśāradaiḥ.»

vacanam ity upalakṣaṇam evaṃ vibhāv'|ânubhāveṣv api draṣṭavyam.

8.40 kv' âhaṃ, kva tvaṃ? kva madhu|samayaḥ,
kutra vā dūtik" âsau,
megha|cchāyā|pravicalam idaṃ
prema vā kutra yūnoḥ?
āyur vāyu|pracala|nalinī|
vāri|bind'|ûpamānaṃ.
mānaṃ, mugdhe, visṛja sakalaṃ—
tuccham eva pratīmaḥ. [12]

atra nirveda|pratipādakam akhilaṃ, tac ca śṛṅgāra|virodhi. an|aucityaṃ sarvath" âvadheyam. tatra prācīna|grantha|kṛtaḥ:

may be true, the fright in the one case and the wonder in the other do not come about in conjunction with a rasa; and even if we were to admit that they did, there is a difference in object: the hero fears not an enemy but a snake; and the man in a fury feels wonder not at the presence of the enemy's overwhelming force but rather at the presence of a portent.

In general, anything that produces a conflict of rasas must be carefully avoided. Earlier teachers have addressed this:

> "Any speech that may produce a conflict of rasas must not be spoken, according to those skilled in dramaturgy, men who know rasas and feelings."*

"Speech" is meant to comprise factors as well as reactions.

What have we in common, you and I? 8.40
The spring, that go-between,
a young couple's love, more changeable
than a shadow cast by a cloud,
while life is like a droplet on a lotus
buffeted by the breeze.
Give up your anger, innocent girl—nothing
has any meaning at all.

In the above poem, the entire speech communicates dispassion, and that is contradictory to the erotic. Impropriety must by all means be carefully avoided. The ancient writers have addressed this:

«an|aucityād ṛte n' ânyad
  rasa|bhaṅgasya kāraṇam.
prasiddh'|āucitya|bandhas tu
  rasasy' ôpaniṣat parā.»

iti. udvega | karam an | aucityam. loka | yātrā | prasiddhi | siddhatvam† aucityam. tasmād dvayor yūnor yatra mitho ratis, tatr' âiva rasaḥ. ekasy' âiva ratiś ced, ras' | ābhāsa ev'; âikasyā eva ratiś ced, ras'|ābhāsa eva. krameṇ' ôdāharaṇam:

Sītā|samāgama|ślāghā|
  bandhuraṃ Daśa|kandharam
prahartuṃ kṣamate Kāmo—
  Rāmo vā—niśitaiḥ śaraiḥ. [13]

8.45 atra Rāvaṇasy' âiva ratir na tu Sītāyāḥ.

nidhuvana|vana|
    prānte yāntaṃ calair nayan'|âñcalaiḥ
  kim iti valita|
    grīvaṃ, mugdhe, muhur muhur īkṣase?
viphalam akhilaṃ,
    yūnor no ced udeti parasparaṃ
  ratir. atha mano|
    janmā devaḥ sa eva niṣevyatām. [14]

8.43 *prasiddhisiddhatvam* J : *-prasiddham* Ś

"There is nothing that destroys rasa more than impropriety. Composing in a way that keeps to the canons of propriety is the priceless secret of rasa."*

Impropriety causes disruption, whereas propriety confirms the currency of the general state of affairs. Thus we can have rasa only in the case of a young couple who feel desire for each other. If only the man feels desire, we have what is known as the semblance of rasa, and so also if only the woman does. An example of each, in order:

Rávana is so delirious with desire
at Sita's arrival
that only the sharp arrows of Love can quell him—
or those of Rama.

In the above poem, only Rávana feels desire, not Sita. 8.45

Simple girl, why crane your neck and look again
and again with fluttering glances
at that fellow as he passes by the woods
where people go to make love?
It's all in vain unless a young couple feels
desire for one another.
So there is nothing to do but worship the god
who takes birth in the heart.

atra nāyikāyā eva ratir na tu nāyakasya. evam ekasy' ân|eka|viṣayā ratī ras'|ābhāsa eva. paran tu eṣa viśeṣaḥ. yasya vyavasthitā bahvyo nāyikā bhavanti, tatra na ras'|ābhāsas; tathā sati Kṛṣṇasya sakal'|ôttama|nāyakasya bahu|kāminī|viṣayāyā rater ābhāsat" | āpatteḥ. tasmād a | vyavasthita | bahu|kāminī|viṣayaka|vaiśika|nāyaka†|param etat. ata eva vaiśikānāṃ veśyānāṃ ca ras'|ābhāsa iti prācīna|matam. ekasyā an|eka|viṣayā ratir yathā:

sampat kasy' âdya tārā,
bhavati taralitā yat|puro netra|tārā?
dṛṣṭā ken' âdya Kāñcī,
yad|abhimukha|gatā vepate ratna|kāñcī?
Ugraḥ kasy' âdya tuṣṭaḥ,
sakhi, yad|anugame kaś cid ugro 'bhitāpaḥ?
snātaṃ ken' âdya Veṇī|
payasi, vilulitā yat|kṛte k" âpi veṇī? [15]

atra kimo bāhulyena veśyātvam.

8.50 ekasy' ân|eka|viṣayā ratir yathā:

8.47 *-kāminīviṣayakavaiśikanāyaka-* B : *-kāminīkavaiśikaṃ nāyaka-* J : *-kāminīkavaiṣayikabahunāyaka-* Ś

In the above poem, only the *náyika* feels desire, not the *náyaka*. Similarly, if one man feels desire for many women at the same time, we have a semblance of rasa. But there is one distinction to be drawn: For someone who has a determinate number of multiple *náyika*s, there is no semblance of rasa. Otherwise, Krishna, the supreme *náyaka* of all, whose desire is directed to multiple lovers, would turn out to have a semblance of desire. Hence the definition concerns a *náyaka* who is a libertine, whose object of desire is an indeterminate number of lovers. Accordingly, the view of the ancients is that semblance of rasa applies to libertines and courtesans. An example of one woman feeling desire for many men:

> Who just acquired so vast a fortune to make
> you bat your eyes in front of him?
> Who just saw holy Kanchi, that the gems
> on your belt should shimmer before him?
> Who just appeased the awful Shiva, my friend,
> that you feel such awful pain when he leaves?
> Who just bathed at the River Braid that your braid,
> your gorgeous braid, should be loosened for him?*

The multiple use of "who" shows this is a courtesan.*

An example of one man feeling desire for many women: 8.50

pañc'|êṣu|kṣitipa|pratāpa|laharī|
prītis tvadīyā punaḥ:*
kāsāṃ na stana|kāñcan'|âcala|taṭe
kāśmīrapaṅkāyate?
kāsāṃ mūrdhani n' âiva paṅkaja|dṛśāṃ
sindūralekhāyate?
kāsāṃ vā na ca karṇayoḥ, priya|sakhe,
māṇikyabhūṣāyate? [16]

atr' âpi vaiśikatā prāgvad eva.

yatra rasā bahavaḥ sa rasa|śabalaḥ. yatra bhāvā bahavaḥ sa bhāva|śabalaḥ. atra rasa|śabalo darśitaḥ. bhāva|śabalo yathā:

pravrajy" âiva śubhāya me! śruti|pathaṃ
jāyeta tasyā vacaś!
cakr'|âgre mama kaḥ Smaras? tri|jagatī
śūnyā vinā Rādhayā.
nirmukt" âiva manas|trapā? mṛga|dṛśo
lāvaṇyam anyādṛśaṃ.
dhig janma! kva gat" âsi? kiṃ vilapitaiḥ?
kv' âsi? prasannā bhava! [17]

8.55 nirved' | āutsuky' | âmarṣa | bhrama | mati | smṛti | viṣāda | dainyānāṃ* bhāvānāṃ sāṅkaryād eṣa bhāva|śabala iti.

---

[i] Krishna speaks.

Your passion is a wave of the power
of the king, the God of love:
what women's golden moundlike breasts
has it not stained like saffron,
what women's heads, with their lotus eyes,
has it not marked like vermilion,
and on what women's ears, my friend,
has it not hung like earrings?

In the above verse, too, we are presented with a libertine, for the reason stated for the previous example.

Where there are many rasas we have a mosaic of rasas, and where many emotions, a mosaic of emotions. The mosaic of rasas has already been shown. An example of a mosaic of emotions:[i]

Renunciation is my one salvation!
If only I could hear her voice!
Who is Love in the face of my discus? The universe
is utterly empty without Radha.
Have I completely lost all shame? The woman's
beauty is without equal.
A curse on my birth! Where have you gone?
What use is weeping? Where are you? Be kind!

This mixture of despair, longing, vindictiveness, confu- 8.55
sion, wisdom, remembrance, depression, and despondency produces a mosaic of emotions.*

atha rasa | bhāv' | âlaṅkārāṇām abhivyaktiḥ. rasas tri | vidho 'bhimukho vimukhaḥ para | mukhaś c' êti. vyaktair bhāva|vibhāv'|ânubhāvair yasy' âbhivyaktiḥ so 'bhimukhaḥ. bhāva | vibhāv' | ânubhāvānām an | uktatvāt kaṣṭ' | âvagamo vimukhaḥ. para | mukho 'pi dvi | vidho 'laṅkāra | mukho bhāva | mukhaś c' êti. alaṅkāra | mukhe 'laṅkāro mukhyo mano|viśrāma|hetutvād, raso gauṇaḥ. bhāva|mukhe bhāvo mukhyo mano|viśrāma|hetutvād, raso gauṇaḥ. atra prācīna| sammatiḥ:

> «alaṅkāre ca rucire
>   mano|viśrānti|kāriṇi
> alaṅkārasya mukhyatvaṃ,
>   gauṇatvaṃ rasa|bhāvayoḥ.»

iti. abhimukhāḥ sva|sva|prakaraṇa udāhṛtā eva. vimukho yathā:

> Maithilī, Lakṣmaṇo, Rāmaḥ,
>   Sugrīvaḥ, Pavan'|ātmajaḥ
> Laṅkā|puraṃ parityajya
>   pāraṃ vāri|nidher yayuḥ. [18]

8.60 atra saṅkaṭam akhilaṃ samuttīry' âite samāgatā, ity adbhuto rasaḥ kaṣṭād avagamyate.

---

[i] Sita [ii] Hánuman

Finally, we turn to the manifestation of rasas, emotions, and figures of sense. Rasa is three-fold, being direct, oblique, or mediated. Rasa is direct when it is manifested by emotions, factors, and reactions that are themselves clearly manifest. It is oblique when emotions, factors and reactions are not clearly stated, and it is therefore hard to understand. It is mediated in two ways: by means of either a figure of sense or an emotion. When rasa is mediated by means of a figure, the figure is primary because it is there that the mind comes to repose, and the rasa is secondary; when it is mediated by way of an emotion, the emotion is primary because it is there that the mind comes to repose, and the rasa is also secondary. The ancients are in consensus on this point:

> "When there is a striking figure that causes the mind to pause, the figure is primary and the rasa and emotion secondary."*

The direct rasas have been exemplified each in its own section. An example of an oblique rasa:

> Máithili,[i] Lákshmana, and Rama,
> Sugríva, and the son of the Wind,[ii]
> abandoning the city of Lanka
> crossed to the ocean's further shore.*

In the above poem the amazing rasa—which derives from the fact that the persons mentioned overcame all adversity and were reunited—is very hard to grasp. 8.60

alaṅkāra|mukho yathā:

eṣā na lekhā bhramatām alīnāṃ
bhāti prabhāte nava|kairaviṇyāḥ.
āliṅgataḥ kin tu tuṣāra|bhānoḥ
kāntiḥ kalaṅkasya vapur|vilagnā.* [19]

atr' âpahnuter alaṅkārasya mukhyatā.

bhāva|mukho yathā:

8.65 sapt'|âmbho|nidhi|nīra|hīra|paṭal'|â-
laṅ|kāriṇīṃ medinīṃ
dātuṃ vipra|kulāya yojitavataḥ
saṅkalpa|vāky'|ôdyamam
nābhī|nīraruhāt saroruha|bhuvā
tat|kālam āviṣ|kṛte
hast'|âmbhoruhi Bhārgavasya kim api
vrīḍā†|smitaṃ pātu vaḥ [20]

atr' âdbhuta|bhāvasya mukhyatā. dāna|vīra|raso gauṇaḥ.

vidvad|vāridharāḥ *snehaṃ* tathā varṣata santatam,
labhate vipulāṃ vṛddhiṃ yathā Rasataraṅgiṇī. [21]

8.65 *vrīḍā-* J : *krīḍā-* Ś

---

[i] The blue lotus blossoms in moonlight.

An example of mediation by means of a figure of sense:

Those can't be bees on the blue lotuses—
bees do not appear at dawn.
It must instead be the mark of the moon[i]
left on their bodies from its embrace.

In the above poem the figure known as denial is primary.

An example of mediation by means of an emotion:

When Bhárgava undertook his declared intention 8.65
to bestow as a gift upon the brahmins
the whole world adorned with those masses
of diamonds, the seven seas,
at that moment the god born in the lotus
reached out from the navel lotus
his lotus hand, which brought a smile of shame
to Bhárgava—may it protect you.*

In the above poem, the emotion of amazement is primary and the heroic rasa, of the munificence subvariety, is secondary.

May those rain clouds—men of learning—
forever pour down their *moisture : affection*
so this "River of Rasa" will grow
ever greater in grandeur.

avagāhasva, vāg|devi, divyāṃ Rasataraṅgiṇīm;
asmat|padyena padmena racaya śruti|bhūṣaṇam. [22]

yāvad Bhānoḥ sutā k" âpi Kālindī bhuvi vartate,
tāvat tiṣṭhatu me Bhānor eṣā Rasataraṅgiṇī. [23]

8.70 iti śrī|Bhānudatta|miśra|viracitāyāṃ
Rasataraṅgiṇyāṃ prakīrṇakaṃ nām' âṣṭamas taraṅgaḥ.

Goddess of Language, plunge
into this "River of Rasa"
and make of this lotus, my verse,
an ornament for your ear.

As long as the Kálindi flows on earth,
the daughter of Bhanu the sun,
may this work of mine stay current,
Bhanu's River of Rasa.

The end of the Miscellany, the Eighth Wave of Bhanu·datta's "River of Rasa." 8.70

NOTES

Bold *references are to the English text;* ***bold italic*** *references are to the Sanskrit text. An asterisk (*) in the body of the text marks the word or passage being annotated.*

Bouquet of Rasa

2 [1] Ś reports the v.l. *dadāti* (for ***dadhāti***) in *a*. There is some disagreement about the accusative reading ***antaḥpremabharālasām***. For A, N (disputed by V; G reads *antaḥpremarasālasām*), this emphasizes Gaurī's love for Śiva, which establishes the reciprocity between lovers that is required if the erotic rasa is to be successful. It would also explain why Śiva is worried about Gaurī's fatigue. Ś reads the nominative *-bharālasaḥ* (N reports the reading *-rasālasaḥ*) and criticizes the accusative reading, claiming that a cause for Śiva's actions must be provided.

2 [1] The verse plays upon the image of the androgynous Śiva. His wife Gaurī occupies the left half of his body, and Śiva does everything possible with the other half to spare her any discomfort. I add **right to side** with A. The **flower** is something Gaurī herself wants as an ornament (N) or for their lovemaking (Ś).

4 **Husband**: *svāmin*, "master" or even "owner." The word is probably used to allow for the possibility that the woman and man are not married. All related terms used here, including "husband" (*bhartṛ*, *pati*) and "married," are often rendered ambiguous by the commentators and cannot be translated uniformly throughout the poem; attention to context often requires flexibility.

4 **This definition** ...: the ŚM (p. 3) critiques the RM's position here at length.

5 **Obedience**, *śuśrūṣā*, is missing in some MSS.; *ārjavam* is offered by all MSS. and editions; but OG understands "sweet

temper" (*komalabhāva*), suggesting that the Sanskrit before the eyes of the translator was *mārdavam*. But the verse seems to mention (as we expect it to do) the four traits of the definition one after the other. "Obedience" is therefore required, and there is no room for OG's "sweet temper," which is also made redundant by *kṣamā*.

6 [3] **Highborn women**: taking *natabhrū* in the sense of woman, and *kulanatabhrū* as equal to *kulavadhū*. Alternatively: "those who lower their eyes even in the presence of family members," let alone others (A). The translation attempts to capture both senses. Such women never look around to see what is going on (since they are preoccupied with obediently serving their husbands, so A), and they never bare their teeth when they smile (see RT 7.1). The verse is cited (without being recognized as such) in *Ain-i Akbari* (trans. JARRETT), p. 256.

7 **She may or may not understand its manifestations**: according to A: whose manifestations are not understood, i.e., by another, or whose manifestations are understood by her, and he calls attention specifically to the girl's understanding in 13 [6].

7 **Of her actions**: commentators disagree on whether *kriyā* is in compound. N is adamant, and I follow him.

9 [4] The syntax of the first two *pāda*s allows other constructions (I follow Ś; V understands *ājñaptam* as impersonal passive). *Pāda*s *c–d*, literally, "the play of the wagtail is commanded [to be provided] by her glance..." Commentators strive here, without great success, to find the three kinds of characteristics of the new bride (behavior enchanting for its modesty, moderate love-anger, eagerness for new ornaments) in her glancing eye, her ambrosial glow, and the constantly changing waves of her speech. What is not clear is how the verse illustrates (as it should, in view of the typology and the following verse) the naïve *nāyikā* who does not understand the manifestations of

puberty. The wagtail bird is a common sexual symbol in Sanskrit poetry; some commentators here connect it with the girl's black darting eyes or her bashfulness (since the bird shows itself only infrequently) or her hidden excellences, since there is a tradition that the wagtail appears over buried treasure (V, N). For *d*, cf. Byron: "There be none of Beauty's daughters / With a magic like thee; / And like music on the waters / Is thy sweet voice to me" ("Stanzas for Music"). OG understands that womanhood is commanded by the God of love to dwell in the body itself. All the commentators take the king, the Love god, to be preparing a fortress where he himself can reside and launch his conquest of the world.

11 [5] N, V rightly remark that it is self-evident that the *nāyikā* would have seen the **lotus petal** in her reflection in the water. The **line of hair** appearing at the navel with the onset of puberty is a favorite image of Sanskrit poets.

13 [6] How the verse demonstrates the girl's understanding vexes the C. N (as well as Ś) is probably correct: the only reason the friend asks this question is because she knows her friend to be sophisticated enough to answer it. Or rather: the very question presupposes that the *nāyikā* understands the manifestations of womanhood. The verse includes a pun: Since your breasts are **self-existent** and **all-gracious** (and even perhaps "water/milk-bearing," i.e., **Ganga-bearing**), that is, since they are Śiva, they must be crowned with a crescent moon, as Śiva himself.

17 [8] **One hand on her belt**: A, N, and others point out that *nīvī*, "belt," can also signify "treasure."

18 **Because of her extreme compliance**: A notes that this sentence may be an interpolation but he finds ways to allow it (it is given in U). G remarks that the line is a variant and both unexemplified in the treatise and impossible (*yā hy atidhārṣṭyavatī tasyāṃ kathaṃ prayuktavakṣyamāṇamadhyāvyavahārasaṃbhavaḥ*, presumably in reference to the trait in the following sentence,

since the "insolence" of the average *nāyikā* is nowhere else described).

18 Examples of these last two traits are not provided, and they seem out of place, since they are discussed after the second illustration of the "experienced" woman in 23 [11].

19 [9] **My love**: it is her "lover" rather than her "husband," say A and N (being perhaps too clever), and this explains her anxiety of losing the chance to see him. In pl. 9, the twist of the verse is realized in the *nāyikā*'s pulling her sari up around her, indicating sleep (cf. pl. 18 and pl. 65), while her eyes remain wide open.

20 Most commentators read *asyās tu* for ***asyās***.

20 As several commentators point out, what follows are two different subtypes of *pragalbhā nāyikā*, not the behavior of one and the same; as A states, the examples "first" and "second" that follow bear this out.

21 [10] The dual **ears** with the singular **lotus** is hard to explain (A and V claim unpersuasively that the one lotus serves to ornament both ears). The plural **hems** suggests she is hiding all the petals of the lotus (Ś). Blue lotuses bloom at dawn. A observes that the lover desires to know if the **god ... who rules day-blooming flowers**, i.e. sun, has risen for either of two reasons. The first is because it would then be time to cease (according to the injunction, "One should not make love in the daytime"; various commentators point out that the word "god" hints it is time for the morning worship of the sun). This is more likely, and would explain the *nāyikā*'s actions (note that it cannot mean it's time for him to go away, since this is "his own" *nāyikā*, though this is apparently how the OG takes it). The second reason is because the woman is one of the types of *nāyikā* who can achieve climax only in the daylight (the *padminī*, he cites *Anaṅgaraṅga* 1.20 to this effect), and the lover, having performed foreplay

(*bāhyarata*), desires to know whether it is time to begin intercourse (*āntararata*; this interpretation would mean that the *nāyikā* prefers that he continue foreplay rather than begin intercourse, and might construe better with the definition of the first type of "sophisticated" *nāyikā*). Yet another interpretation combines the two: he is not aware that she is a *padminī*-type of woman, though she is, and she does not want him to break off his lovemaking.

23 [11] The v.l. in *a* reported by A (*dale* for ***tale***) and accepted by V (by reason of the alliteration) is found in U (G reads *tale*).

23 [11] ***kva* ... *kva*** are adversative (so Ś), rather than coordinate (thus A, N, V); that is: how could I have remembered (generally), let alone remembered the lovemaking or your advice?

24 **The average and the experienced**: A asks why the types of anger response are not attributed to the naïve *nāyikā* and concludes that they should have been, as least in the case of the naïve *nāyikā* who understands the manifestations of puberty.

26 [12] In *a*, *lola-* could of course be vocative, "inconstant" (so V). One assumes the last line is sarcastic: it is no more likely that he became sweaty from going off to the dark cool forest than that she could cool him down with a single lotus leaf (Sh takes it improbably as an expression of the *nāyikā*'s good will). The implication of the plural "bees"—that there are many lovers (suggested by Ś; A takes *āli*/*ālī* as a *śleṣa*, in the second sense signifying "girlfriends," that is, her rivals)—is not borne out by the painted version (*Lalitkalā* 23; the *nāyikā* in the painting's lower right-hand corner is presumably putting on her jewelry again after lovemaking). V rejects the interpretation (that a single *nāyaka* would be making love with multiple *nāyikā*s in the grove) as violating convention (*asāṃpradāyika*).

28 [13] U reads *bahutaraṃ* for ***hutavaha-*** in *d*.

28 [13] The **redness** in the *nāyikā*'s eyes is from her anger (Ś). Bhānu's verse is cited in the *Ain-i Akbari* (trans. Jarrett) p. 257. The

U illustration of this verse, now in the Kanoria collection, is reproduced in "Indian Paintings from Rajasthan."

30 [14] I read ***nātho*** with G, Ś, Triv. A, and B, U, and OG (which is to be taken ironically, as G notes, *nātho 'si prabhur asi. upatāpako 'sīti vakroktiḥ*); A, N have *yogyo* ("eligible").

30 [14] The first half of the verse shows her steadiness, the second, her unsteadiness. In the first, she could be speaking as easily about the perception of another woman as of her own, hence her sarcastic cleverness. A observes, "In these [foregoing] examples, the coherence (*saṅgati*) of the woman's being an average *nāyikā* is suspect," that is, it is not easy to see how they show the woman to be average. The U illustration of this verse, now in the Cleveland Art Museum, may be found at http://www.clevelandart.org under accession number 1960.52.

32 [15] The woman is angry with her lover, but as an "experienced steady" *nāyikā* she refuses to show it and prefers simply to feign indifference to him (so essentially Ś, V), which constitutes the "indifference to lovemaking" in the definition. N, Ś are correct, I think, in believing that the speaker is the lover (not a girlfriend, as per G, and A, first interpretation); there is no difficulty in the lover's referring to himself as *dayite* (A unnecessarily takes this as a feminine vocative). Ś, Triv. A, U read *parijanakrodha-*, which removes the repetition with *c*.

34 [16] V notes that the descriptor **daughter of the Mountain** (i.e., the Himālaya) would normally be used to indicate that she is firm and steadfast, though here the opposite is implied. For N, the shimmering glow of the bracelet is meant to suggest the terrifying quality of her fury.

36 [17] Ś thinks the lover misinterprets each of her gestures as a sign that she is mollified, and so he proceeds to the next step. The final image is an imaginary one (technically a kind of *utprekṣā*, or poetic fantasy: while a woman's eyes are often compared to

the small, darting *śaphari* fish, here such a fish could compare with her angry glances only if its back were painted with red lacquer.

37 And a "steady more loved" and a "steady less loved" [experienced] *nāyikā*, etc., as well.

39 [18] The woman **wrapped in her veil** (who thereby shows her indifference to lovemaking) is an average *nāyikā*, the other, experienced; they are both angry at his infidelity, which has made them momentary allies (A, N).

43 [20] The U illustration of this verse is published in "Indian Miniature Paintings" (WIENER), p. 47.

44 **Kept hidden**: except from her friends or other perceptive people. ŚM disputes the adequacy of the definition precisely on this point, the knowledge of the *parakīyā*'s attachments—especially since in two of the subvarieties, the discovered and the promiscuous, such knowledge is essential—and therefore rejects the condition "hidden." See also RAGHAVAN 1951: 76.

44 **Total secretiveness**: the unmarried *parakīyā* is never shown to be marked or promiscuous or any of the other varieties.

46 **All three types**: A notes that the third type is implicit in the other two (*arthasamājasiddha*) and does not actually constitute a separate category.

47 [22] The *nāyikā* is attempting to hide the reason for the scratch marks on her body left by her lover. The verse is cited in *Ain-i Akbari* (trans. JARRETT), p. 258. The U artist has produced a striking painting, in narrative terms (see pl. 22). Bhānu says this verse illustrates all three types of *guptā nāyikā*. The commentators say there can be only two types, for the third must be comprised within the second. The lover sucking on a blade of grass (as in pl. 11) is presumably the continuing lover.

51 [24] **The jujube tree** would be the place where she meets her lover.

53 [25] The friend is advising the *nāyikā* (so Ś, V), rather than the reverse (so A, N); this seems to be corroborated by the *ko 'pi* in *d*, which the *nāyikā* would not attribute to herself. (N reports the v.l. *gopi* for *ko 'pi* in *d*.) The verse presented a challenge to the U painter, given the exiguous narrative situation. The question of who speaks is a problem here, too. The hand gestures are no doubt key to the painting, the *nāyikā* perhaps making a denial to her friend, who is showing amazement.

55 [26] The rainy season is conventionally associated with the erotic rasa, and it is therefore meant as an irony that the clouds disappoint the promiscuous girl. **In all the universe**: even the wish-granting trees of heaven do not produce what she most treasures, which adds to her sense of being cursed (N). Ś seems to want a crescendo in her complaints (humans, men, lovers), but that is not easily read out of the text.

56 **Lover**: *bhartuḥ* cannot have its normal sense of "husband," since this is another's *nāyikā*. For V, the three types intimate that the *parakīyā* is not concerned with any particular lover.

57 [27] V tries to justify the compound ***nipatitapatre***, which has an awkward *sāpekṣā* relationship with *-latikāyāḥ*, and suggests either that the latter may be ablative, or, more persuasively, that the correct reading may be *nipatati* (though no MS. offers this).

58 [28] The qualifications in the last two lines indicate, among other things, that the forests are undisturbed by people and offer good camouflage.

59 [29] The **mango** tree would be where the lovers had their meeting place. V: "Rādhā is another's *nāyikā* insofar as she is an unmarried girl, not because she is a married woman, which would be completely inappropriate for someone who is an avatar of Mahālakṣmī." But this is clearly not the view of Bhānu, who does not deal with the unmarried *parakīyā* until 63 [31] (see 44).

61 [30] The situation suggested is that the *nāyikā*'s girlfriend is speaking to a passing stranger. Some commentators understand *taruṇīkuca-* in compound, taking *ātatāna* intransitively, but this makes the construction of *niśamya* awkward.

63 [31] Some commentators read *karṇasya* for *gaṇḍasya* in *c*.

63 [31] The girl is trying to signal her lover while at the same time hiding her message from her nearby friends (Ś, A). A and N provide specific messages intended by each of her movements (e.g., by hiding her bright-white smile she means to indicate that her lover is not to come while the moon is bright). That she is a princess indicates how closely guarded she is and how secretive she must be.

64 **Airávati**: presumably the reference is to Kālidāsa's *Mālavikāgnimitra*, but there Irāvatī (*sic*, so read here only by J) is King Agnimitra's second wife, and I do not see what evidence Bhānu had for thinking of her as a courtesan. At the end of the prose section here A and N include an additional sentence: "Passion for a holy man based on physical beauty is a sporadic condition, whereas with respect to what is invariably concomitant it would appear that wealth is the sole condition." If the *sāmānyavanita* falls in love, with money playing no part, she ceases to be a *sāmānyavanitā*. Passion based on money is therefore invariably concomitant with the definition of the *sāmānyavanitā*, passion based on physical attraction is not, and therefore cannot pertain to the definition.

65 [32] Her **breasts** are, so to say, overjoyed at the thought that they will be receiving a new necklace (A). The U painter here (see pl. 32) exhibits remarkable delicacy in the depiction of the dropping flowers.

66 A notes that the naïve *nāyikā* is not subject to these three additional states.

68 [33] The implication is that the go-between has gone to the man's house and has made love with him; the **garland of flame-tree**

flowers is a euphemism for the love scratches on the girl's body. (It is slightly odd to use a *vakrokti* verse as illustration, since the definition does not require it.) N distinguishes between this *nāyikā* and the *khanditā*, that is, the *nāyikā* whose lover has cheated on her: the latter sees on her lover's body the evidence of lovemaking with another woman, whereas this *nāyikā* sees such evidence on the other woman's body.

73 [35] **His insults**: she is saying that her eyes and speech are incomparable, and yet her lover has the temerity to compare them to such mundane things.

74 That is, her anger is revealed by behavior showing she is aware of her lover's infidelity (A, N).

74 **A semblance of rasa**: love that produces the *śṛṅgāra rasa* must be capable of being consummated. A: such an anger is not real.

75 [36] The variant *bhūṣayati* ("gave her jewelry") for ***bhāṣayati*** ("spoke with her") is found in the U illustration, where the rival is shown pointing to her necklace (pl. 36).

75 [36] **Slender girl**: even her waist affords no place for anger to stand.

77 [37] B: *bhramam* for ***bhramo***.

77 [37] The commentators assume that **swearing an oath by a snake** was a common ordeal, but I know no parallel.

79 [38] I follow V in my interpretation of *c-d* and in reading ***koṇabhāsā*** (this must also be G's reading, given his gloss *prāntakāntyā*). A and N, reading *koṇabhāsaḥ* (which V reports but takes as ablative singular), understand *c-d* as "flashes from the corner [of her eye] released near her ear," or "the flashes from the corner [of her eye] became pearls redder," or "the pearl earrings [brought by the *nāyaka*]," or, "worn by the *nāyaka* who is bowed at her feet". V denies that the pearls at her ear are supposed to be gifts from the lover meant to assuage her anger (so A, and in accordance with the definition and in conformity with the two previous verses that illustrate appeasement), since the lover is not

supposed to be aware of the lac on his forehead and therefore could not have anticipated the *nāyikā*'s anger. On V's interpretation the conciliation (falling at her feet, giving her jewelry) is only implicit in the verse. G interprets ***śikhara*** as "pomegranate seeds," a meaning I have not found for the word.

79 [38] The lover's **forehead** would have become marked either through the inverted position of lovemaking or through bowing to his mistress's feet in an attempt to assuage her own anger (N).

80 **Sixteen types**: that is, the thirteen subtypes comprised of "one's own" (the naïve, the average, and the sophisticated, the latter two of which can be steady, unsteady, or steady-unsteady, and either more loved or less loved), the two types of another's (married and unmarried), and the one type of "common."

80 The three types are described below, from 192. See also ŚT 1.88; NŚ (KM ed.) 23.34ff., pp. 268ff., where the category refers to personality traits, especially degrees of quarrelsomeness. So in the case of some *nāyaka*s (231). Different is the social hierarchy to which the terms refer in RT 5.16 and RT 7.1.

81 The logic here is unclear to me. Presumably, as various commentators point out, once the criterion of species is allowed there would be no end to categories, since species are innumerable: one could differentiate according to place (A) or according to subspecies such as *vidyādhara*s (among the divine) or castes (among the nondivine) (V). This would force us, as A and N torturously explain, to ascribe all other subtypes such as "the jealous one" to the *nāyaka* as well; but since that would be contrary to literary convention—we never find verses on a *nāyaka* whose mistress has cheated on him (despite the presence of the category another's *nāyikā*)—we determine that *nāyikā*s are not to be differentiated according to *jāti* (this is Bhānu's own position, see 249). Commentators point out that Vātsyāyana and others do accept differentiation based on species. Indrāṇī is the wife of Indra, king of the gods;

Mālatī, the betrothed of Mādhava, in an eighth-century drama of Bhavabhūti; and Sītā, the wife of Rāma. The semidivinity of Rāma was a problem for many manuscripts, which replace him with Arjuna or Kṛṣṇa.

86 [40] I follow V here: A friend is trying to dress the *nāyikā* for the spring festival and finds that everything is **too big** (*adhika*), since the *nāyikā* is wasting away with loneliness. The fact that she does not tell her friends the truth of the matter is a sign of her modesty, while her thinness is a sign of her passion (the defining trait of the *madhyā nāyikā*, see 18). Less satisfactory Ś: "Before the start of spring the woman would wear her jewelry and so on to conceal her loneliness; but with the start of spring she became too distraught with her intense passion and found the jewelry and the rest too much to bear (another possible meaning of *adhika*)—which implies that her desire and modesty are in balance."

88 [41] V reports the variant *kiṃ ca tvayi yadupate prasthite* for ***yāte prabhavati harau subhruvaḥ***, as well as a locative singular, *pravasati*, which I cannot easily construe.

88 [41] The lotus garland and the pearl necklace would have been expected to cool down the *nāyikā*'s sorrow for her lover's absence, but she abandons them because they do the opposite; and she has grown so thin that she cannot keep the armlet on her upper arm.

90 [42] She is burning with the pain of separation, which would reveal itself to her mother-in-law by reducing the lotus to ash if she were to touch it, and to her friends if they were to feel the heat of her breath. Her mother-in-law would have offered the lotus as a good-luck charm for the well-being of the *nāyikā*'s husband (V). According to G's interpretation of *b*, the "dry sound" of the leaf—presumably, the sound of the leaf having become desiccated by her mere touch—would give away her feelings (*yā marmaraśaṅkā śuṣkaparṇadhvaniśaṅkā tayā. sparśamātreṇaiva*

śuṣke 'smin dale mama virahatāpaṃ mā jñāsīd iti śaṅkayā ity arthaḥ).

95 [44] **Jug marks:** his mistress's breasts would have been smeared with saffron paste; so in the next verse. The girl does not actually ask because of her shame, and this illustrates her "muttering" (N). B reads *draṣṭum* for *praṣṭum* (the ed. of V prints this in error). V unpersuasively criticizes A's interpretation that the *nāyikā*, being naïve, wouldn't think these are the marks of breasts but mistakenly believes they're the marks of jugs, and equally unpersuasively insists the girl is asking her girlfriend, not her husband.

97 [45] The U illustration of this verse is published in Ehnbom 1985: 47.

99 [46] **The mirror she carried mornings for good luck**: glancing in a mirror first thing in the morning was considered auspicious. In *c* B's reading *vyaktaṃ* for *rūkṣam* (cf. 101 [47]*b*) admittedly fits better with *asphuṭālāpam* in the definition but has no other MS. support. V has two extra verses here, which I omit.

101 [47] In *d* V reads *rurudhire* for ***nidadhire***, which he seems to want to interpret as "her tears being held back."

101 [47] She is **afraid others might hear** and thereby realize she is having an affair with the man (so N). It is unclear whether she stares at the go-between because she suspects her of having embraced the man (probable) or because she wants her to reprove him (so G, *svadūtyasya phalavaicitryam avalokayeti dhiyā*). U interpreted it in the latter sense, placing another woman at the lower left of the painting, see pl. 47.

106 [49] **Learns how heavy an empty heart can be**: literally, "she bears an empty heart for a long time."

110 [51] **When fate's not on your side**: literally, "those bitten by fate," a rare expression (G, Ś, V read more banally *-duṣṭāḥ*). **Tongue:** *rasajña*, literally, "knower of taste," used to imply that while the

hand and eye don't "have taste" and so would be expected to do what they have done, this is not the case with the tongue.

112 [52] I take *bhartṛ* in the sense of **lover**, with V (who effectively critiques the other possible constructions). The **river** is that leading to their secret meeting place. The vocative **mother** is often used as an exclamation (see *Uttararāmacarita* (Pollock 2007) 2.58 and 4.32 n.)

114 [53] **The lucky letters on my forehead**: the lines on the forehead were thought to be writing foretelling the person's fate (see also 185 [85]). The other two signs also portend good fortune (the lucky astral house is the ninth, according to C).

115 The **characteristic behaviors** listed here do not clearly line up with the examples in the three verses that follow.

117 [54] A, N read *ruṣā* and seem to construe it with the following compound (since it makes little sense in the case of a naïve *nāyikā*). G, Ś read instead *tṛṣā*, "with longing," but also connect it with the compound (the bees are longing for flower-nectar); I follow V, who reads similarly but more sensibly understands the word *apo koinou*.

117 [54] The naïve *nāyikā* cannot leave because it would be embarrassing if her girlfriends knew that she knew they brought her to see her lover; and she sees no purpose in staying if her lover is not there (so V, who reports the simpler interpretation that if she goes she might miss him and if she stays she would feel the pain of his absence). **Glances like bees**: the compound in *d* literally means "her glances attaining the beauty of wild swarms of bees growing languid." The commentators offer a variety of reasons for her looking toward the grove, including scanning the area for a lover, avoiding having to see her girlfriends, and searching for a way out since staying there is intolerable.

121 [56] She prays to Śiva as the traditional enemy of the God of love (V appears to suggest instead that she invokes him because she

now feels enmity, not love, toward her lover). The various epithets are imaginatively interpreted by the C. "*Śrīkaṇṭha*" ("possessing a throat of glory") is generally taken to refer to Śiva's drinking the cosmic poison produced at the primal churning of the milk ocean. "*Bharga*" (possibly "Destroyer") is associated with the death of Kāma.

123 [57] A, N, V report (U reads) the v.l. ***khala*** for *ghana* ("dense," or "of clouds"), which I accept, since it parallels the first two images (as V sees).

123 [57] **The wild bull of Death**: the buffalo bull is the mount of Yama, god of death. As Ś says simply, the sight of clouds, for a woman separated from her lover, is like death.

125 [58] The U painter (pl. 58) represents the courtesan waiting in the trysting grove, with the glances turned into actual bees.

126 Bhānu's requirement that this *nāyikā* should be thinking about a meeting outside the home is ignored in U in the next two paintings (pls. 59 and 60).

130 [60] *Nāyaka*s are never shown to be frightened of anything, and so it is impossible to understand *bhīto bhujaṅgāt* as a masculine participial phrase. I therefore essentially agree with V, in understanding *bhīto* as ablative and seeing two different reasons (but I take *bhujaṅga* literally, while V understands the word as referring to her preoccupation with her own lover). I also agree with V in taking *navoḍha-* as the *pūrvapada* of a *karmadhāraya* compound.

132 [61] There is no suggestion here that the *nāyikā* is talking about hiding her transgressions (as N believes), since one's own and not another's *nāyikā* is speaking (recall that one's own does not have to be married, only faithful to her lover). V sees this and rightly interprets more complexly. He suggests an allusion to *Yājñavalkyasmṛti* that requires a father, grandfather, brother, kinsman, and mother in that order, the previous one failing,

to be responsible for giving away a girl in marriage (1.63). The bower and so on are compared to each of these relations as things capable of bringing her together with her lover. Presumably her "experience" consists in her knowing who is responsible for her happiness. Dāmodara's dark complexion should make it even easier for him to come in the night (so most C).

134 [62] Each act can be interpreted simultaneously as erotic and religious (sandalwood cream, for example, would be smeared on the woman's breasts as well as on the image of the deity). **Renounced:** *kṛtā dakṣiṇā*, literally, "made the sacrificial fee," continuing the ritual trope. A, N point out that something given away as a sacrificial fee can never be reclaimed—which suggests the degree of the *nāyikā*'s attachment. Commentators do not convincingly explain how the *nāyikā*'s being another's is expressed in the verse. Note the U painter's solution to the problem of "the god born in the heart," pl. 62.

136 [63] G, Ś, V read *akṣālayan* (for ***asrāvayan***) in *c* and (excepting G) ***dhanābhilāṣān*** (for *dhanābhilāṣāt*) in *d* (U *akṣālayan* ... *-dhārā* ... *dhanābhilāṣāt*; B *akṣālayan* ... *-dhārām* ... *dhanābhilāṣāt*). Ś's original reading in *c* was (*pace* the printed edition), ***-vārā*** (instrumental of *vār*), which I believe is correct (he lists *-dhārā* as a v.l.; so apparently G [*pace* the MS.], who glosses *nipatadaśrujalena*). R calls the accusative *dhanābhilāṣān* "completely incoherent," arguing unpersuasively that we should supply "her chest" or "the grove (that she would be cleaving to)" as the direct object.

137 There is disagreement among *ālaṅkārika*s about the term ***vāsakasajjā***. Bhoja, for example, interprets it more credibly as "a woman who, 'once the bed chamber has been prepared,' adorns herself and awaits him, reclining on the bed" (*Sarasvatīkaṇṭhābharaṇa* 5.117).

139 [64] Various commentators (and U) read *tārakānti-* for ***tārakāti-***.

139 [64] V (and N, second interpretation, and U) alone understand the syntax of the verse correctly.

141 [65] Both A and N say the verse illustrates her average character by the mix of embarrassment and smiling. But the **smile** is that of the Love God, however much the love is actually inside of her (as Ś points out, only Love knew what was going on, since Love is "born in the heart"). V again correctly: her being average is shown by Love's recognizing that even while he is growing in her she cannot abandon her embarrassment.

143 [66] The U illustration of this verse is published in BAUTZE 1991: 135.

144 N is rightly troubled that among the various types of behavior of the *nāyikā* who "prepares for the occasion" only "wishing" is illustrated. But all editions and commentators carry the prose and following verse.

145 [67] V reads in *c* more easily *smitasphītam* (adjective to *anyonya-vīkṣaṇam*) instead of ***smitaṃ sphītam.*** V appears to have read *aṅga yad* for ***aṅgayor*** in *a*.

145 [67] That is, because their embraces are deep and constant. The "wish" presumably lies in how the *nāyikā* can avoid both "difficulties" (so T) though the latter is of course only an apparent one.

150 Bhānu's definition, especially the qualification "always," is disputed in the ŚM, p. 15. Those criticisms are answered by T.

150 Contrast RT 5.17 [5] and RT 5.15.

152 [70] For A and N the verse shows the *nāyikā*'s egotism (so in the following two verses as well). Far from being charmed by the poet's wordplay, Ś, A, and N are troubled by the use of the morpheme *-man*, which in some of the cases (according to Ś, grammarian's son that he was) no grammatical rule sanctions. The U illustration of this verse, now in the Kanoria Collection, Patna, Bihar, India, can be found at the Huntington Archive

of Buddhist and Related Art under scan number 0060468: http://huntington.wmc.ohio-state.edu/public/index.cfm?fuseaction=showThisDetail&ObjectID=30029295.

154 [71] In the U album, the entire power of the painting seems to be concentrated in the birds (see pl. 71). Part or all of the human narrative is re-presented in the bird narrative.

156 [72] The U painter here achieves something remarkable in his quest for turning text into image, see plate 72.

158 [73] The reading in *a*, *gṛhe gṛhe*, is faulty: the lover doesn't have a woman "in every house," but "right at home" (this phrasing may have been infected by 160 [74]). In *d*, J's reading (which is also G's, according to my MS., and not *bhrāmyantyā mama*, as JHA reports, p. 133; N offers the also possible *bhrāmantyā mama*) makes no sense: the gaze cannot "wander" yet "never leave." U's *purato* may be preferable to ***parito*** as the latter would seem more appropriate to the false reading *bhrāmyantī*.

158 [73] V notes the crescendo of intimacy in the places mentioned, where the lover's attentions might be exposed. The U illustration of this verse is published in PAL 1978, p. 7.

160 [74] V shows a sophisticated understanding of the verse, noting for example that the stress "pays *me*" (and not "*pays* me") indicates that it would be false to assume he would pay his own *nāyikā* but rather that the courtesan wants to praise her own skills by indicating that her lover is prepared to pay her alone for quality services when he could get common services elsewhere.

161 Despite what is printed in the edited text, V reads ***prakṛta eva kramaḥ*** (and not *sa eva kramaḥ*), and omits the explanatory clause that follows. Yet he wants to take this to mean that the behavior of one's own and of another's *nāyikā* are "identical," that the very fact of her going on a secret rendezvous demonstrates she has something to hide—otherwise she would be

"preparing for the occasion." This interpretation is confirmed by much other Sanskrit poetry.

161 **Clothing appropriate to the time of the month**: that is, dark during the new moon, white during the full.

165 [76] The U illustration of this verse may be found at the University of Michigan Museum of Art (accession number 1980/2.242): http://quod.lib.umich.edu/cgi/i/image/image-idx?id=S-MUS ART-X-1980-SL-2.242%5D1980_2.242.JPG.

171 [79] **She left with a sly smile on her face**: the *nāyikā* smiles (her smile or laughter, being conventionally represented as white, can easily be hid, according to V) because she thinks she can outwit Love, who has been tormenting her in her absence from her lover. She therefore goes out on a rendezvous undetected, thanks to the ruse of hiding her white body—already pale from the pain of separation—in the white moonlight. Love responds with his **jasmine arrows**, which increase her longing even more (so generally Ś, A). The flowers are white to show her that Love can defeat her with her own weapons (A, V suggest that it is because Love does not want to disturb her accoutrements, but this makes no sense to me). N does not see the point in Love's attempt to harm her, and so tries to interpret the verb *ni-han* differently, and unsuccessfully.

173 [80] This verse is missing in Ś, G, T but found in A, N, and V. The meter is in the rare *svāgatā*, with *yati* (typically) after the third syllable.

175 [81] **Village headman**: literally, "headman of the villages," the plural implying even greater authority. The commentators disagree on how this verse illustrates a woman who goes on a secret rendezvous. T, for example, imagines that the *nāyikā* had alerted her lover in advance and advised him to stay home and then arrives. V merely says this is a different kind of secret rendezvous.

177 [82] The poet stresses the courtesan's grand display on her rendezvous in order to contrast it with the secrecy of the previously described *nāyikās* (so too essentially V). Commentators disagree on the meaning of *nyañcat*, either tightly drawn (V) or slipping (A, N).

179 [83] *Amaruśataka* (ed. NSP), v. 35.

180 See ŚT v. 147 (one of the "earlier writers" Bhānu is referring to). For a long critique of the category see ŚM pp. 32–33. Ś, A, N remark on the solecism *proṣyat* (*patikā*) (strictly, the form should be *pravatsyat-*, as J has corrected everywhere); V attempts to justify it by assuming its source in a denominative *proṣyati*.

183 [84] The **cuckoo**'s passionate call is a sign of spring, a time when the lover would wish to remain with his beloved. The U illustration of this verse is published in BINNEY and ARCHER 1968: 19.

185 [85] The **lifeline** was written on the forehead, see note to 114. According to Ś, her hair comes undone from her torment at the thought of the coming separation; for V, her veil and then her hair are disturbed when she drops her head in shame.

187 [86] V reads, and other commentators report, *atraiva* for ***atreva*** (i.e., do they burn only here or also in the other world?).

187 [86] The things the *nāyikā*'s friends give her to assuage her grief are similar to what the bereaved **offer the dead** at the funeral ceremony. So even if she were to die from her suffering, death would bring her no relief. The suffering woman here is presumably Kṛṣṇa's lover Rādhā (though for A it is an undefined *gopī*), and it is his departure from Vraja for Mathurā that is intended (A claims it is the departure for Dvāravatī, but that is not typically the source of *virahakāvya* in the Kṛṣṇa cycle), though that is not the sort of "traveling" the genre presupposes.

189 [87] She imagines that her emotional suffering is the punishment of hell for the transgressions she has acknowledged. **Elders:**

guror (which I take as *jātyekavacana*) need not specifically be the father-in-law (Ś, A, N), since another's *nāyikā* is not always married (see 44). V takes it to mean husband. **Infernal pain in my eyes ... thousand tortures in every limb ... torment of my heart:** T is probably right to connect the three sufferings with the three infractions: the torture of her limbs is result of her treading on snakes (which, like kings and brahmins, are not to be shown disrespect, so *Yājñavalkyasmṛti* 1.153 cited by V); the pain of her eyes is the result of her lack of veneration for her elders; the torment of her heart is the result of her giving up all modesty.

191 [88] Women wither away in grief for their absent lovers, and their bracelets slip from their wrists. Her wrists will be so thin that even a small ring would fit (so V, correctly). Presumably her strength in holding him back belies her protestations about her growing weakness.

192 I must omit here discussion of the long and complicated argument in some C, especially T, on the propriety of this category.

195 [90] In *c*, V reads *-peśala-* for ***-kesara-***, thereby disrupting the extended metaphor (which curiously none of the commentators adequately glosses).

195 [90] **Reached for her blouse**: as V points out, the lover should have been reaching not for the *nāyikā*'s blouse but for her feet, in order to appease her. The **wish-granting vine** grows in heaven.

196 **Irascible:** *caṇḍī*, also the proper name of a destructive goddess, though that is probably not meant here.

197 [91] V reads *-ambhoruhi* for ***-ambhoruhe*** in *a*.

197 [91] In the final, rather unexpected image the petals are comparable to her eyes and the red sap of the tree to her anger.

198 **Each of the various types:** that is, each of the 128 types of *nāyikā* enumerated earlier (80).

200 [92] The syntax of G's commentary (if not the MS.) and the gloss of Ś (if not the printed ed.) indicate that both read ***likhantīm*** in *c*.

200 [92] **The usual design** is *makarikā*, a pattern of fern-like leaves, presumably of the sort seen today in the art of mehendi. T is not extant from this point on.

202 [93] The **rainy season** was viewed as an especially romantic time of the year, but the verse depends on the pun in the word *(niḥ)sneha*: "(without) moisture" / "(without) affection."

204 [94] Beyond the fact that the *nāyikā* is being compared to a sweet flower and the full white moon (*cakora* birds live on moonbeams), the implication of the verse is unclear. Some commentators suggest that the noise of the swarming birds and bees might alert observers that she is on a rendezvous; others, that the birds and bees stand for meddlesome people.

206 [95] The **seventh incarnation** of Viṣṇu is Rāma, son of Daśaratha, hero of the *Rāmāyaṇa*, and husband of Sītā. As the commentators imply, the friends are trying to get her to say the name of her husband, which Indian wives typically avoid doing since it is considered unlucky.

210 [97] The verse has the form of *maṅgalācaraṇa*, suggesting it was borrowed from some other work of the poet's (though one I have been unable to identify). Śiva is prepared to swear by water, fire, or snakes (that is, by undergoing an ordeal of one of these three forms) that he did not steal Pārvatī's necklace, as she is facetiously claims he did, by cheating at their cosmic dice match. V suggests that the irony here lies in the fact that, as the last line intimates, Śiva himself is the granter of all blessings.

212 [98] It is unclear who the speaker is, whether the *nāyikā*, *nāyaka*, or go-between. Most commentators report the v.l. in *b* … *idaṃ dūti cañcati* (changing the verse from an *upagīti* to a standard *āryā*), making clear it is the first (A, V; so G, but without the

v.l.) or second (N). The **solemn promise** is the go-between's assurance that she would find a way to unite the two lovers.

214 [99] The same pun on *sneha* as in 202 [93]. Her **final hour** refers to the last of the ten stages of the pain of separation (listed below in 265).

217 [100] The **moon**, the cosmic **serpent**, and the Gaṅgā **river** are all accoutrements of Śiva, so he has complete command over them (A). Possibly the androgynous form of Śiva is intended here (as in 2 [1]).

218 As V points out, there are additional classifications of *nāyaka*s (principally according to the fourfold scheme romantic, dignified, impulsive, and serene), but these are the four pertinent to the erotic mood.

219 [101] The **Dándaka forest** is the scene of Rāma's exile in the *Rāmāyaṇa*. Although Rāma tried to prevent his wife, Sītā, from accompanying him, she insisted. A points out that though Sītā was born of the earth, who would naturally be kind to her, Rāma's invocation shows the depth of his love; moreover, there is special propriety in Rāma's invoking the sun since he is a scion of the solar dynasty.

221 [102] This subcategory refers strictly to husbands (and not lovers), so the **women** here should be thought of as Kṛṣṇa's wives (N, V). Although for a *nāyikā* to have more than one lover produces a "semblance of a rasa" (*rasābhāsa*), the reverse is generally not true, and so a *nāyaka* can be shown to have multiple *nāyikā*s (thus N and V, arguing implicitly against Ś).

223 [103] **They**: the implied subject of the first line is the *nāyikā*'s attendants. It is not clear why she is not wearing her bracelet. Ś, R suggest that it is improper to sleep with jewelry on; N, that it came off because she was wasting away from separation from her lover, scoundrel though he is.

224 V explains that the gallant *nāyaka* is in love equally with his wife and mistress, the faithful only with his wife, whereas the

deceptive is inconstant in his love to both. He goes on to argue that this differentiation might appear to render empty the category of "brazen" or require that it be included either in the gallant or the deceptive. But the greater or lesser degree of love on the part of the deceptive *nāyaka* is necessarily dependent on particular circumstances; when there is no such regular condition the *nāyaka* would be classified as brazen.

225 [104] The action of a *nāyaka* is described here. The collocation *bhāla-phalake … patrāvalīm* is awkward since "designs" are never painted on the forehead. MSS. require keeping the reading of the first compound; I reinterpret the second with V.

226 **A man who causes**: literally, "a husband who causes." The word *pati* is used to suggest the etymology of *upapati* and should not be taken *strictu sensu*.

227 [105] V understands the verse correctly: **what kind of love** refers to the nature of domestic sex, where all is boringly licit, in contrast to the excitement caused by the restrictions imposed on illicit lovers, who must avoid discovery (*tat svīyādiratam kim? parakīyāratāpekṣayāpakṛṣṭatvam*). The alternative interpretation ("what an inferior kind of love is stolen love," see Ś, *tat kiṃratam sa kiṃsambhogaḥ kutsitaḥ sambhoga ity arthaḥ*) is absurdly censorious. V is also correct to say that those (and he is referring to A) who argue that the self-control shown to be required in illicit love demonstrates that it cannot be all-consuming and hence cannot produce *rasa*, are talking pure nonsense (*pralapitam*).

228 Since the faithful *nāyaka* is defined as "constant in affection toward his wife while constant in his indifference to the wives of other men," commentators ask how there can be a subtype "faithful" of the "lover." Ś thinks it a category error. A and N answer that "wives" (and presumably "wife") in the definition here refers to mistresses.

230 [106] **Love's playhouse:** *anaṅgaraṅga-*. Commentators gloss merely "love's festival" (or "battle"), but I stress the theatrical image, especially in view of the fact that courtesans were often actresses. The **bells ringing** on her belt suggests that the woman is making love on top, for if she were on the bottom it would be her anklets ringing (R). The **wild eyes** (an indication of her lack of modesty, V) are likened to *cakora* birds since they are waiting to drink in the beams of her lover's moon-face (for *cakora* see note to 204).

232 [107] **Corner,** *-prāntam*: for V this implies that her sidelong glance is being directed at the lover. He does not smile in order to indicate that he too is downhearted. And he only approaches the edge of the bed, since she would be angrier still if he tried to climb up, yet if he did nothing, he would appear indifferent. Restringing her pearls is something the *nāyikā*'s girlfriend would do, and the action indicates the *nāyaka*'s deep love.

238 [110] Ś inexplicably understands this as an account reported by one man to another.

240 [111] The musicality in the verse is remarkable in Bhānu's oeuvre.

242 [112] The **lemon** refers to the *nāyikā*'s breasts, and the *nāyaka* is indicating he wants to make love with her; the **circle** refers either to zero, that is, the setting of the sun, or to the spot on the moon (the Western "man in the moon"), that is, the rising of the moon. (V observes that it is the *nāyaka*'s action in suggesting a rendezvous that is central here—since the verse is an illustration of his cleverness—not the *nāyikā*'s determination of the exact time.) **Full-moon** refers to the woman's face beaming at her lover's suggestion (A). Note also the rich alliteration in the verse, /k/ six times.

248 [116] **The house was empty . . . so I took him to the woods:** she does not succeed in the house, even though it is empty, because the young man fears someone may come. She then takes him to

the woods, but even there he worries that she may be interested in someone else, so she looks at him with love in her eyes (V).

249 R alone reads *anyathā* (for ***anyac ca***), though the sentence is as likely to be offering an additional argument as it is to be elaborating on the one just made.

249 There appear to be additional corruptions in this passage that unfortunately none of the MSS. available allows us to correct. G offers a number of apparent emendations, reading ***asaṃpradāyād*** (which I believe to be necessary), but also (contrary to my understanding) taking ***-śaṅkā*** in compound with ***dhūrtatvam*** and reading at the end: *pratyuta* [for ***tān prati***] *saṃpradāyam anādṛtyety arthaḥ. tattadudbhāvane teṣāṃ nāyakānāṃ tāsām utkādyavasthānāṃ.*

249 See 81 along with note to 81, both for the subvarieties and for the argument that classification of the *nāyikā* is based on temporary states.

249 **It is only the *náyaka*...**: this seems like a non sequitur, but perhaps the point is to show that the reverse is not true, that is, a *nāyaka* cannot be either jilted or cheated on.

251 [117] **Or let it be**: that is, forget about giving up your anger (so correctly V).

253 [118] V's *apy avandhyodyamo* for ***anavadyotsavo*** (G, A, Ś) is not really required, given that *utsava* can be used in the sense of "effective remedy" (cf. G gloss, *tattadbhayavyādhināśakavaidyacikitsārambhaḥ*).

253 [118] The terms in the first half of the verse, *kumudeśvara* (**the lord of lotuses**) and the rest, also refer to types of alchemical practices.

255 [119] **Met one day by chance**: V notes that "by chance" can mean either that their love is fated or that having met by coincidence, the lovers have nowhere else to go to be alone together.

257 [120] The early morning call of the **rooster** is a favorite topos in love poetry globally (as demonstrated in A.T. Hatto, "Eos" [London: Mouton, 1965]), usually indicating that it is time for the (illicit) lover to depart. Here, the idea is either that the mistress is being told to stop her usual coyness and proceed directly to lovemaking (N), or the lover, in recollection, is laughing at himself for being fooled and frightened away by the friend's trick (so essentially Ś), or both lovers are being told to hurry and are thus amused. The reference to the rooster's being young is meant to indicate that his call is protracted (N, V).

260 [121] The ninth reaction here, *ālasyam*, is not one of the canonical number but is usually considered a transitory feeling (see RT 5.2). A identifies "the earth-protector Nijāma" as "king of Devagiri" (see introduction for further discussion). Triv. A and G replace the reading with a reference to Kṛṣṇa (*vrajendratanayaḥ kṛṣṇas tayā* [G, *tvayā*]; similar B), but G's reading in particular, given his relationship to the Vaiṣṇava reformer Caitanya, is suspect.

262 [122] A woman is making love on top of her lover ("in the sky" modifies all the verbs: the point of view is that of the *nāyaka* below). The **cloud** represents the mass of her dark hair; the **moon**, her fair face; the dove's **coos**, her moans of pleasure; **stars shooting**, the flowers falling from her hair; **waves** of the river of the gods, i.e., the Gaṅgā as it flows in the sky, either her pearl necklace or the beads of sweat on the folds of skin at her waist. The asyndeton of *b* is possible but improbable, but no commentator or MS. reports a variant. I follow V, or what I take to be his general implication.

264 [123] **First cloud of the rains**: the coming of the monsoon rains marked the time for lovers to return home to their beloved. **Cooling lotus stalks** would be applied to reduce the fever caused by the pain of separation.

265 In the RM, both men and women are subject to these ten states; elsewhere it is usually only women. Most of the following are

spoken by men; the commentators who remark on the matter agree that 275 [128] is spoken by a man and 277 [129] by a woman, though there are no markers in the poems to this effect. If the reading *-kāntā-* in 272 is correct (and it is supported by all C), then for Bhānu "glorification" is only done by a man in reference to his beloved. A and N similarly in their glosses (dividing *priyā-āśrita*) restrict "raving" (277 [129] and 276) to the *nāyaka*; V appears to allow it for both. R is very clear in 278 that "madness" pertains to both men and women, so, too, in his comment on "remembering" (271 [126]).

267 [124] **My heavy heart sank down, but my eye is light and floats about**: that is, his heart, heavy with desire, is lost in the woman, while his eye continues to feast on her sight. An additional implication is suggested by V: The eye engages directly with its object whereas the cognitive faculty (*cetaḥ*, here translated "heart") engages in a mediated way via association with the eye; it is as it were borne by the eye. In the real world, not only lightweight things such as boats float on the water but so do the heavy things they carry. Here, however, this is not the case. R reads *saṃplutam* for *sarvato*.

269 [125] **Garland**: for the unusual *netrotpalatoraṇāni* I follow G and Ś, who gloss *vandanamālā* and *toraṇamālikāḥ* respectively.

271 [126] One might have expected *-vivardhamāna-* for ***-vivartamāna-***, but no MS. and none of the commentators read this.

275 [128] **What am I supposed to do now?** or, "What else do you have in store for me?"

278 **Which comes from mental derangement produced**: V seems to understand, "which comes … and is produced." I agree with G and R.

281 [131] The **moon**, the **God of love**, and the **bee** are not functioning here as standards of comparison for the beloved; they are, rather, stimulant factors of the erotic rasa. V persuasively reads

the verse as an example of the rasa type called "a mosaic of feelings" (*bhāvaśabalatva*, see RT 8.53). (Thus, the first line expresses first the lover's resentment toward the moon and then his pride in the beloved; the second, the lover's bitterness toward the Love God and then his joy in his beloved; the third, his sadness [at the sign of spring represented by the bee?] and dejection at not being able to be with his beloved; the fourth, his disgust with the world and his longing.) The lack of logical-syntactical connection between the two sentences in each line is the sign of the lover's madness. On *karmāṇi* in *d*, I agree with N, V that these are the "labors" that take the lover from home; less likely, with A, the "troubles" of trying to find somewhere a likeness of his woman.

283 [132] N finds an additional meaning: Kāma cannot tolerate rivals and destroys them, so the lover is being besought to protect his beloved from the Love God's wrath lest she, too, becomes bodiless. V reports the reading *tava* (for *tayoḥ*) in *c*, which produces a much different ending: since you (the *nāyaka*) and Kāma are so similar—since like Kāma you have a bow and arrow in her beloved's brows and glances, and you dwell in her heart—don't diminish your power by allowing your beloved to lose her body.

287 The connection with what precedes is noted by A, who claims that these **three modes** form the basis of the aforementioned ten states. But those are states only of frustrated eroticism, and these modes are much broader (not unrelatedly Ś).

288 [134] G, Ś, A, and V all assume the *nāyikā* herself to be speaking. But she would not use *kucagireḥ* of herself, or refer to her friend as *tanvi*, and so I find their explanation odd. For *saṃdadhānaḥ* V. also suggests "attaching to me a garland" (instead of "garlanded"), since it is "more in keeping with the prefix *sam*."

292 [136] **Blessed love** is asked to be still so the *nāyikā* can collect her thoughts (N; so essentially V). V notes that the *śāstra*(*kāvya*) of Bhānu concludes with an auspicious invocation in accordance

with the *Mahābhāṣya*'s requirements for beginning and ending such works.

294 [137] **Flowing nectar**: *mādhvīkasyanda-*. For V the two terms also can refer to the literary qualities of sweetness and clarity.

River of Rasa

1.1 [1] I read ***upaharan*** (for *upahasan*, "mocked") in *a* with N (who clearly read this, glossing *ānayan*). This is a much-disputed variant. The phrase must identify another avatar and so cannot construe with the following (so G with obvious semantic logic but with equally obvious formal difficulty); in the Matsya avatar Viṣṇu recovered the Vedas after slaying the demon Hayagrīva, the humor here lying in God's having taken the form of a fish.

1.1 [1] **His reddened eye**: redness indicates passion, usually romantic passion, but sometimes, as here, the passion of anger.

1.1 [1] In this verse Viṣṇu's eight incarnations are linked with the eight rasas. The avatars and their associated rasas may be apportioned as follows (see N): **He looked at Lakshmi**: Nṛsiṃha (the Man-Lion), the erotic rasa (*śṛṅgāra*); **recovered the Vedas**: Matsya (the Fish), the comic rasa (*hāsya*); **grieved for the victims**: the Buddha, the sorrowful rasa (*karuṇa*); **beheld the kshatriyas**: Paraśurāma, the furious rasa (*raudra*); **looked upon Rávana**: Rāma, the heroic rasa (*vīra*); **stole the fresh butter**: Kṛṣṇa, the fearful rasa (*bhayānaka*); **bedaubed the horizons**: Kalki, the disgusting rasa (*bībhatsa*); **balanced the earth**: Varāha (the Boar), the amazing rasa (*adbhuta*). The **God of the yellow robe,** Viṣṇu, is not to be associated with any particular rasa (*pace* N, who links with *śānta*), since Bhānu generally concerned himself with only eight (though see Bhānu's remarks on RT 7.63).

1.4 [4] ***vimalo***: G and N read the less persuasive *viralo* and take the whole clause as a negative purpose ("lest its water be turbid and sparse").

1.5 The definition of emotion is "transformation," and there are physical as well as mental transformations.

1.6 **Better yet**: to avoid the vicious circle of the previous statement, which essentially defines a stable emotion in terms of itself (V).

1.6 **Climax**: that is, of the scene or work.

1.8 **Not fully matured**: in other words, it has not reached the state of a developed rasa (G, V). Bhānu uses *parimita* below in the same sense.

1.9 [5] The **tree of love** is tended by the play of eyebrows insofar as the mistress's girlfriend communicates only by signals and not directly lest anything be divulged (N).

1.10 I assume this means: the word "delicate" is the author's way of signaling that the verse is *bhāvakāvya*, rather than *rasakāvya*, and not that the word "delicate" itself somehow makes the verse the one rather than the other.

1.11 **My honored father**: Bhānudatta's father was also a poet, see 295 [138], RT 3.18 [4].

1.12 [6] In his **Dwarf** incarnation Viṣṇu disguised himself as a mendicant.

1.14 **There is still hope of life**: V adds, "through, for example, the intervention of a divine power," though this is not really necessary.

1.14 **"The Birth of Kumára"**: *Kumārasaṃbhava* of Kālidāsa (trans. by David Smith, CSL, 2005). **"Princess Kadámbari"**: *Kādambarī* of Bāṇa (trans. by David Smith, CSL, 2009). **"The Lineage of Raghu"**: *Raghuvaṃśa* of Kālidāsa. **"Jewel Lamp of Rasa"**: *Rasaratnapradipikā* of Allarāja 5.50. The citation that follows is from *Kumārasambhava* 4.3.

1.19 **Rama when shown disrespect**: As the next verse shows, such an insult fills Rāma with energy, not with rage.

1.22 **The heroic**: it is clear from RT 2.28 that Bhānu means by *vīra* the rasa and not the hero himself.

1.23 [10] The compound ***utsāhavicāramūḍha-*** puzzles N and G, for whom it seems to mean "confused about what to do and what not to do prior to [the coming into being of] his energy," that is, when he was filled with anger (which accounts for the underdevelopment of the emotion mentioned next). This may be overreading the verse; very likely, it is simply meant to illustrate the *utsāhādhyavasāya* in RT 2.20. The main point, however, is that Rāma is planning what to do, not actually doing it—so this is an illustration of the *bhāva* of *utsāha*, and not of *vīra* itself.

1.29 [12] **Káustubha jewel**: a magic gem obtained by Viṣṇu (literally, "foe of the demon Kaiṭabha") at the churning of the milk ocean.

1.31 See NŚ 7.22. **Transgression** would include an infraction against a teacher or a king; cf. RT 2.30. It is unclear to me where the stable emotion of fear resides in this case, in the onlooker or (more likely) in the perpetrator.

1.32 [13] **Káliya** is a serpent slain by Kṛṣṇa (**joy of the Yadus**), whose mount is the eagle Garuḍa.

1.34 V's reading shows that the otherwise universally attested *smaraṇa* (memory) is an old corruption (perhaps dittography from what follows). "Hearing" is clearly what is at issue in the illustration.

1.35 [14] **Horns**, *śṛṅga-*: So G, N, whom I accept *pace* V. ("peak" of the mountain), since we need something to be crunched.

1.38 [15] G, O specify that this concerns Arjuna's fight with Kṛṣṇa's kinsman Kṛtavarman, but the point still escapes me.

1.41 [16] What is dominant here is the description of the woman's beauty, hence the wonder is subordinate to it (V).

1.43 [17] *nirātaṅkaḥ*: "has no spot," so N; G, "freed from any attack by Rāhu"; V, oddly, *nirbhayaḥ*.

1.43 [17] Unlike the moon, the woman's face sheds no light in the sky; black hair increases the darkness. The **bow** is her eyebrows, the **lotuses** her eyes. The **spot** is what is known in the West as the man in the moon.

2.7 The underlying factors and stimulant factors are treated jointly from this point on to the end of the chapter.

2.8 **Grotesque things**: *vikṛtair arthaviśeṣair*. G takes as "grotesque beings," such as dwarfs and hunchbacks. But compare RT 2.12.

2.14 [4] **The coils of this snake**: or "the coils that are this snake" (N, V).

2.18 [5] **It spreads a gleaming darkness**: as N observes, it is conventional to describe a shining sword as black; here the idea is that the sword also spread darkness over the eyes of the enemy.

2.18 [5] **Chakra birds**: the *cakravāka* bird, which is separated from its mate every night.

2.18 [5] **Pearls scattered about from the splitting forehead lobes**: elephants are conventionally said to contain pearls in their foreheads.

2.20 **Without ... pride or confusion**: see NŚ 6. 67, where the reading of Abhinavagupta is *avismayāmohāt*, taken as a *dvandva* (p. 319), and this is confirmed in the preceding prose. Commentators read *mohāt*, "frenzy," so essentially V, who glosses *viparyaya*, "misapprehension," and says that to deny its role in the heroic rasa is an empty assertion on the part of the ancients; N interprets unjustifiably as "anger." From the use of *mūḍha* in RT 1.23 [10], one might infer that Bhānu himself actually understood the tradition as V interprets it. **Events**, *-artha-*. See note to RT 2.8 (V. hopelessly interprets "wealth").

2.30 I follow Abhinavagupta here (p. 320).

2.31 **Night watchman**: V glosses *rājakīyapuruṣa*.

2.32 [9] This can only refer to the Man-Lion avatar (G). As N points out, **Bali** has no part in this narrative, but attempts by N and V to interpret as referring to the Dwarf avatar are completely unconvincing. I therefore follow G, who understands *bali* as *balisadma*, i.e., the underworld. The first half of the verse is not a *rūpaka*; although saying that the clouds were split by the lion's mane may seem to make little sense (G), this signification is certified by RT 2.40 [11].

2.36 [10] I agree with V that *purabhid* refers to **Indra** (rather than Śiva), since it is Indra who welcomes dead soldiers into heaven.

2.38 NŚ 6.75. Abhinava takes *b* as "an extraordinary act of artistry," which seems to me improbable in view of the conjunctions.

3.1 The reading ***phal'|âyoga|vyavacchedena*** is certified by Prakāśikā on *Tarkasaṃgraha* 47 *phalāyogavyavacchinnaṃ kāraṇaṃ karaṇam*.

3.3 One might easily conjecture *kāmino* here on hints provided in V and N, as also on the evidence of the next paragraph, where the use of the dual ***kāminoḥ*** may seem inappropriate: Presumably what is meant is that the *nāyikā*'s glances are observed not only by the *nāyaka* directly but by the *nāyikā* herself indirectly as she sees her lover's reaction. This may be what V implies (ad *viṣayatvena*, glossed *parasparaṃ dṛṣṭigocarībhūtatvena*).

3.4 [1] The reading reported by N, *-smitaprekṣitair*, looks like an attempt to avoid the rather awkward anacoluthon.

3.4 [1] *Rasaratnapradīpikā* 5.9.

3.4 [1] Presumably Bhānu thought of the **glances** and so on as stimulating the lover's desire, not "causing it to be experienced" by the beloved (or the audience), though note that in the *Rasaratnapradīpikā* (5.9) the verse is cited as an example of *saṃbhogaśṛṅgāra* produced through *anubhāvas*. Erotic references to the underarm are very rare in Sanskrit poetry, but see RT 4.21 [9]. V is probably right to understand the vague *droṇī* (a favorite word of Bhānu's) as merely pluralizing the preceding noun (it cannot mean *patra*, as N often suggests, because it is typically in compound with *dala*).

3.5 MSS. are very confused here, the confusion resulting from the fact that both *nāyikā* and *nāyaka* are meant to be as involved in the reactions as they are in the stimulants (cf. note to RT 3.3). I follow the astute V, who glosses *ātmani rasānubhavapātre nāyakaṃ prati nāyikānirūpitakaṭākṣādayaḥ*.

3.8 NŚ 6.48. Abhinava takes *dhṛti* and *pramoda* as *vyabhicāribhāvas*. If J is correct, this may be why Bhānu suppresses *dhṛti*, which can hardly been taken as a physical reaction.

3.10 [2] **Since all would pale in comparison**: the *nāyikā* knows that nothing can adorn her and she puts aside her ornaments *paribhavabhayāt*, (literally) "out of concern [for them] that they would be disgraced." Commentators are oddly confused: V: *saukumāryātiśayenāṅgānāṃ kleśabhayāt*; O: *mālinya saṃbhāvanā ke udvega se*.

3.14 [3] The **skull** and **crescent moon** are attributes of Śiva; **serpents** were believed to have jewels embedded in their hoods. **Mother** refers to Śiva's wife, the **child** either to Gaṇeśa or Kārtikeya.

3.18 [4] There is a surprising and irremediable violation of caesura in *a* (***nirga/cchati***). One might have thought it a sign of the poet's grief, but there are comparable metrical problems elsewhere in the work (e.g., RT 3.22 [5], RT 7.7 [3], RT 7.22 [10], RT 8.11 [3]).

3.18 [4] The **bangles** slip off because she has grown thin in grief; the moist **saffron paste** is dried by her sighs.

3.20 The entire first line is very weak. The reading ***-saṃkulaśirasaḥ*** is a legitimate v.l. in the NŚ, but the whole tenor seems off. NŚ gives: "By wielding various weapons, by severing the head or the arms of a headless trunk." What distinguishes *raudra* from *vīra*, according to Abhinava, is blind rage, whereby one seeks to kill even what it already dead, and the desire to kill, which is absent in *vīra*. In *raudra*, personal greed is primary, which renders any war both illegal and immoral (p. 319).

3.20 **Pounding the fist**: or "slapping with the palms of the hand" (V).

3.22 [5] It is considered a metrical fault for the enclitic-like particle ***iva*** to follow a caesura, as here in *c*.

3.24 **Laden with double meanings**, *ākṣepa/kṛtair*: one might have thought, in the context of a discussion of *vīrarasa*, that this means "filled with defiant exclamations," rather than "filled with hints, i.e., statements that are deep and hard to fathom," as Abhinava takes it (ad NŚ 6.68, p. 319). But his view seems borne out by other evidence; see, for example, the definition of the dramaturgical feature called *gaṇḍaṃ* (NŚ 18. after 118: *bahuvacanākṣepakṛtaṃ gaṇḍaṃ pravadanti tattvajñāḥ*).

3.25 **Force**, *bala*: Abhinava glosses "army components," but that would be fitting in a discussion of *vibhāvas*, not *anubhāvas*.

3.25 I do not fully grasp Bhānu's point here. One might have expected *na virodhaḥ* for *na viśeṣaḥ*, but no MS. offers this, and so I follow V: *vṛttijanyopasthiteḥ smaraṇātmakatve mānasam; pratyabhijñānātmakatve aindriyakam* ("When a cognitive event is remembered, it is 'mental'; when it is recognized, it is 'perceptible'"). N: "So long as the reaction is cognized it makes no difference whether this happens through inference [his gloss on 'mental'] or direct perception."

3.37 **By indistinct footfalls**, *avyaktapādapatanaiḥ*: this phrase was apparently already obscure by Abhinava's time (he offers two explanations, neither very persuasive, p. 323).

3.39 [10] On ***kapaṭaharer*** I follow B (*nṛsiṃhasya*). V mistakenly understands a reference to baby Kṛṣṇa, which causes him problems in interpreting "Lakṣmī" here.

3.41 The NŚ reads the rare *-ullukasanair* (*sparśagrahollukasanaiḥ*), glossed by Abhinava as a "joyful raising and shaking of the arms" (p. 324).

3.43 [11] **Unblinkingly awake**: the eyes of the gods by nature do not blink.

4.3 **Despair, remembrance, and fortitude**: as Bhānu goes on to say, these feelings also arise in connection with "sympathy."

4.4 Either **property of the body** means "property of the enlivened, conscious body," or, less likely, Bhānu thought of *nidrā* and *apasmāra* (RT 5.51 [22] and RT 5.53 [23]) as mental properties. NŚ 7.93ff. has a rather different interpretation of the term (*iha hi sattvaṃ nāma manaḥprabhavam*, etc.).

4.8 N remarks that whereas **cold** may be a factor of horripilation, it is not a factor of the involuntary physical reaction of that name. There are similar problems in the preceding verse and in RT 4.14 and elsewhere below (e.g., RT 4.16, where N again remarks that factors of tears are being listed that are not necessarily *sāttvikabhāvas*). But see NŚ 7.98 and *passim*.

4.9 [3] A *nāyikā*'s friend is commenting on Kṛṣṇa's reaction to her arrival in the grove. **Bees darting in anger**: presumably at being disturbed by Kṛṣṇa.

4.22 **"Forehead Ornament of the Erotic"**: *Śṛṅgāratilaka* of Rudra (or Rudra Bhaṭṭa). See Introduction, p. xxxiv.

4.22 N rejects Bhānu's reasoning here with great vigor.

4.23 [10] V: "The yawning is produced by her fatigue at the unbearable delay of embracing Śiva caused by her love-anger." O notes that the yawn is a sign that her anger would be easily assuaged.

Snapping the fingers is even today a way to awaken the deity in temples.

5.9 In accordance with V, who argues that the first property is physical, the second internal. As N points out in RT 5.19 [6] below, the distinctions between fatigue, exhaustion, and torpor are vague.

5.9 One factor of fatigue is excessive drinking of alcohol, to which the **rolling of the eyes** is a reaction (NŚ 7.30–31).

5.12 [3] **Snake**: *cakṣuḥśravāḥ*, literally, "famed for its sight." Snakes were attributed with great knowledge derived from their sharp sense of sight.

5.14 [4] Pārvatī is jealous of the **crescent moon** (feminine in gender in Sanskrit) in Śiva's headdress. **The demon Eclipse** was represented as swallowing the moon.

5.16 The categories refer to social hierarchy, contrast 80.

5.16 The verse is untraced.

5.25 [9] Curiously, V, N, B all construe the particles ***kiṃ nāma*** with the preceding clause; I agree with G.

5.27 [10] V reads *ajñāta-* (unrecorded) instead of ***a/jñāna-***. His intended reference to marriage is very far-fetched (*ramāparivārakṛtavivāhanimittabhujagapāśapatanarūpa ācāro na jñāta iti bhāvaḥ. nāgapāśa iti varasya (?) ācāro lokānāṃ prasiddhaḥ*). See the use of *pāśa-* in RT 2.14 [4], RT 7.22 [10]).

5.28 ***sadṛś'/âdṛṣṭa-***: among the multiple variants here the most attractive is *sadṛśatādṛṣṭi-* (reported by Ś).

5.28 So Abhinava (who glosses *praṇidhāna*), p. 357.

5.29 [11] There are deep confusions about this verse, and it is hard not to suspect corruption; none of the commentators explains it in a way I find acceptable. The four line-final verbs require a parallelism impossible according to the syntax of the first two lines as transmitted, and the asyndeton is almost intolerable. One might suppose separating off *kālindī* from the compound (and perhaps conjecturing *rabhasā* [cf. RT 5.88 [41]] or *rabhasāt* [cf. 169 [78]] for *nabhasaḥ* [though see RT 5.58 [25]]), but even this is hardly compelling since there is no *kavisamaya* about the Yamunā uniting with a pond; nor does conjecturing *visphūrjatīm* for *visphūrjati* help much. It is also entirely unclear what "recognition" is taking place, since the "similarity" behind recognition concerns two experiences of the same entity, not an analogy between entities. And the attempt to supply this similarity via quasi *śleṣa* (N, O) or to find some parallel between the Yamunā and the sky, the birds and the moon, etc., strikes me as desperate.

5.29 [11] Kṛṣṇa recognizes Rādhā, who has returned to their rendezvous spot in the hope of meeting him by day.

5.31 [12] Kṛṣṇa is so enchanted with Rādhā's beauty that he places on her upper arm an ornament meant for her ear (less likely, head, V), which is what makes her smile (so in part N).

5.32 The compound ***jñānaśakti*** is a *tatpuruṣa*, not a *dvandva* (*jñānaśakti* in NŚ 7.56 is followed in the prose by *śrutivibhava*, which Abhinava glosses as *bāhuśrutyam*).

5.36 V glosses ***itar'/êtara/kriyā/karaṇaṃ*** as *avyavahitadvitrikriyākaraṇam*.

5.36 V argues forcefully that the reading ***vairi-*** is an error for *vaira-*. We clearly have to distinguish this reaction from the underlying factors *vairidarśana* in RT 5.40. (In a roundabout way this is V's point, though he does not cite the later occurrence.)

5.38 **Mental radiance**: that is, *sattva* unmixed with either *rajaḥ* or *tamaḥ* (N).

5.39 [16] **Fragility**: I follow N, but hesitantly. V is unfortunately illegible in both MSS. (*saṃtrudyapatanam*?), B impossibly imagines this to be some sort of gesture (*bhaṅgo lakṣaṇayā bhaṅgābhinayas tasya bhītiṃ tajjanyaceṣṭām*), G glosses *bhaṅga* weakly as *vyathā*.

5.40 **Internal transformation**: I follow V here.

5.40 A second definition is given since the first might be confused with "being dumbfounded" (*jaḍatā*) in the next verse. (O).

5.43 [18] The monkeys first laugh thinking the task will easy to accomplish. The commentators have various problems with this verse (in part perhaps because *pāra* is used not in the normal sense of "further shore" as explicitly defined by Amara but simply as "shore"), and offer various unsatisfactory solutions (such as impossibly understanding *āgacchataḥ* as nominative plural, so V, N).

5.45 [19] **The sage born in an urn**: Agasti (usually Agastya) drank the ocean empty to expose the demons dwelling therein and help the gods to slay them. **Ganga prepared to consign her body to Shiva's forehead fire**: the ocean is represented as the husband of rivers; the Gaṅgā is here about to commit sati because of the "death" of her husband. **I created oceans ... of tears**: shed by the widows of the kshatriyas slaughtered by Paraśurāma. B, V are troubled that oceans in the plural are restored to the Gaṅgā (instead of just a second ocean) and suggest alternate readings or interpretations, unnecessarily.

5.49 [21] **Games and jokes and wishing**, *keli/kautuka/mano/rājyaiḥ*: I see no reason (*pace* V, N, O) not to take this as a *dvandva*, parallel to the compounds in *b* and *c* (so V).

5.51 [22] Of course **dreams** are preceded by sleep (V), but still the verse is an odd choice for illustrating sleep.

5.53 [23] Hanumān brought to Laṅkā a **mountain peak** with a healing herb to revive Lakṣmaṇa (he brings the whole peak at one point because the herbs are hiding, and at another because he is unsure which are the right ones).

5.58 [25] This use of ***daridraṃ kṛ***, which here means only something like "surpassed," is somewhat unusual. N's reading, *-droṇyādaridram*, is attractive but not widely represented.

5.62 [27] I follow V and N in interpreting *Kīra* as the name of one of Rāvaṇa's counsellors, who are explicit in their identification of Kīra. G, B, and O see instead a reference to a parrot: Rāvaṇa places the pearls before the bird to see whether it will mistake them for seeds.

5.64 [28] According to the C, the transgression here is Rāma's breaking of the bow of Śiva, of whom Paraśurāma was a devotee.

5.65 **Raising one's eyebrows when teaching students**: see Abhinava, *śisyopadeśalakṣaṇena prayojanena dehavikārāḥ* (p. 369).

5.66 [29] **Lata women**: the women of Lāṭa (southern Gujarat) are famed in Sanskrit poetry for their seductiveness.

5.67 B takes ***naya|vinay'|ânunay'|ôpadeś'|ôpālambhāḥ*** as a *dvandva*, which forces him to explain why no examples are given of good judgment and the other two.

5.72 [32] **Cool the whole world with your liquid nectar**: or: make the world as cool as liquid ambrosia (V).

5.73 The term *upadrava* (let alone *daśopadrava*) appears nowhere in the rasa literature. V argues powerfully for ***deha|kārśy'|ādayaḥ***, the conjecture adopted.

5.74 [33] **To get a golden ring instead**: see note to 191.

5.76 [34] I am satisfied with none of the C's constructions (G is closest). To me it is clear that Kṛṣṇa is attempting to revive Rādhā. We need therefore to supply *latām* with *siñcati* and *saṃbhāṣate*, and *latāyām* with *vyātanute*.

5.80 [36] **Mainâka** sought refuge in the ocean when Indra was cutting off the wings of the primordial mountains to keep them in place. **Hari** can refer to "monkey" in addition to Indra and Viṣṇu;

Rāma could easily be expected to mention the word in reference to Hanumān and his other simian allies, though it is not clear on what occasion Rāma would have spoken the name in the hearing of Maināka. (V suggests, unpersuasively, that on the occasion when Rāma's passage across the ocean was blocked and he flew into a rage, Maināka [assuming his location to be in the ocean near Laṅkā] would have been expected to be overcome with fear as well [*samudraṃ prati krodhakaraṇasamaye mainākasyāpi saṃbhāvyate bhayam*]).

5.82 [37] The context is the marriage contest prior to Rāma's attempt to string the **bow of Shiva**. Commentators disagree about the speaker; I am in accord with G, who says it is Sītā's father, Janaka (N ascribes the verse to Sītā, B to Viśvāmitra). Janaka's concerns are about the pledge he made (to give Sītā in marriage to whoever is able to string the bow of Śiva), and the consequences of the pledge being violated by its very impossibility. He takes refuge in the sun presumably as the primal ancestor of Rāma's clan.

5.83 [38] **Charm itself craning its neck to behold the world**: I am uncertain of this translation, which agrees with V (first interpretation; his second is unintelligible), N, G. Possible is B's reading *trijagatām*: "the beauty of the triple world craning its neck to look about" (*kiṃ ca vilokituṃ sāmānyato draṣṭuṃ trijagatām trilokānāṃ lāvaṇya[sya] saundaryasya udgrīvikā*). For the rare *udgrīvikā* as a substantive see *Subhāṣitaratnakośa* 3.856 and *Naiṣadīya* 14.53.

5.84 [39] V makes a strong case that *a* and *b* are syntactically independent, but that seems a harder construction.

5.87 This is apparently Bhānu's innovation, despite his attribution to others in RT 5.89 below.

5.88 [41] *Amaruśataka* v. 17.

5.93 [43] **Painfully fixed his eyes**: somehow G understands that Rāma is hereby hiding his own feelings. I do not find this in the Sanskrit, but I also do not otherwise understand the nature of the deception in this verse. The tradition of Rāvaṇa's having **seven magical lakes** or moats built around Laṅkā (to which commentators refer) is post-Valmiki and unknown to me.

6.1 One would have assumed ***upanīyamānaḥ*** to be a corruption of *upacīyamānaḥ* (the latter is read by B, which V records as a *pāṭha*), but I believe the dominant reading may be authenticated by the use of *aupanayika* in 6.2.

6.2 **Ordinary and extraordinary**: B improbably glosses these two terms as *svakīya* and *parakīya*.

6.2 **Ordinary contact is of six types**: contiguity, inherence, and the rest (see *Tarkasaṃgraha* 43). V is certainly correct to add: "contact, i.e., of the *nāyaka* and the *nāyikā*."

6.2 **The last is found in the beauty of drama...**: this refers to an onlooker's experience of rasa, whereas the rasas of dream and the imagination refer to the *nāyaka* or *nāyikā*, and accordingly may have an admixture of sorrow (N, V). Dev's *Bhāvvilās* 3.8 illustrates *aupanayika* rasa in a verse where a *nāyikā* dresses up as Kṛṣṇa and plays a flute, and thereby relieves the onlooking *gopīs*' sorrow of separation from their beloved (I thank Allison Busch for this reference).

6.3 [1] Bhartṛhari 3.14 (in the edition of Rāmacandra Budhendra).

6.4 **In authoritative texts:** Bhānu's reference is unclear. He may have in mind Praśastapāda's analysis, which includes *ātmamanaḥsaṃyoga* (see *Nyāyakośa* s.v. *sukha*). Ś, like others assuming *śāstra* means Vedanta, points to *Pañcadaśī* 11.87, which lists three types of bliss (*brahmānanda*, *vāsanānanda*, *pratibimbānanda*), and presumably *vāsanānanda* is implicated in *mānorathika* rasa.

6.7 **The tranquil**: for *śāntarasa*, see RT 7.63 and note to RT 7.62.

6.7 *vyabhicāri/raty/ātmakatvāt*: V glosses *vyabhicārabhāvarūpa-rasasvarūpa-*.

6.7 V: *paratra vātsalye; kḷptatvāt karuṇasyāntarbhūtatayā kḷptatvāt.* B: *paratra śṛṅgāre* [*sic*, but must be false]; *kḷptatvāt sthāyitvenāṅgīkṛtatvād atra karuṇe....*

6.7 V: *dharmikalpanātaḥ karuṇarasarūpadharmikalpanātaḥ dharmakalpanāyāḥ karuṇarasasya vyabhicāribhāvasvarūparatirūpatvakalpanāyāḥ.*

6.7 V: *upakṣayāt anyathāsiddhāt.*

6.10 The two types of enjoyment are illustrated sequentially.

6.13 [3] Her eyes would be **closed** in the pretense of sleep in order to see what her lover would do (V).

6.18 **Factors**: again Bhānu seems to mix underlying factors and stimulant factors in the examples that follow.

6.18 **Reactions**: Bhānu appears not to be using *anubhāva* in the technical sense here.

6.24 **Pride of wealth**: for *dhanamada* see RT 6.36.

6.27 Compare NŚ 22.18.

6.28 Since turmoil is both a physical and a mental phenomenon (see earlier), two examples are given.

6.29 [8] **Bending:** N: *caṇḍimā vakratāviśeṣaḥ.*

6.31 [9] V appears to take ***krodh'/āgāra*** as synonymous with *kopabhavana*, "anger room" or boudoir, a place to pout; in this context it would be the eye, which as V notes would be red.

6.31 [9] The goddess's glances appear to be figured as a woman's morning toilette (the interpretation here is owing to Dániel Balogh, and, I now see, partially confirmed by B). **Mounting concern** is uncertain; perhaps she is supposed to be remorseful at her show of anger.

6.33 [10] Perhaps we should accept the variant *-paṭi* for ***-kaṭi***, which poeticians often regard as obscene.

6.40 The entire textual tradition of the RT reads *abhilāṣa*, which is not only almost unintelligible in the context of a discussion of the *hāva*s, but, what is more important, contradicts the entire tradition of poetics (NŚ 22.24–25; SD 3.105cd; and in vernacular poetics, *Rasikapriyā* 6.33). B's gloss, however, supports my emendation ***abhilāpa*** (*avasarāgatavacanaṃ vyjājādinā viśeṣeṇa hṛtam* (or *hatam*) *vihṛtam* (or *vihatam*).

6.41 [14] **Bhaváni grew angry**: her anger, according to N, stems from Śiva's having a moon for a crest and wanting to offer her only a *tilaka* mark. Surely it arises from her impatience at his delay in making love, which she remedies with her ruse.

6.44 The much-attested reading *muditatvābhāvāt* requires a very forced interpretation: because their senses are not joyous then—i.e., only at the initial moment of love-anger. The reading accepted, ***muditatvāt***, indicates that the woman, though angry with her errant lover, still wants to be with him: she is simply punishing him.

6.49 [17] **Fainting**: B finds a *śleṣa* here (*mūrchanā* also meaning musical scale), but that strikes me as awkward and unnecessary.

6.51 [18] To obtain the punning translation "moon," the word ***doṣ'/ ākaro*** must be analysed as *doṣā/karo*.

6.55 [20] The use of ***prabhavati*** here is peculiar. B helpfully glosses *prabhavati tadrūpeṇa pariṇamati*.

6.57 [21] N and V remark that this verse does not illustrate separation through a curse but rather illustrates a threat from a mistress to keep her lover from going away (B's desperate attempts to explain otherwise fail).

6.59 [22] So B. Or: "(the woman) hanging her head like a *cakravāka* bird" (N, V). The second translation would require some explanation for the separation, which is proverbial in the case of the *cakravāka*.

6.61 [23] I emend in accordance with what seems to have been V's reading, given his gloss: (*atra jīve [']sati viśleṣas tu bhavatu nāma. paraṃ viśleṣe sati jīvanaṃ daivād evety āśayaḥ. athavā kasya cit sukṛtino yāvajjīvanaṃ viyogābhāvaḥ, anyasya tu viyoge jīvanābhāva eva. te jagatyāṃ sulabhā eva. mādṛśas tu viyogaṃ jīvanaṃ cobhayam api prāpto durlabhaḥ*).

6.62 B, reading ***viḍvara*** (cf. RT 6.45), calls it "a vernacularism (*deśabhāṣāśabda*), like *iṅgāla* [= *aṅgāra*]," though the normal Prakrit form would be *viddava* (= *vidrava*), which is what I am assuming this word means here and earlier (V glosses *upadravīyam*).

6.63 [24] We must follow V (implicitly) and B (explicitly), who take "couple" in a general sense, referring to all the young lovers who had to abandon Laṅkā and each other in the aftermath of the fire caused by Hanumān.

7.1 Generally speaking, the difference here is whether the motivating factor of the emotion is located in the subject or in someone else. When someone has done something funny himself, the comic rasa is **self-directed**; when someone else has done so, it is **other-directed**. Or in case of the fearful rasa (RT 7.31–37 [17]), when someone has committed a transgression himself, the fearful rasa is self-directed; when someone else has committed the transgression, it is other-directed.

7.1 **High, average, and low**: the reference is to the character's social class.

7.5 [2] Laughter in Sanskrit literature is conventionally represented as white (even when, as here, the teeth are not supposed to be showing).

7.6 It is not easy to infer, as we must, from the narrative of the following verse that the first half provokes a smile from Pārvatī, the second half a laugh. And the verse itself confuses the C, none of whom explains it convincingly (e.g., V: "the lampblack enables the serpent to see its enemies clearly, which makes it afraid; or perhaps: as a result of the application of the lampblack, tears come to the serpent's eyes so that it cannot see the enemy at all"). It is also unclear what is funny about this verse. In the case of Śeṣa, it may be the fact that the snake has two thousand eyes. But the significance of the golden leaf on Nandi is completely dark to the commentators and to me.

7.7 [3] ***āyo/jayati***: the violation of end-line caesura is considered a gross metrical defect, but it is irremediable in the manuscripts.

7.11 [5] **I cunt begin**: The joke depends on the segmentation of the Sanskrit: *yo nirodho*, "which constraint," or *yoni-rodho*, "a straining of the vulva."

7.13 [6] **Sacred thread**: brahmins at all times wear a thread over their left shoulder and under their right.

7.15 [7] The **datura** plant is also known as jimsonweed and thornapple. An interesting description of the effects of datura comes from Van Linschoten in 1598: "Out of this blossome groweth a bud, much like the bud of Popie, wherein are certaine small kernels like the kernels of Melons, which being stamped, and put into any meate, wine, water, or any other drinke or composition, and eaten or drunke therewith, maketh a man, in such case as if hee were foolish [or out of his wittes,] so that he doth nothing else but laugh, without any understanding or sence [once] to perceive any thing that is done in his presence" (Jan Huyghen Van Linschoten, "The Voyage of John Huyghen van Linschoten to the East Indies" [London: Hakluyt Society, 1885 (original 1598)], p. 69).

7.22 [10] The caesura ***Duryo/dhana*** is considered a metrical fault.

7.22 [10] Bhīma is making two claims: his arm is weapon enough to slay Duryodhana, and if he so wished he could turn the sun and the rest into weapons for his use (so V).

7.24 [11] The word *ṭāpa* is probably a Maithili dialect word meaning "hoof," cf. Nepali *ṭāp*.

7.24 [11] Unidentified soldiers speak (there is no need to assume this is Bhīma, so B). With V I assume that the horses belong to the enemy. By poetic convention, snakes have jewels in their hoods. The cosmic serpent Śeṣa holds up the world, but the force of the elephants has caused him to bow. The war elephants are "competing" with the war horses (V).

7.28 [13] **I will inevitably be bereft:** by poetic convention, rivers and seas are thought of as wives and husbands. **The river cleaves to his feet:** the Gaṅgā is sometimes represented as flowing from Viṣṇu's feet.

7.29 The hero in the following verse is Viṣṇu himself, who showed compassion in taking embodiment in the forms of Rāma and Lakṣmaṇa (so V).

7.31 **Self-directed or other-directed**: on this distinction see note to RT 7.1 above. Here and elsewhere V points out that it is the stable emotion of fear that is *sva-* or *paraniṣṭha*, not the rasa, for the latter is always located in the audience member (but see introduction on the history of the question of rasa's location).

7.40 [18] **Vultures**, *jhillī*: so implied by commentators (normally the word means cricket). For B, the sky is reflected in the river of blood. I take the phrase literally (so N).

7.47 [21] **Like an age-worn pigeon**: the image is odd, but none of the commentators remarks on it.

7.48 This four-fold division seems to be an innovation of Bhānu's.

7.52 [23] **Divine Lion**, *divyahari*: I am in agreement with B; V, G, O oddly take this as a reference yet again to the *varāhāvatāra*.

7.52 [23] **Betel leaf ... cutch juice**: the various ingredients of the Indian delicacy known as paan.

7.58 [26] An extended fantasy on a woman's body after lovemaking, referring successively to her breasts (the pearls are beads of sweat, according to B), eyes, face, eyebrows (though I see no additional reference to her breathing, with G and O), and hair. I believe V is wrong to supply *vamati* with the second half of *a* (while N's transmission of the verse is completely confused).

7.62 The v.l. *adbhutākhyaḥ paraniṣṭha eva* would make this a separate sentence, and one that logically should have preceded the foregoing sentence, which would make perfectly good sense. But no MS. gives this order. The present order and reading can admittedly be made to bear some meaning: SD (p. 78) reports the view ascribed to one Dharmadatta that all rasas are, in the end, the amazing, for which the motivating factor (see note to RT 7.1 above) can obviously only exist outside of oneself, for otherwise it would not prompt amazement. Nonetheless, the opening sentence (where the *ca* remains somewhat awkward no matter what the order) is meant to set up a contrast with the definition of *śānta rasa*, which Bhānu, continuing a tradition that begins with the DR, allows only in poetry, not in drama (see below), and this does require the explanation of the two types of mentality immediately following it.

7.63 **Rasa of phenomenal reality**, *māyārasa*, is Bhānu's invention, necessitated, in his thinking, by the existence of *śānta rasa* in poetry. My grasp of the sense of the following two paragraphs is imperfect.

7.65 [28] **O lord of the world**: the addressee is surely God (Brahmā, B), and not a king (V); nor is the compound *bandhurāga* in apposition to *lokeśa* (V). The "false consciousness" in the verse should be evident.

7.67 [29] I accept the v.l. of G, ***śreyam***, which must be taken as an anomalous gerund of the root *śri*. Note that V reads *yogyam*, which he glosses as *saṃgrāhyam*.

7.67 [29] **Life should be lived**: less likely, "'one's birth should be brought,' sc., to an end" (B).

8.1 According to B, these **looks** are discussed in treatises on dance-music-singing (*saṃgītaśāstra*). The only place I have found them treated is Bhoja's *Samaraṅgasūtradhāra* ch. 82, which is concerned with painting.

8.1 The repetition here is Bhānu's fault; there are no MS. variants.

8.4 [2] **Fanned her with his crescent moon**: commentators are uncertain about the interpretation of this image and want to find some way around the obvious (the fan is in the shape of the moon, for example). V argues that Śiva nowhere removes the moon from his headdress, so such an image would be unprecedented. But this is clearly what Bhānu is saying.

8.7 NŚ 6.39.

8.9 Untraced.

8.11 [3] The quasi-demon **Thousand-armed Árjuna** lusted after the mother of Bhārgava (the "descendent of Bhṛgu" or Paraśurāma) and killed his father, Jamadagni. There is a bad (but again irremediable) caesura in *c*.

8.12 The rasa of pity is generated by the sight of his mother's sorrow, that of disgust by the sight of his father's mortal wound.

8.18 ŚT 3.21.

8.20 Untraced.

8.24 [7] The **churning of the primeval ocean** produced the goddess Lakṣmī, along with the drink of immortality (which the demon Rāhu began to drink before Viṣṇu cut off his head with his discus) and the cosmic poison that Śiva swallowed in his mercifulness.

8.32 [10] V (Baroda MS.), B understand the two rasas to be the heroic (dominant) and the erotic frustrated (subordinate), though these are not usually seen as contradictory. For G and O, less persuasively, the rasas are the heroic (subordinate) and the fearful (dominant).

8.34 [11] **Enemy of the City**: Śiva, who uses a skull for a begging bowl and wears an animal skin as a loin cloth, destroyed the Triple City of the demons.

8.38 Untraced.

8.42 *Dhvanyāloka* 3.14ff., p. 330.

8.48 [15] **Kanchi** refers both to the holy temple city in south India, and to a woman's jeweled belt. The **River Braid** is the confluence of the Gaṅgā and Yamunā at Prayāga.

8.49 V here asks how to understand the type of *nāyikā* who is not a courtesan but has many lovers, for which he cites 55 [26]. His answer, if I understand correctly, is that there is no rasa in the case of (a poem about?) a promiscuous woman; if the word "rasa" is used in reference to such a woman (he cites a *sūtra* he attributes to Vātsyāyana), it only refers to the pleasures of lovemaking, not to the aesthetic experience.

8.51 [16] ***pratāpalaharī***: an obscure collocation, explained by none of the commentators (N reads *-pracāra-* for *-pratāpa-*, though this is not much of an improvement).

8.55 We must assume ***bhrama*** is a synonym (or error) for *moha*. No one, including Bhānu, lists *bhrama* as a *bhāva*.

8.55 Although there is some disagreement among C, compounded by v.l.s, concerning which sentence corresponds with which emotion, the only problematic instance is wisdom, which requires some stretching to relate to the recognition of his shamelessness. (For the others: "renunciation" (despair), "if only" (longing), "who is love" (vindictiveness), "the universe" (confusion), "the woman's beauty" (remembrance), "a curse" (depression), "where have you gone," etc. (despondency).)

8.57 Untraced.

8.59 [18] B notes that the rasa here is oblique in part because no underlying factors are mentioned.

8.62 [19] V remarks on the unusually awkward syntax of this verse (*kaṣṭānvaya*).

8.65 [20] The verse plays on both the fact that Brahmā, the **god born in the lotus**, is a brahmin and should therefore receive the gift, and the fact that Bhārgava (Paraśurāma) is an incarnation of Viṣṇu, the god of the **navel lotus** from whom Brahmā is born. What remains unclear is whether Bhārgava's response should be embarrassment (so the reading of J, which I have adopted) or playfulness (Ś). V, B have *-tīra-* for *-nīra-* in *a*, thereby understanding the diamonds concretely, as spread out on the shores of the seas; the metaphorical usage is unusual.

THE CLAY SANSKRIT LIBRARY

Current Volumes

For further details please consult the CSL website.

1. The Emperor of the Sorcerers (*Bṛhatkathāślokasaṃgraha*) (vol. 1 of 2) by *Budhasvāmin*. Sir James Mallinson
2. Heavenly Exploits (*Divyāvadāna*) Joel Tatelman
3. Maha·bhárata III: The Forest (*Vanaparvan*) (vol. 4 of 4) William J. Johnson
4. Much Ado about Religion (*Āgamaḍambara*) by *Bhaṭṭa Jayanta*. Csaba Dezső
5. The Birth of Kumára (*Kumārasaṃbhava*) by *Kālidāsa*. David Smith
6. Ramáyana I: Boyhood (*Bālakāṇḍa*) by *Vālmīki*. Robert P. Goldman
7. The Epitome of Queen Lilávati (*Līlāvatīsāra*) (vol. 1 of 2) by *Jinaratna*. R.C.C. Fynes
8. Ramáyana II: Ayódhya (*Ayodhyākāṇḍa*) by *Vālmīki*. Sheldon I. Pollock
9. Love Lyrics (*Amaruśataka, Śatakatraya & Caurapañcāśikā*) by *Amaru, Bhartṛhari & Bilhaṇa*. Greg Bailey & Richard Gombrich
10. What Ten Young Men Did (*Daśakumāracarita*) by *Daṇḍin*. Isabelle Onians
11. Three Satires (*Kaliviḍambana, Kalāvilāsa & Bhallaṭaśataka*) by *Nīlakaṇṭha, Kṣemendra & Bhallaṭa* Somadeva Vasudeva
12. Ramáyana IV: Kishkíndha (*Kiṣkindhākāṇḍa*) by *Vālmīki*. Rosalind Lefeber

13. The Emperor of the Sorcerers (*Bṛhatkathāślokasaṃgraha*) (vol. 2 of 2) by *Budhasvāmin*. SIR JAMES MALLINSON
14. Maha·bhárata IX: Shalya (*Śalyaparvan*) (vol. 1 of 2) JUSTIN MEILAND
15. Rákshasa's Ring (*Mudrārākṣasa*) by *Viśākhadatta*. MICHAEL COULSON
16. Messenger Poems (*Meghadūta, Pavanadūta & Haṃsadūta*) by *Kālidāsa, Dhoyī & Rūpa Gosvāmin*. SIR JAMES MALLINSON
17. Ramáyana III: The Forest (*Araṇyakāṇḍa*) by *Vālmīki*. SHELDON I. POLLOCK
18. The Epitome of Queen Lilávati (*Līlāvatīsāra*) (vol. 2 of 2) by *Jinaratna*. R.C.C. FYNES
19. Five Discourses on Worldly Wisdom (*Pañcatantra*) by *Viṣṇuśarman*. PATRICK OLIVELLE
20. Ramáyana V: Súndara (*Sundarakāṇḍa*) by *Vālmīki*. ROBERT P. GOLDMAN & SALLY J. SUTHERLAND GOLDMAN
21. Maha·bhárata II: The Great Hall (*Sabhāparvan*) PAUL WILMOT
22. The Recognition of Shakúntala (*Abhijñānaśākuntala*) (Kashmir Recension) by *Kālidāsa*. SOMADEVA VASUDEVA
23. Maha·bhárata VII: Drona (*Droṇaparvan*) (vol. 1 of 4) VAUGHAN PILIKIAN
24. Rama Beyond Price (*Anargharāghava*) by *Murāri*. JUDIT TÖRZSÖK
25. Maha·bhárata IV: Viráta (*Virāṭaparvan*) KATHLEEN GARBUTT
26. Maha·bhárata VIII: Karna (*Karṇaparvan*) (vol. 1 of 2) ADAM BOWLES
27. "The Lady of the Jewel Necklace" and "The Lady who Shows her Love" (*Ratnāvalī & Priyadarśikā*) by *Harṣa*. WENDY DONIGER

28. The Ocean of the Rivers of Story (*Kathāsaritsāgara*) (vol. 1 of 7)
    by *Somadeva*. Sir James Mallinson
29. Handsome Nanda (*Saundarananda*)
    by *Aśvaghoṣa*. Linda Covill
30. Maha·bhárata IX: Shalya (*Śalyaparvan*) (vol. 2 of 2)
    Justin Meiland
31. Rama's Last Act (*Uttararāmacarita*) by *Bhavabhūti*.
    Sheldon Pollock. Foreword by Girish Karnad
32. "Friendly Advice" (*Hitopadeśa*) by *Nārāyaṇa* &
    "King Víkrama's Adventures" (*Vikramacarita*). Judit Törzsök
33. Life of the Buddha (*Buddhacarita*)
    by *Aśvaghoṣa*. Patrick Olivelle
34. Maha·bhárata V: Preparations for War (*Udyogaparvan*) (vol. 1 of 2)
    Kathleen Garbutt. Foreword by Gurcharan Das
35. Maha·bhárata VIII: Karna (*Karṇaparvan*) (vol. 2 of 2)
    Adam Bowles
36. Maha·bhárata V: Preparations for War (*Udyogaparvan*) (vol. 2 of 2)
    Kathleen Garbutt
37. Maha·bhárata VI: Bhishma (*Bhīṣmaparvan*) (vol. 1 of 2)
    Including the "Bhagavad Gita" in Context
    Alex Cherniak. Foreword by Ranajit Guha
38. The Ocean of the Rivers of Story (*Kathāsaritsāgara*) (vol. 2 of 7)
    by *Somadeva*. Sir James Mallinson
39. "How the Nagas were Pleased" (*Nāgānanda*) by *Harṣa* &
    "The Shattered Thighs" (*Ūrubhaṅga*) by *Bhāsa*.
    Andrew Skilton
40. Gita·govínda: Love Songs of Radha and Krishna (*Gītagovinda*)
    by *Jayadeva*. Lee Siegel. Foreword by Sudipta Kaviraj
41. "Bouquet of Rasa" & "River of Rasa" (*Rasamañjarī & Rasataraṅgiṇī*)
    by *Bhānudatta*. Sheldon Pollock

To Appear in 2009

Bhatti's Poem: The Death of Rávana (*Bhaṭṭikāvya*)
by *Bhaṭṭi*. Oliver Fallon

Garland of Past Lives (*Jātakamālā*) (vol. 1 of 2) by *Āryaśūra*
Justin Meiland

Garland of Past Lives (*Jātakamālā*) (vol. 2 of 2) by *Āryaśūra*
Justin Meiland

How Úrvashi Was Won (*Vikramorvaśīya*) by *Kālidāsa*
Velcheru Narayana Rao & David Shulman

Little Clay Cart (*Mṛcchakaṭikā*) by *Śūdraka*.
Diwakar Acharya. Foreword by Partha Chatterjee

Maha·bhárata VI: Bhishma (*Bhīṣmaparvan*) (vol. 2 of 2)
Alex Cherniak

Maha·bhárata XII: Peace (*Śāntiparvan*) (vol. 3 of 5) Part Two: "The Book of Liberation" (*Mokṣadharma*). Alex Wynne

Maha·bhárata XIV: The Horse Sacrifice (*Āśvamedhikaparvan*)
Greg Bailey

On Self-Surrender, Compassion, and the Mission of a Goose: Sanskrit Poetry from the South (*Ātmārpaṇastuti, Dayāśataka & Haṃsasaṃdeśa*) by *Appaya Dīkṣita* and *Vedāntadeśika*.
Yigal Bronner & David Shulman

Princess Kadámbari (*Kādambarī*) (vol. 1 of 3)
by *Bāṇa*. David Smith

The Quartet of Causeries (*Caturbhāṇī*)
by *Śūdraka, Śyāmilaka, Vararuci & Īśvaradatta*.
Csaba Dezső & Somadeva Vasudeva

Seven Hundred Elegant Verses (*Āryāsaptaśatī*)
by *Govardhana*. Friedhelm Hardy